# Innovation Diffusion Process

## A Case Study: Automotive Supplier Industry

### Ibrahim Uzpeder

NEW YORK
CITY BOOKS

Copyright ©2019

All Rights Reserved

Including the right of reproduction in whole or in part in any form.

Uzpeder, Ibrahim

Innovation Diffusion Process. A Case Study: Automotive Supplier Industry

ISBN-978-605-66603-0-6

Published by New York City Books

www.nycitybooks.com

**ISBN:** 9781099592133

Cataloging-in-Publication

Keywords: diffusion, innovation, system dynamics, technology lifecycle, technical change

# Innovation Diffusion Process

## A Case Study: Automotive Supplier Industry

### Ibrahim Uzpeder

# TABLE OF CONTENTS

1 **INTRODUCTION** ................................................................................................. 1
   1.1 BACKGROUND ................................................................................................ 1
   1.2 PURPOSE OF THE STUDY ................................................................................ 3
   1.3 SIGNIFICANCE OF THE STUDY ........................................................................ 4
   1.4 SCOPE OF THE STUDY .................................................................................... 5
   1.5 STRUCTURE OF THE THESIS ........................................................................... 6
   1.6 DEFINITIONS .................................................................................................. 6
   1.7 METHODOLOGY ............................................................................................. 7

2 **LITERATURE REVIEW** .................................................................................... 11
   2.1 INNOVATION ................................................................................................ 11
       *2.1.1 Technology and Innovation* ............................................................... 12
       *2.1.2 Technology Lifecycle and Technological Change* ........................... 16
       *2.1.3 Characteristics of Innovation* ............................................................ 22
       *2.1.4 Stages of Innovation* ........................................................................... 23
   2.2 TYPES OF INNOVATION ................................................................................ 25
   2.3 INNOVATION DIFFUSION ............................................................................. 28
       *2.3.1 Adoption of Innovation* ...................................................................... 32
       *2.3.2 Technological Innovation Adoption* ................................................. 33
   2.4 INNOVATION DIFFUSION MODELS ............................................................... 34
       *2.4.1 Epidemic Diffusion Models* ............................................................... 37
       *2.4.2 Bass Model* ......................................................................................... 41
       *2.4.3 Diffusion Models with Marketing Mix Variables* ........................... 45
       *2.4.4 Probit Models in Economics* ............................................................. 48
   2.5 CAUSAL LOOPS REGARDING INNOVATION DIFFUSION ................................ 51
       *2.5.1 Technology* .......................................................................................... 51
       *2.5.2 Industry* ............................................................................................... 57
       *2.5.3 Technology Suppliers* ......................................................................... 60
       *2.5.4 Social Networks* ................................................................................. 71
       *2.5.5 Public Policies* .................................................................................... 74

3 **METHODOLOGY** ............................................................................................... 88
   3.1 SYSTEM THEORIES OF ORGANIZATION ....................................................... 88
   3.2 SYSTEMS THINKING .................................................................................... 90
   3.3 SYSTEM DYNAMICS .................................................................................... 95

4 **PROPOSED MODEL** .......................................................................................... 99
   4.1 INTRODUCTION ............................................................................................ 99
   4.2 EXPERT EXECUTIVE INTERVIEWS .............................................................. 102
       *4.2.1 Executive Interview with Automotive Parts Manufacturer* ......... 103
       *4.2.2 Executive Interview with Machine Tool Supplier* ........................ 106
   4.3 CAUSAL LOOP MODULES .......................................................................... 109
       *4.3.1 Technology Causal Loop Module* ................................................... 109
       *4.3.2 Market Causal Loop Module* .......................................................... 117
       *4.3.3 Customers Causal Loop Module* .................................................... 126
       *4.3.4 Technology Suppliers Causal Loop Module* .................................. 127
       *4.3.5 Social Networks Causal Loop Module* .......................................... 131

- 4.3.6 *Public Policies Loop Module* .................... *132*
- 4.4 TECHNOLOGY SUPPLIERS .................... 138
  - 4.4.1 *System Dynamics Model of Technology Diffusion* .................... *145*
  - 4.4.2 *Simulation Results of Technology Diffusion* .................... *148*
- 4.5 MODEL VALIDITY .................... 155
  - 4.5.1 *Dimensional Consistency Check* .................... *159*
  - 4.5.2 *Extreme Condition Test* .................... *159*
  - 4.5.3 *Applying Lai and Wahbar's Checklist* .................... *160*
  - 4.5.4 *Formal Inspections / Reviews* .................... *161*
  - 4.5.5 *Replicability* .................... *161*
  - 4.5.6 *Behavioral Tests* .................... *161*
- 4.6 SENSITIVITY ANALYSIS .................... 162
  - 4.6.1 *Expenditure Budgets* .................... *162*
  - 4.6.2 *Process Quality and Production* .................... *171*
  - 4.6.3 *Capacity and Backlog* .................... *172*
  - 4.6.4 *Marketing and Demand* .................... *183*
  - 4.6.5 *Price and Revenue* .................... *192*
  - 4.6.6 *Comprehensive Results* .................... *196*
  - 4.6.7 *Extended Model* .................... *199*

# 5 CONCLUSION .................... 201

- 5.1 BRIEF OVERVIEW OF STUDY .................... 201
- 5.2 DISCUSSION OF RESULTS .................... 203
- 5.3 LIMITATIONS OF THE STUDY .................... 206
- 5.4 RECOMMENDATIONS FOR FUTURE RESEARCH .................... 207

**REFERENCES** .................... **209**

**APPENDIX I: MODEL EQUATIONS** .................... **221**

**APPENDIX II: SENSITIVITY ANALYSIS OUTPUTS OF COMPREHENSIVE RESULTS** .................... **229**

**APPENDIX III: SENSITIVITY ANALYSIS OUTPUTS OF EXTENDED MODEL** .................... **233**

# LIST OF FIGURES

Figure 1 Diagram of technology cycle (Gaynor, 1996) .................................................. 18

Figure 2 Disruptive change from one S-curve to another (Christensen, 1998) ............................ 19

Figure 3 Use of a Process Innovation (drawn from Mansfield, 1961) ........................................... 39

Figure 4 Negative Exponential Distribution (Meier, et al., 2007) ...................................................... 40

Figure 5 Balancing Loop of Market Penetration (drawn from Fourt and Woodlock, 1960).......... 41

Figure 6 Adoptions in Bass Model (Mahajan, Muller and Bass, 1990) ........................................... 42

Figure 7 Bass Model: Analytical Structure (Mahajan, Muller and Bass, 1990) .............................. 43

Figure 8 Drawn from Bass (1969) .................................................................................................... 44

Figure 9 Causal Relationships of Technology and Change (drawn from Drejer, 2002): ................ 52

Figure 10 Technology lifecycle (drawn from Drejer, 2002) ............................................................. 53

Figure 11 Technological innovation (drawn from Drejer, 2002) ..................................................... 53

Figure 12 Competitive advantage (drawn from Drejer, 2002) ........................................................ 54

Figure 13 Management of Technology Theory (drawn from Drejer, 2002) ................................... 54

Figure 14 Network externalities (drawn from Mahajan, Muller and Wind, 2000)........................ 55

Figure 15 Product compatibility (drawn from Mahajan, 2000)...................................................... 56

Figure 16 Diffusion of process technologies (drawn from Stoneman, 2002:56).......................... 57

Figure 17 Firm size and price on adoption (drawn from Stoneman and Ireland, 1983) ............... 58

Figure 18 Firm size and adoption cost (drawn from Götz, 1999) ................................................... 59

Figure 19 Stock effects of adoption (drawn from Reinganum, 1981) ............................................ 60

Figure 20 Causal relationship between User Experience and Diffusion (drawn from Yeon et al., 2006) ................................................................................................................................................. 61

Figure 21 Impact of Technology Hype on Diffusion (drawn from Swann, 2001) .......................... 61

Figure 22 Customer Satisfaction andDiffusion (drawn from Mahajan, Muller and Wind, 2000 and Yeon et al., 2006)................................................ 62

Figure 23 Diffusion models' assumption drawn from Yeon et al. (2006) ...................................... 62

Figure 24 Technology Acceptance Model (drawn from Davis, 1989) .............................................. 63

Figure 25 Analytical framework for customer Satisfaction (Anderson and Sullivan, 1993) .......... 64

Figure 26 Customer Satisfaction (drawn from Anderson, Fornell and Lehmann, 1994) ................ 65

Figure 27 Price and adoption (drawn from Karshenas and Stoneman, 2003) ............................... 65

Figure 28 Reservation price (drawn from Kalish, 1985) ................................................................ 66

Figure 29 Price and new product (drawn from Kalish, 1985; Tam and Hui, 1999) ....................... 67

Figure 30 Dynamic price model (drawn from Robinson and Lakhani, 1975) ................................ 68

Figure 31 Innate innovativeness ................................................................................................... 69

Figure 32 Sales of successive generations (drawn from Norton and Bass, 1987) ......................... 69

Figure 33 Market Power (drawn from Quirmbach, 1986) ............................................................. 70

Figure 34 Price and Firm Entry (drawn from Bayus, Kang and Agarwal, 2005) ............................. 71

Figure 35 Information flow (drawn from Krackhardt and Hanson, 2003; Borgatti and Cross, 2003) ................................................................................................................................................... 71

Figure 36 Information spread (drawn from Hargadaon, 1998) ..................................................... 71

Figure 37 Interaction on adoption (drawn from Wejnert, 2002) ................................................... 73

Figure 38 External pressure on adoption (drawn from Tung and Rieck, 2005) ............................ 74

Figure 39 Supply and Demand Interaction (drawn from Stoneman and Diederen, 1994) ........... 75

Figure 40 Diffusion Path (drawn from Stoneman and Diederen, 1994) ....................................... 76

Figure 41 Public policies (drawn from Jaffe, Newell and Stavins, 2005) ....................................... 77

Figure 42 Imperfect information and diffusion (drawn from Stoneman and Diederen, 1994) ..... 78

Figure 43 Imperfect information and government (drawn from Stoneman and Diederen, 1994) 78

Figure 44 Diffusion of new technology (drawn from Reinganum, 1981a) .................................... 79

Figure 45 Adoption under perfect information (drawn from Reinganum, 1981b; Quirmbach, 1986) ............................................................................................................................................. 80

Figure 46 Market Structure and Diffusion of New Technology (drawn from Reinganum, 1981b) 81

Figure 47 Diffusion capital equipment as process innovation (drawn from Quirmbach, 1986) ... 81

Figure 48 Market power and diffusion (drawn from Quirmbach, 1986) ............................ 83

Figure 49 Technology transfer (drawn from Bessant and Rush, 1993) .......................... 85

Figure 50 Relationship between innovation and entry barriers (drawn from Bayus, Kang, Agarwal, 2007) ............................................................................................................ 86

Figure 51 Industry Attractiveness (drawn from Thacker and Handscombe, 2003) ........ 87

Figure 52 Five Forces of Competition (Porter, 1980) .................................................... 87

Figure 53 Event-oriented view of the world (Sterman, 2000) ........................................ 90

Figure 54 Feedback view (Sterman, 2000) .................................................................... 91

Figure 55 System dynamics steps from problem symptoms to improvement (Forrester, 1994) . 95

Figure 56 The diagram of causal relationship ................................................................ 97

Figure 57 Stock-flow diagram; ....................................................................................... 98

Figure 58 General configuration on innovation diffusion ............................................ 100

Figure 59 General configuration on innovation diffusion ............................................ 101

Figure 60 Innovation Diffusion Structure and Material/Information Flows ................ 102

Figure 61 Manufacturing cycle of aerospace and defense industry (drawn from executive interview) ..................................................................................................................... 107

Figure 62 Adoption of technology ................................................................................ 111

Figure 63 Cost Loop ..................................................................................................... 112

Figure 64 Productivity Loop ......................................................................................... 113

Figure 65 Technology Lifecycle ................................................................................... 114

Figure 66 Technology Diffusion ................................................................................... 116

Figure 67 Stock Flow Diagram – Technology Diffusion ............................................. 116

Figure 68 Market vs.Innovation Orientation (Source: Berthon, Hulbert and Pitt, 1999) ............ 118

Figure 69 Diffusion of an Industrial Innovation (drawn from Mansfield, 1961) ......... 119

Figure 70 Bass Mixed Influence Model (modified from Sterman, 2000 and Maier, 2002) ......... 120

Figure 71 Simulation Results for Bass Mixed Influence Model .................................. 121

Figure 72 Simulation Results for Adoption ................................................................. 122

Figure 73 Technology Diffusion and Contact Rate ..................................................... 123

Figure 74 Sensitivity Analysis – Technology Diffusion and Adoption Fraction .......... 124

Figure 75 A causal loop of technology diffusion in any industry ................................ 126

Figure 76 Customers .................................................................................................. 127

Figure 77 Technology suppliers .................................................................................. 128

Figure 78 R&D Loop ................................................................................................... 129

Figure 79 Revenue Growth Loop ................................................................................ 129

Figure 80 Marketing Loop .......................................................................................... 130

Figure 81 Social networks .......................................................................................... 132

Figure 82 Lifecycle of ideas in good currency ............................................................ 133

Figure 83 Public policies ............................................................................................ 134

Figure 84 Public policies Affecting Firms' Innovation Activities ................................ 135

Figure 85 Public funds ............................................................................................... 136

Figure 86 Public funds and procurement .................................................................. 137

Figure 87 Law enforcement ....................................................................................... 137

Figure 88 Public Policies ............................................................................................ 138

Figure 89 Cause-Effect Relations in Production ........................................................ 139

Figure 90 Stock-and-flow Relations in Production .................................................... 139

Figure 91 Revenue and Cost of Production ............................................................... 140

Figure 92 Production Loop ........................................................................................ 141

Figure 93 Stock-and-flow production loop ................................................................ 142

Figure 94 Production Loop ........................................................................................ 143

Figure 95 Production Loop with non-negative stock ................................................. 144

Figure 96 Effect of production budget allocation and profit on sales ....................... 145

Figure 97 Supplier's System Dynamic View on Innovation Diffusion ............................................. 147

Figure 98 Simulation Results for Demand, Backlog, Production and Capacity ........................... 151

Figure 99 Price and Cost of New Technology ................................................................................ 152

Figure 100 Simulation Results for Revenue and Budget Allocations............................................ 153

Figure 101 R&D – Process Quality and Marketing – Customer Awareness ................................ 154

Figure 102 Overall nature and selected tests of formal model validation (Barlas, 1996) ........... 157

Figure 103 Sensitivity Analysis: Effect of Allocation Fraction on Production .............................. 163

Figure 104 Sensitivity Analysis: Effect of Allocation Fraction on Backlog ................................... 163

Figure 105 Sensitivity Analysis: Effect of Allocation Fraction on Capacity .................................. 164

Figure 106 Sensitivity Analysis: Effect of Allocation Fraction on Process Quality ...................... 165

Figure 107 Sensitivity Analysis: Effect of Production Budget Fraction on Production .............. 166

Figure 108 Sensitivity Analysis: Effect of Production Budget Fraction on Backlog .................... 166

Figure 109 Sensitivity Analysis: Effect of Production Budget Fraction on Capacity ................... 167

Figure 110 Sensitivity Analysis: Effect of Reference R&D Budget Fraction on R&D Process Budget Ratio ................................................................................................................................... 168

Figure 111 Sensitivity Analysis: Effect of Reference R&D Budget Fraction on Process Quality .. 169

Figure 112 Sensitivity Analysis: Effect of Reference R&D Budget Fraction on Production Cost . 169

Figure 113 Sensitivity Analysis: Effect of Marketing Budget Fraction on Customer Awareness. 170

Figure 114 Effect of Marketing Budget Fraction on New Customers.......................................... 171

Figure 115 Sensitivity Analysis: Effect of Process Quality Outflow Fraction on Process Quality 172

Figure 116 Sensitivity Analysis: Effect of Process Quality Outflow Fraction on R&D Process Budget ............................................................................................................................................ 172

Figure 117 Desired Production and Potential Production............................................................ 173

Figure 118 Sensitivity Analysis: Effect of Capacity Step on Capacity .......................................... 174

Figure 119 Sensitivity Analysis: Effect of Capacity Step on Backlog............................................ 174

Figure 120 Updated System Dynamics Model ............................................................................. 176

Figure 121 Effect of Initial Capacity on Capacity Adjustment .................................................. 178

Figure 122 Effect of Initial Capacity on Capacity ....................................................................... 179

Figure 123 Sensitivity Analysis: Effect of Reference Time to Adjust Capacity on Capacity Adjustment ................................................................................................................................. 180

Figure 124 Sensitivity Analysis: Effect of Reference Time to Adjust Capacity on Capacity ......... 180

Figure 125 Sensitivity Analysis: Effect of Reference Time to Adjust Capacity on Production ..... 181

Figure 126 Sensitivity Analysis: Effect of Reference Time to Adjust Capacity on Revenue ......... 181

Figure 127 Sensitivity Analysis: Effect of Technology per Customer on Backlog ....................... 182

Figure 128 Sensitivity Analysis: Effect of Technology per Customer on Capacity ...................... 183

Figure 129 Sensitivity Analysis: Effect of Technology per Customer on Production .................. 183

Figure 130 Effect of Customer Awareness Adjustment Time on Customer Awareness ............. 184

Figure 131 Effect of Customer Awareness Adjustment Time on Demand (i.e. New Customers) 185

Figure 132 Effect of Forgetting Fraction on Customer Awareness ............................................. 186

Figure 133 Effect of Forgetting Fraction on Demand (i.e. New Customers) .............................. 187

Figure 134 Effect of Forgetting Fraction on Backlog .................................................................. 187

Figure 135 Effect of Sociability on Demand ............................................................................... 189

Figure 136 Effect of Sociability on Backlog ................................................................................ 189

Figure 137 Effect of Sociability on Production .......................................................................... 190

Figure 138 Effect of Fruitfulness Adjustment on Demand ......................................................... 191

Figure 139 Effect of Fruitfulness Adjustment on Revenue ......................................................... 192

Figure 140 Effect of Delay in Customer Payments on Revenue ................................................. 194

Figure 141 Effect of Delay in Customer Payments on Total Expenditure Budget ...................... 194

Figure 142 Effect Price Adjustment Time on Revenue ............................................................... 195

Figure 143 Effect of Initial Number of Firms Using New Technology on Revenue .................... 196

Figure 144 Sensitivity Analysis: Effect on Revenue .................................................................... 197

Figure 145 Sensitivity Analysis on Demand ................................................................................ 198

Figure 146 Sensitivity Analysis on Number of Firms Using New Technology ............................. 199

Figure 147 Sensitivity Analysis of Extended Model on Revenue ................................................. 200

Figure 148 Sensitivity Analysis of Extended Model on Demand ................................................. 200

Figure 149 Sensitivity Analysis on Total Expenditure Budget ..................................................... 229

Figure 150 Sensitivity Analysis on Production Budget ............................................................... 229

Figure 151 Sensitivity Analysis on Marketing Budget ................................................................ 230

Figure 152 Sensitivity Analysis on Process Quality .................................................................... 230

Figure 153 Sensitivity Analysis on Capacity ............................................................................... 231

Figure 154 Sensitivity Analysis on Backlog ................................................................................ 231

Figure 155 Sensitivity Analysis on Customer Awareness ........................................................... 232

Figure 156 Sensitivity Analysis of Extended Model on Total Expenditure Budget ..................... 233

Figure 157 Sensitivity Analysis of Extended Model on Production Budget ............................... 233

Figure 158 Sensitivity Analysis of Extended Model on Marketing Budget ................................ 234

Figure 159 Sensitivity Analysis of Extended Model on Process Quality .................................... 234

Figure 160 Sensitivity Analysis of Extended Model on Capacity ............................................... 235

Figure 161 Sensitivity Analysis of Extended Model on Backlog ................................................ 235

Figure 162 Sensitivity Analysis of Extended Model on Customer Awareness ........................... 236

# PREFACE

The prime objective of this book is to explore mechanisms for the diffusion of industrial innovations within industries. Technological change is a main factor of economic growth, and innovation diffusion, a major research area in technological change, is presented in a framework by synthesizing innovation diffusion literature from marketing, management and economics.

Understanding structures and forces driving the processes of innovation and diffusion require complex models. In this study, an industrial innovation or new technology is both a product innovation from the aspect of supplier firm and a process innovation from the perspective of buyer firms who adopt and use it in their processes. Often well intentioned efforts to solve pressing organizational problems such as technological change cause unanticipated side effects which are termed as "counterintuitive behavior of social systems". System dynamics provides the use of feedback loops with mutual or recursive causality when studying complex systems.

The innovation diffusion framework consists of six areas: technology, market (i.e. firms in an industry), suppliers, customers (end users) and public policies. Causal loop diagrams (CLDs) have been drawn for each area. Based on CLDs, system dynamics model is established primarily focusing on suppliers and secondarily on market. The model consists of 11 stock variables and 23 parameters. Automotive parts industry has been selected for executive interviews in order to provide meaningful values for model parameters while building the system dynamics model.

Model results and testing have been carried out such that it reproduces the behavior seen in the real world. Sensitivity analyses are done for policy formulation and evaluation. The model enables managers of technology suppliers to investigate complex relationships among demand, backlog and capacity. Determining approriate sales price is one of the most important conclusions for lifecycle profit of a certain technology. The system dynamics model enables managers and policy makers to apply and change various pricing policies over time. Both word-of-mouth demand and demand from advertising influence decision for adoption/use of technology.

# ACKNOWLEDGEMENTS

The completion of a book or thesis dissertation is an overwhelming task, requiring an amount of effort that can not be imagined until one has gone through the process, especially when the author is a full time professional in a company like in my case. I am grateful to everybody who influenced and improved the quality of this study.

First and foremost, I would like to thank to my thesis advisor Asst. Prof. M. Atilla Öner, who provided extensive effort, guidance and support to enable this dissertation which turned into a book in time. He taught me, through word and deed, the real meaning of being a scholar and an investigator at the same time. My grateful appreciation is to Prof. Dr. Atilla Dicle and to Prof. Dr. Ülkü Dicle, who inspired me in my personal life many ways deeper than anyone in addition to their highly qualified academic teachings. I extend my special thanks to Prof. Dr. Nuri Başoğlu who had contribution on literature and research methods. Thanks to Assoc. Prof. Lütfihak Alpkan and Asst. Prof. Senem Göl for accepting to be my committee members and for the contributions on the dissertation. I would also like to sincerely thank each and every one of my tutors of the Doctorate program seminars.

Special thanks goes to my cohorts Dr. Hakkı Yıldırmaz, Dr. Ömer Livvarçin, Dr. Özgür Zan, Dr. Mehmet Dudaroğlu for being friends and their support during this research. They injected me hope about completing this Ph.D. study. They did not hesitate to share all their knowledge and valuable time during workshops and other meetings at home, work and else where.

Finally, I would like to express my deepest gratitude to my parents and my sister İpek, who supported me with their continued loving patience. I dedicate this dissertation to my family.

# CLAIM FOR ORIGINALITY

According to our reviews in the literature, this is the first study to explore the effects of industrial innovations and technological change on buyer/user firms within a specific industry, industries.

1. System dynamics modeling, which is used in this study, will contribute to the realization of systems school in management and organization theory.
2. The system dynamics model provides a useful tool for managers of technology suppliers for policy/strategy formulation and evaluation without costly real life experiences.
3. The thesis combines six different causal loop sectors (technology, market, suppliers, customers, public policies and social networks).
4. The developed model allows the use of different pricing policies (full cost coverage, skimming price, penetration pricing, myopic profit maximization) for decision analysis.
5. The model allows gaming approach to the timing of capacity investment decisions.
6. The model allows the study of impact of marketing budget on demand for new technology.

These six features aim at providing a holistic approach for understanding diffusion of industrial innovations, as well as bringing a significant impact on public policies that aim on development and use of new technology.

İbrahim Uzpeder                                              Asst. Prof. M. Atilla Öner

# 1 INTRODUCTION

## 1.1 Background

It is inevitable that organizations have to adopt changing market conditions in order to remain at the competitive edge (Cagan, Oner and Basoglu, 2003). Innovation and the management of technology is becoming crucial to corporate success due to the increased competition and accelerated product development cycles (Wheelen and Hunger, 2004). Consequently companies and industries need to know about the mechanisms that motivate the innovation and diffusion processes (Rogers, 1995).

The major studies on innovation diffusion were established during 1960s and 1970s predicting the diffusion speed (process technology, Mansfield, 1961; television, Bain, 1963; hybrid corn, Rogers, 1962; consumer products, Bass, 1969). However, these models have been on the explanation of past behavior rather than on forecasting future behavior. According to Rogers (2003), the diffusion theory is organized around four basic components:

1. Innovation
2. Communication
3. Time
4. Social System

The modeling developments continued so far with the purpose of having greater flexibility to include aspects such as different generations of technology and different stages of innovation in different countries (dynamic price, Robinson and Lakhani, 1975; successive generations of high-tech products, Norton and Bass, 1987; effects of competition, Gatignon and Robertson, 1989). Although diffusion models become analysis instruments to formulate strategies, they do not provide the understanding of the structures and forces driving the processes of innovation and diffusion (Yeon et al., 2006). System dynamics methodology can contribute to the development of more complex models to investigate innovation diffusion at an industry level.

Since competitive differences between firms and between countries have come to depend on their abilities to acquire, develop, and focus new technologies on market need, the following question needs to be elaborated in more systematic ways: *Why do companies need to innovate?*

There are two major competitive strategies to gain competitive advantage: *cost leadership* and *differentiation.* (Porter, 1980). The competitive environment is more dynamic and characterized by change in products and markets driven by technology and information (Brown and Blackmon, 2005). The essence of strategy is about creating new competitive advantages, before competitors mimic the existing ones. A new product that creates/satisfies market demand brings about competitive advantage, until it is imitated. Hence some companies such as Sony, 3M made innovation an indispensable part of their strategies. (Prahalad and Hamel, 1989)

Investigating the effects of innovation diffusion across industries requires a broader term for innovation covering both product and process innovations. The processes involved in organizational diffusion and assimilation can be highly unpredictable and complex. Therefore the study of organizational technology diffusion (the process by which technology spreads across organizational adopters) and assimilation (the process by which technology is eventually deployed within an adopter organization) are key areas of interest as a multidisciplinary field. (Fichman, 2000)

Schumpeter (1934) defined the stages of innovation as follows:

1. Invention
2. Innovation
3. Diffusion or imitation

The majority costs along the innovation process are incurred in the second and third stages. Therefore both companies and industries need to improve innovation management by understanding the structures and forces driving the processes of innovation and diffusion. (Maier, 1998)

Innovation diffusion converts newly created knowledge into the increase of firm value. For management questions, intra-firm diffusion, inter-firm diffusion and overall diffusion were stated as three aspects of innovation diffusion (Yang and Liu, 2006). Bandwagon effects contribute to the explanation of firms' innovation diffusion, it is mainly about intra-firm diffusion due to the focus on product innovation. (Abrahamson and Rosenkopf, 2003) The proposed research aims to provide a rational model incorporating the above aspects of innovation diffusion from the perspective of industrial characteristics. This research intends at answering how suppliers make the suitable and well-timed decisions in diffusing new technology to adopters within the context of automotive supplier industry.

The next section introduces research question which is mainly about the outcomes and intentions of this study. This section basically converts managerial questions into research questions. It explains the methodology and approaches that are anticipated for the development of the proposed strategy model and appropriate managerial solutions.

## 1.2 Purpose of the Study

The title of thesis study is "Assessment of Innovation Diffusion Process Using System Dynamics Modeling" with a particular focus on automotive supplier industry.

The proposed research will provide a system dynamics model as a direct or indirect tool for evaluating the following generic questions (adapted from: Stoneman, 2002; Mahajan et al., 2000):

1. How do firms decide on investment for new technology?
2. How soon do other firms use a particular process innovation when it is introduced by one firm first?
3. What are the policies which influence diffusion of a particular industrial innovation in a specific industry?
4. Which factors do technology suppliers take into account in order to promote new technology?
5. How do technology suppliers make suitable and timely decisions in order to diffuse new technology to firms as adopters?
6. Which classification can be used in order to categorize companies with respect to their approach towards innovation?

Yang and Liu's (2006) following definition of innovation diffusion will be the guideline to deal with the term via the system dynamics methodology: *"A tacit knowledge transfer process turning innovation into new products in an effort to foster and advance the innovation"*

Based on the above management questions, two major research questions arise:

1. What is the relationship between the speed of diffusion of a firm's product and its certain strategic actions?
2. How will the structure of the adopter industry change over time? What will be the impact on the diffusion path?

The first research question can further be elaborated as follows:

1. How will suppliers price new products embodying new technology?
2. How do marketing decisions affect the diffusion of a new product?
3. How does competition among incumbent suppliers or potential entry affect the diffusion of a new product?
4. What will be the impact on the diffusion path?

A sub question based on the second research question can be:

- Which classification can be used in order to categorize companies with respect to their approach towards innovation?

## 1.3 Significance of the Study

This study provides companies selling innovation/technology a dynamic model to evaluate their strategic decisions by analyzing its effects on diffusion of that particular technology. It provided answers to the following research questions on page three:

1. How will suppliers price new products embodying new technology?
2. What is the relationship between speed of diffusion of a firm's product and its certain strategic actions?
3. How do marketing decisions affect the diffusion of new product?
4. How will supplier behavior develop, and what will be the impact on diffusion path?

The system dynamics model provides a tool easy to use for managers of technology suppliers about setting prices for new product launch and later on. The study showed clear ways of alignment between firms' actions and speed of diffusion which provide managers new insights about market dynamics.

## 1.4 Scope of the Study

This study seeks to explore dynamics of new technology adoption by companies in a particular industry, in this study, automotive supplier industry. This study aims to develop a generic system dynamics model for the evaluation of innovation diffusion process.

According to Association of Automotive Parts & Components Manufacturers in Turkey (TAYSAD, 2008), automotive supplier industry will be more consolidated. There are around fifteen worldwide first-tier automotive suppliers, whereas the remaining suppliers will have no choice of becoming second, third and fourth-tier automotive suppliers. Consequently, primary automotive suppliers become "system suppliers" rather than "commodity suppliers" in a price-sensitive market. Therefore automotive suppliers need to utilize technology such that they achieve product innovation.

That automotive suppliers invest in new technology, is mainly process innovation for a firm. The rate of diffusion of new process technologies differs across technologies, industries, firms, nations. Technology suppliers need to consider main factors impacting innovation diffusion process (Stoneman, 2002:102):

1. Expected profitability or benefit from technology adoption;
2. Cost of adopting new technology;
3. Firm characteristics: e.g. size;
4. Government involvement.

Further the interaction between adopter industry and technology supplier industry is another factor that results in complex relationships among factors affecting innovation diffusion process. Therefore existing quantitative diffusion models had limited applications so far to aid in decision making (Lilien and Rangaswamy, 2000).

The scope of the study does not include the effects of innovation diffusion on competitiveness of companies and industries. It also does not incorporate competition explicitly, since diffusion of new technology, i.e. innovation, usually originates from one supplier firm at least during the initial stages of lifecycle.

## 1.5 Structure of the Thesis

In Chapter 2 Literature Review including comprehensive analysis of existing approaches will be discussed. Chapter 3 covers in-depth literature review of system dynamics and its applications in innovation diffusion. In Chapter 4, proposed model for innovation diffusion process will be introduced. It includes expert executive interviews in automotive supplier industry and analyzes the results. Contributions of the research, possible application fields in the future and research outcomes will be discussed in Chapter 5.

## 1.6 Definitions

The definitions given in this section are related to innovation and technology.

**Innovation**

A new product, service or technology that has been commercially launched to the market. In this study, innovation and technology are used as equivalent terms pointing out industrial innovations and excluding innovations for consumers and households.

**Market / Industry**

Group of firms that establish an industry, regarded as market for selling technology to those firms.

**Product Innovation**

The introduction of a good or service that is new or significantly improved with respect to its characteristics or intended uses.

**Process Innovation**

The implementation of a new or significantly improved process technology, which is used by firms (not consumers) in their manufacturing and/or core business processes.

**Technology Supplier**

Firm that sells its products/services as technology to other firms in a particular industry.

## 1.7 Methodology

This research is concerned about providing a rational approach to identify the diffusion patterns of innovation. There is a significant amount of quantitative models and relatively few system dynamics models for innovation diffusion.

As a general rule in social research, different research problems require different research approaches (Singleton and Straits, 1999). The present research design is based both on an exploratory and conclusive research. It is exploratory, because the research aims to provide significant insight into the dynamics of innovation diffusion process. It is also conclusive, because automotive supplier industry is the focus of the study in reaching useful conclusions.

Although most researchers do either quantitative or qualitative research work, some researchers have suggested combining one or more research methods in the one study (called triangulation) (Gable, 1994; Kaplan and Duchon, 1988; Lee, 1991; Mingers, 2001; Ragin, 1987; Myers, 1997). System dynamics modeling, which is a good example of triangular approach, will be used in this research. Historical analysis, conceptual modeling and case studies will also be conducted in the study. These stated research methodologies are marked as bold in

Table 1. Meredith et al. (1989) introduce a useful review of two key dimensions that shape the philosophical basis for research. The first dimension is the "rational/existential" and concerns the nature of truth and whether it is purely logical and independent of man or whether it can only be defined relative to individual experience. The second is "natural/artificial" dimension and concerns the source and kind of information used in the research.

Meredith et al. (1989) try to put each research in one of the cells. At rational/existential dimension this research is both logical/positivist/empiricist and interpretive. However at natural/artificial dimension all of the three columns match the philosophy of this study. Highlighted (bold) items of three cells in Table 1 summarize the research methodologies that will be used in this study.

Table 1 A Framework for Research Methods (Meredith et al., 1989)

| | | Source of Information used in the Research | | |
| --- | --- | --- | --- | --- |
| | | NATURAL | | ARTIFICIAL |
| | | Direct Observation of Object Reality | People's Perceptions of Object Reality | Artificial Reconstruction of Object Reality |
| RATIONAL | Axiomatic | | | *Reason/Logic /Theorems<br><br>* Normative Modeling<br><br>* Descriptive Modeling |
| RATIONAL | Logical Positivist/ Empiricist | * Field Studies<br><br>*Field experiments | *Structured Interviews<br><br>* Survey Research | * Prototyping<br><br>* Physical Modeling<br><br>*Laboratory experiments<br><br>* **Simulation** |
| EXISTENTIAL | Interpretive | * Action Research<br><br>* **Case Studies** | *Historical analysis<br><br>* Delphi<br><br>***Intensive Interviews**<br><br>* Expert panels<br><br>* Futures/ scenarios | ***Conceptual Modeling**<br><br>* Hermeneutics |
| EXISTENTIAL | Critical Theory | | *Introspective Reflection | |

(Epistemological Structure of the Research Process)

First research method is called "simulation" and in this approach, an artificial reconstruction of object reality is attempted in almost all the modeling and systems analytic efforts in operations. These approaches recast the object reality, as originally determined from one of the above two categories (usually the researcher's own belief concerning the object reality), into another form that is more appropriate for testing and experimentation, such as analytical models, computer simulations, or information constructs. System dynamics research methodology incorporates both conceptual modeling and simulation. As previously discussed, the aim of the proposed research is to build rational model of innovation diffusion patterns displaying industrial differences.

Historical/archival analysis is the second research method. This approach looks into less formally recorded data such that a situation is analyzed frequently over some period of time. Empirical studies on innovation diffusion will be investigated by making comparisons and inferences and gaining insight, and generally analyze a situation from a particular perspective, frequently over some period of time. Particular evidence, factors will be interpreted while building proposed model on innovation diffusion.

Another research method that will be utilized in this study is intensive interviews. It will be used for descriptive and exploratory phases of research before building a simulation model. As a summary, four research methods described in Meredith et al. (1989) will be used as sub tools in this study. However, the study's main methodology will be literature review based system dynamics modeling.

# 2 LITERATURE REVIEW

The literature review will synthesize all major mathematical models of innovation diffusion from the perspective of system dynamics modeling. The prime objective is to explore mechanisms for the diffusion of innovations and/or new technologies within industries; in this study, automotive supplier industry.

## 2.1 Innovation

Innovation is defined as *"the change that creates a new dimension of performance"* (Drucker, 1995 cited in Hesselbein, 2002). Another interpretation of innovation specifies that the first use of an idea by a given set of organizations with a common goal constitutes innovation (Kimberly and Evanisko, 1981). According to another approach the definition of innovation should include success as a qualifier, arguing that use of the term should be limited to the commercial development of a new idea, process, or technology (Krasner, 1982).

Innovation involves creativity, but is not identical to it; innovation involves acting on the creative ideas to make some specific and tangible difference in the domain in which the innovation occurs (Amabile et al., 1996). Innovation is also defined as the embodiment, combination, or synthesis of knowledge in original, relevant, valued new products, processes, or services (Luecke and Katz, 2003).

The classic dictionary definition of **innovation** is *"the act of introducing something new: something newly introduced"* (Pickett et al., 2006). The narrowest definition of the term views innovation and invention synonymously (Cooper, 1998). In this context, both terms refer to creative processes involving the application of existing ideas to create a unique solution to a problem (Duncan, 1972). In this perspective the innovation occurs very infrequently and involves very few organizations (Cooper, 1998). In theory this approach of innovation could help identify firms that achieve sustained competitive advantage through radical change. In practice on the other hand the inventor organizations often seek to develop new process of outputs as ends in them, choosing to refrain from commercial use of the invention for long periods (Utterback, 1973).

Several studies claim that a firm may be the first or among the first in an industry to adopt or commercialize an innovation as a matter of luck or happenstance. Some scholars (Midgley and Dowling, 1978, 1993) even claim that adoption is not a strategic choice.

Every year, tens of thousands of new technologies are created by businesses, research labs, universities, and private individuals (Saffer, 2006). This can be referred as innovation; however innovation is not limited to products in terms of scope. Innovation refers to both radical (Christensen, 1997) and/or incremental (Von Hippel, 1988; Scotchmer, 2004) changes to processes, products, or services. Further, innovations are also classified with respect to the amount of knowledge incorporated (Betz, 1994:20):

1. Radical innovations: e.g. transistors, computers;
2. Incremental / continuous innovations: e.g. improved memory device in computers;
3. System innovations: new functional capability by reconfiguring existing communication technologies, e.g. automobile communication networks;
4. Next generation technology innovations.

In this study, innovation is characterized as product innovation from seller perspective who is introducing it to the market. However, it is defined as process innovation from the perspective of buyer firms who adopt and use it as new technology in their business (manufacturing) processes in order to provide product (service). Basic needs of societies such as food, public safety, transportation, clothing, education need to be fulfilled via goods and services provided by government and industries. Technologies change in order to provide more efficient and effective goods and services to the society (Betz, 1994:248). Some industries die, since their technologies are not any more effective for societal functions.

### 2.1.1 Technology and Innovation

The following quote from IBM's Business Leadership Forum states the roles and relationships between technology and innovation (Milsberg, 2006):

> "*Technology plays a leading role in innovation, but it isn't the only factor. What were once disruptive technologies now are commodities. Technology can be the*

*establishing base for innovation, but people are the ones that drive it forward. Technology is really only the mechanics of the process. Real innovation is about great people generating and then implementing new ideas."*

As an innovation is adopted in a system, a feedback loop occurs in the diffusion process as observability and other attributes of the innovation process reduce uncertainties associated with the new idea, process, or technology (Rogers et al, 2005).

Technology has various definitions. Woodward (1965) defines technology as the collection of plant machines tools and methods available at a given time for the execution of the production task. Lowe (1995) distinguishes science and technology. The border between technology and science is vague and dynamic. Contrary to science, whose outputs are regarded as public good in economic terms, technology has both public and private properties. Since technology provides solution to specific problems or opportunities, ownership of such proprietary knowledge is marketable.

The rate at which a new technology penetrates into a market is described as technology diffusion; this rate of diffusion is critical factor when firms try to estimate the rate of return on investment in new technology (Betz, 1994:255). When new technology provides similar functionality but improves performance and/or reduces cost, it replaces current technology in existing markets. However, new technology can create new market when they provide new functionality, which depends on performance improvement to open new applications and improvement in performance/price ratio. Technology substitution is significantly affected by many external forces such as specialized demands for the capability provided, funding, societal attitudes, compound substitutions, and legal procedures (e.g. environmental laws & regulations). Further, some well-justified residual usage may nullify the notion of maturity. (Kumar and Kumar, 1992)

Technology diffusion does not always result in complete substitution for the following reasons (Betz, 1994:258):

1. Cost savings of a new technology must justify the capital costs of implementing new technology. In brick making, tunnel kiln replaced traditional types of kilns by 90% in France, Germany and Italy from first introduction in 1955 to 1985, whereas it peaked at 78% only in United Kingdom, since its higher capital cost

did not rationalize its energy saving advantage with respect to fletton bricks (Ray, 1989).

2. Until a new technology is improved with many incremental innovations to adapt to most conditions of production, technology substitution will not progress to 100% replacement of older processes. A good example is the diffusion of shuttleless loom technology in U.S. textile industry, which is introduced in late 1950s. Technology developments intending to widen the looms, reduced noise level, increased speed. Apart from increasing loom efficiency, its capabilities in processing fabric increased: e.g. more colors, more complex design. The percent substitution of shuttleless looms in U.S. textile industry increased from 20% in 1980 to 40% in 1985 (Ray, 1989).

3. When a new technology as a process innovation is the result of many incremental improvements, technology substitution will start later and only after a certain level of progress. Numerically control (NC) technology is about the use of software on machine tools to control machining operations in metal shaping industrial processes. The development of numerically controlled machine tools (NCMTs) started from 1950s till mid-1970s (Mazzoleni, 1997). Numerically controlled machine tools were originally considered to perform operations on single units and small batches. Improvements in NC technology both enabled machining operations in larger batches and also increased applications of manufacturing processes. Initially numerically controlled machine tools were mainly used for turning, milling and drilling, but later on they were utilized practically for all metal cutting and forming processes (Ray, 1989). Therefore number of numerically controlled machine tools started to increase from 1997. Japanese machine tool industry took the lead, since they focused more on commercial applications, whereas U.S. machine tool industry had concentrated on complex numerically controlled machine tools towards military and defense industries (Kalafsky and MacPherson, 2006).

4. Even if new technology is a radical process innovation, its superior process may not completely replace other processes, since existing technology incorporates sunk capital cost for smaller markets/firms. Therefore they will prefer to utilize

existing technology. In flat glass manufacturing, float glass process had been introduced in 1960 replacing former glass sheet-making processes. The percent substitution reached 50% around mid-1970s and 83% by 1987. (Ray, 1989)

5. When new technology is available, the following types of firms need to be distinguished (Meade, 1989)

   N: firms who use the new technology,

   O: firms who the use old technology,

   N': firms that are potential adopters for the new technology but not using the old technology,

   df: adoption rate.

   When there is certain number of adopters at time (t), the conditional probability (p) for adoption of new technology can be formulated as follows:

   df = p (O+N') / (O+N+N')        [1]

   Available data in substitution process is bivariate (firms using the new technology and firms using the old technology) which differs from a diffusion process depending on population of adopters only.

6. The decision criteria for adoption of new technology might differ with respect to industries and countries. A very good empirical study about variability of adoption decisions is the introduction of industrial robots into several industries in Japan and United States (Mansfield, 1989). Taking 1961 as the starting point for innovation, Table 2 summarizes when half the firms in an industry adopts began using industrial robots. They examined the rate of return as a decision variable and argued that Japanese firms had a faster adoption pattern due to lower expected rate of return on production investment.

**Table 2** Number of years until half the firms use industrial robots (Mansfield, 1989)

| Industry | United States | Japan |
|---|---|---|
| Autos and truck | 15 | 6 |
| Auto parts | 8 | - |
| Electrical equipment | 17 | 2 |
| Appliances | 19 | - |
| Nonferrous metals | 20 | 9 |

| | | |
|---|---|---|
| Steel | 3 | - |
| Machinery | 16 | 15 |
| Aerospace | 7 | - |

### 2.1.2 Technology Lifecycle and Technological Change

Empirical studies indicate that information about advanced technology is primarily communicated through external discussion sources and technical literature (Allen, 1967). According to Kumar and Kumar (1992), the technology is better understood and applied around the middle range of S-curve and the performance increases more rapidly as the technology reaches its most well-developed shape. As technology becomes mature, performance increases narrow since improvements become more difficult and costly. The universal growth curve developed by Floyd (1968) is as follows:

$f(t)$: probability density function

$F(t)$: cumulative density function

$q$: propensity to purchase influenced by the amount of previous purchasing

$$df/dt = q\, f\, (F-f)^2 \qquad [2]$$

Equation 2 attempts to explain growth towards an upper limit on the basis of efforts expended. His model was well fitted to aircraft speed and was found suitable for forecasting the progress of a single technical approach. Such growth models facilitate users of technology to elaborate following questions for the substitution of technology (Ayres, 1989):

1. When should a new technology be substituted for an older one? Management may be interested in substituting newer technology just before the maximum growth level is reached.
2. What is the upper limit to growth?
3. Is it possible to forecast the rate and direction of technological change accurately such that useful guidance is available to decision-makers for investment and divestment decisions?

In summary, technologies evolve over time going through a lifecycle (equivalent to product life cycle comprising introduction, growth, maturity, decline; Rogers, 1962).

Technology lifecycle was first termed by Abernathy and Utterback (1978, cited in Betz, 1994). The main stages are birth, low growth, high growth, stagnation and replacement by new technology. Technologies similar to product life cycles can be represented graphically indicating performance of technology as a function of either time or resources. That function's graph results in an S-curved shape. S-curve is also the empirical pattern of technology diffusion (Drejer, 2002). Bhalla (1987) presents these curves as a projective technique for predicting technology and its expected rate of application to problems, and comparing the performance of one technology with another.

As illustrated in Figure 1, technology goes through a cycle which includes following steps: Technology Awareness, Technology Acquisition, Technology Adaptation, Technology Advancement and Technology Abandonment (Gaynor, 1996). Hence technological change is inevitable, since there is dynamics related to knowledge and learning (Drejer, 2002). Based on empirical studies, Christensen (1998) defines technological changes from one life cycle to another in two categories:

4. Sustainable changes that support established firms and knowledge patterns in an industry;
5. Disruptive changes like those categorized by Schumpeter as "creative destruction".

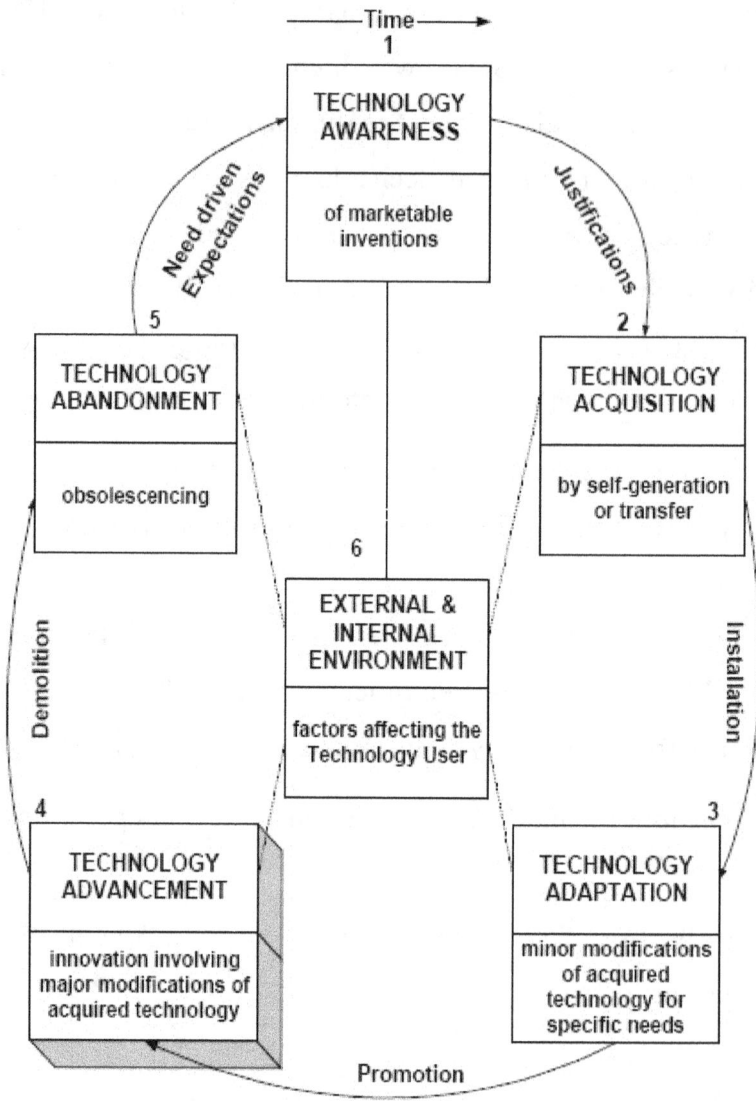

**Figure 1** Diagram of technology cycle (Gaynor, 1996)

Considering technology S-curve, sustainable technological change means a shift from one S-curve to another with respect to same performance parameters, whereas disruptive technological change means jumping to a completely new technology S-curve, which is based on different performance parameters. Sustainable change in terms technology S-curves is displayed in the left-hand side of Figure 2, whereas disruptive change means reaching the end of one technology S-curve and moving to another technology S-curve in a completely different dimension as shown on the right-hand side of Figure 2.

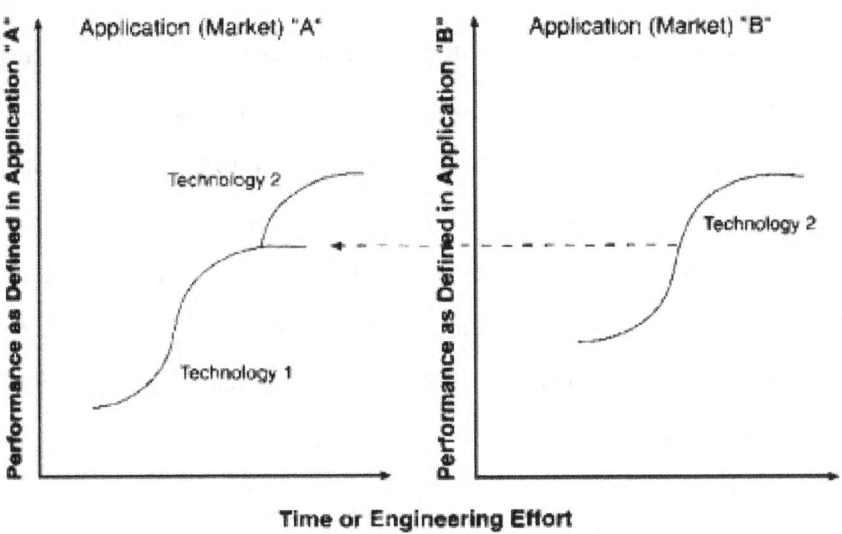

**Figure 2** Disruptive change from one S-curve to another (Christensen, 1998)

In the theory of management of technology, there is the distinction between technology exploitation and creative destruction (Freeman, 1982; Drejer, 1986). Though this distinction appears to be simplistic since not all technological changes are discontinuous ones, as discussed in previous paragraphs. Consequently, Drejer (2002) proposes three situations regarding management of technology:

6. Exploitation of existing technologies
7. Stable technological change
8. Disruptive technological change

The first situation corresponds to movement along the technology S-curve. This means that faster implementation and better use of technology in processes and products. The second situation corresponds to movement from one technology S-curve to another as illustrated on the left-hand side of Figure 2. Technological changes occur, but the value system of a firm does not change. Finally, the third situation is where both market and technology change simultaneously, i.e. the rules of game change.

Regarding technologies, Bower and Christensen (1995) gave the example of hard-disc drive industry that 5.25 inch disc drives were pioneered by Seagate and Seagate was the main supplier to IBM and IBM compatible PC manufacturers. When 3.5 inch disc drives emerged during mid-1980s, it was not valued due to inferior performance with respect to 5.25 inch, since IBM possessed a value system that favored large computers in large firms, and therefore showed no interest in a smaller disc drive. However, as new entrants improve capacity of 3.5 inch disc drives and they are selling them to manufacturers of portable computers and personal computers with smaller space. By the time when Seagate introduced its 3.5 inch disc drives having realized that 3.5 and 5.25 inch drives have equivalent capacities, it was too late for Seagate and lost significant market share. A similar example from computer industry is that Apple created small computers for home use, which had been favored by market. A new product emerged, which was not foreseen by IBM (Drejer, 2002).

The above distinction by Drejer (2002) for management of technology can be regarded from the perspective of use of new technology. From the perspective of supplying and marketing new technology, one can classify technological progress as:

1. Invention: All kinds of major discoveries (Grossman and Helpman, 1991)
2. Innovation: Schumpeterian improvements in machine or production-process quality (Iyimaya, 2006)
3. Learning-by-doing. (Arrow, 1962)

The literature about technological progress reveals that inventions and innovations are complementary in expanding technological frontiers, which is equivalent to Figure 2 described by Christensen (1998). Secondly, major breakthroughs in technology occur once in a while and in clusters. The First Industrial Revolution took place in Lancashire – United Kingdom in 1770s by take-off of textile industry (Iyigun, 2006). It has been caused by the inventions of steam engines, coke blast furnace (iron making process) and spinning machines; however, these inventions were supported by the innovations in machine tools to meet rapid increase in cotton demand and by innovations in transport networks, i.e. river canals constructed from 1760 to 1820 and steamships (Hirooka, 2003). The interactions related to energy and transport infrastructures brought the synergy of innovations. Although James Watt invented steam engine in 1765, it remained principally as water pump until numerous subsequent improvements were made. Compound steam engine was first applied on ships in 1854. The initial advantage of steam engine has been speed and flexibility. As steam engines get better, larger ships were built during the second half of $19^{th}$ century reducing transportation costs and completely replacing sailing ships for transportation by the beginning of $20^{th}$ century. (Mokyr, 1990:126-130)

As a simplification of Figure 1, it can be stated new technology goes through a three period cycle (Iyigun, 2006):

1. *Early stage*: Newly discovered technologies are adopted and the potential benefits of learning-by-doing are largest.
2. *Improvement Phase*: Rapid innovations improve efficiency and attractiveness of existing technology.
3. *Maturity*: Diminishing innovative activities and productivity gains generate discovery for more advanced technologies

New inventions stimulate R&D efforts of even more sophisticated technologies, since productivity is relatively low following the introduction of new technology. As illustrated in the above example of steam engine and coke blast furnace, because productivity gains as learning-by-doing are not realized yet for newly invented technologies, there is increase in probability that a new invention arises soon after the invention of a superior technology. Consequently, clustering of inventions happen (Mokyr, 1990:297). As learning-by-doing happens, the incentives to innovate and improve that existing technology become more than the incentives to developing another new technology. Therefore after the period of inventions, innovative activities intensify by introducing next generation, more efficient machines without changing underlying technology. The introduction of each new generation machine reduces profits of the previous generation monotonically to zero. When productivity gains due to learning-by-doing diminish, there is technological stagnation until new technologies are invented. (Iyigun, 2006)

Hence firms who supply/market new technology, need to direct their R&D activities with respect to both invention and innovation (Metcalfe, 1994). Their learning experience with existing technologies is a key determinant whether incentives for invention or innovation dominate. Therefore firms' decisions about allocation of R&D activities towards invention and/or innovation cycles do generate certain patterns of technological change and economic growth (Iyigun, 2006).

### 2.1.3 Characteristics of Innovation

Important characteristics of an innovation might be listed as follows (Rogers, 2003):

1. **Relative Advantage:** The degree to which it is perceived to be better than what it supersedes. In other words relative advantage is the degree to which a new innovation surpasses current practices. Relative advantage can be operationalized, or measured, in terms of variables such as usefulness in accomplishing work goals, quality of work outcomes, added convenience and social prestige provided by the innovation. (Sonnenwald, Maglaughlin, and Whitton, 2001).

2. **Compatibility:** Compatibility is the degree to which an innovation is perceived to be consistent with adopters' existing values, past experiences and needs. It includes individual, group and organizational goals, needs, culture and structure. It is concerned with the agreement/differences between a group's traditional work patterns and the work patterns required by the innovation (Sonnenwald, Maglaughlin, and Whitton, 2001).

3. **Complexity:** Complexity refers to the perceived difficulty of learning to use and understand a new system or technology. When a system is perceived as difficult to understand, learn and use, it will not be adopted (Sonnenwald, Maglaughlin, and Whitton, 2001).

4. **Trialability:** Trialability refers to the ease of experimenting with an innovation. It includes the level of effort needed and risk involved in observing and participating in small scale demonstrations of the system, including easily recovering from, or "undoing," operations using the systems and the costs involved in reversing the decision to adopt. Experimenting with and exploring system features is also a component of usability engineering (Sonnenwald, Maglaughlin, and Whitton, 2001).

5. **Observability:** Observability is the degree to which the results of the innovation are easily seen and understood. Observability has been operationalized as "results demonstrability," i.e., the ease of telling others the consequences or results of using information technology (Moore and Benbasat, 1991), and thus we selected questions from this scale. Observability also includes visibility, i.e., the degree to which the results of an innovation are visible to others. Observability questions reported in the literature apply to situations where the innovation is observed (over time) within or outside an organization (Sonnenwald, Maglaughlin, and Whitton, 2001).

### 2.1.4 Stages of Innovation

Rogers (2003) introduces five stages for innovation-decision process by which individual or any organizational unit evaluates a new idea and decides whether or not to encompass that particular innovation into practice. Innovation decision making differs in two aspects from other types of decision making:

- Perceived newness of an innovation
- The uncertainty related to that newness

Diffusion scholars have long acknowledged that an individual's decision about an innovation is not instantaneous and arrived at similar set of stages. (Ryan and Gross, 1943)

1. **Knowledge** (exposure to its existence, and understanding of its functions): Knowledge is an increasingly significant factor of production (Rao, 2006). It is widely documented that learning occurs as an associative process in which new knowledge is incorporated cumulatively as a link is established with pre-existing concepts (Gomez and Vargas, 2009). An individual can have a passive role when s/he is exposed to awareness or knowledge about an innovation, whereas other individuals are exposed to communication about an innovation that corresponds to their interests, needs and attitudes such that they avoid messages, information that contradicts with their predispositions (Rogers, 2003).

2. **Persuasion** (the forming of a favorable attitude to it): A consumer or firm develops a favorable or unfavorable attitude to innovation (Cagan, Oner and

Basoglu, 2003). Persuasion is a type of social influence, which might be defined as being able to change one's thoughts and feelings towards a particular subject (Plazo, 2006).

When populations are heterogeneous, differences between individuals can block the process of communication or, more likely, the process of persuasion. To understand diffusion in this context, one needs to understand which adopters are particularly influential and how they meet other potential adopters over whom their influence is decisive. (Geroski, 2000)

3. **Decision** (commitment to its adoption): Decision is a process of coming to a conclusion or determination about something. Therefore, a decision is made in order to adopt or reject the innovation. (Cha, Gregory and Shi, 2004) Similarly, when organizations decide to adopt the innovation, that organizational decision can either be based on either consensus or authority among members of organization (Tung and Rieck, 2005). Rogers (2003) introduces three characteristics of innovation decisions:

- Optional: In this type of innovation decision the organization has a real opportunity to adopt or reject the idea
- Collective: In this type of innovation decision a decision is reached by consensus among the members of a system (the organization)
- Authority-based: In this type of innovation decision a decision is imposed by another person or organization which possesses requisite power, status or technical expertise.

4. **Implementation** (putting it to use): When an individual or organization puts an innovation, implementation follows directly the decision stage, unless the particular innovation is unavailable due to some logistics problems. The consequences of the innovation may still be uncertain. Therefore, an individual, organization wants to know answers to such questions: "how do I use it?", "What operational problems am I likely to encounter?" When an organization adopts, problems are often more serious, since people who implement are usually different than the individuals who were involved in the innovation decision

process (Rogers, 2003). The implementation stage can last a certain period depending upon the nature of innovation.

5. **Confirmation** (reinforcement based on positive outcomes from it): Empirical studies indicate that a decision to adopt or reject a new idea is not the final stage of innovation-decision process. At the confirmation stage, an individual or organization wants to reinforce his/her innovation-decision, but can invalidate it if s/he receives conflicting feedback about the innovation (Rogers, 2003). In that case, s/he can discontinue, i.e. decide to reject the innovation after having adopted it. From customer satisfaction perspective, if an individual or organization intends to use an innovation, s/he subjectively evaluates the discrepancy between expectations and perceived quality; the degree of this positive or negative disconfirmation determines customer satisfaction, i.e. ongoing use or discontinuance of an innovation (Anderson and Sullivan, 1993).

## 2.2 Types of Innovation

There are different innovation typologies in the existing literature. Joseph Schumpeter is credited for being the first economist to draw attention to the importance of innovation. In the 1930's he defined five types of innovation (OECD, 1997, p.28):

1. Innovation of a new product or a qualitative change in an existing product
2. Process innovation new to an industry
3. The opening of a new market
4. Development of new sources of supply for raw materials or other inputs
5. Changes in industrial organization

Four types of innovation are proposed (Tidd et al., 2005):

1. Product Innovation – new products or improvements on products. For example a new or an updated car.
2. Process Innovation – where some part of the process is improved to bring benefit. For example TQM applications.
3. Positioning Innovation – For example "Lucozade" used to be a medicinal drink but was repositioned as a sports drink later on.

4. Paradigm Innovation – where major shifts in thinking cause change. For example during the time of the expensive mainframe, Bill Gates and others aimed to provide a home computer for everyone.

Another typology (Table 3) offers a diagram of the 10 types of innovation is proposed by The Doblin Group, a Chicago-based consultancy.

**Table 3** The Ten Types of Innovation (www.doblin.com, 2008)

| Innovation Category | Innovation Type | Description of type | Business example |
|---|---|---|---|
| Finance | 1 Business | How you make money | Dell revolutionized the personal computer business model by collecting money before the consumer's PC was even assembled and shipped (resulting in net positive working capital of seven to eight days). |
| | 2 Networks and alliances | How you join forces with other companies for mutual benefit | Consumer goods company Sara Lee realized that its core competencies were in consumer insight, brand management, marketing and distribution. Thus it divested itself of a majority of its manufacturing operations and formed alliances with manufacturing and supply chain partners. |
| Process | 3 Enabling process | How you support the company's core processes and workers | Starbucks can deliver its profitable store/coffee experience to customers because it offers better-than-market compensation and employment benefits to its store workers--usually part time, educated, professional, and responsive people. |
| | 4 Core processes | How you create and add value to your offerings | Wal-Mart continues to grow profitably through core process innovations such as real-time inventory management systems, aggressive volume/ pricing/delivery contracts with merchandise providers, and systems that give store managers the ability to identify changing buyer behaviors in and respond quickly with new pricing and merchandising configurations. |
| Offerings | 5 Product performance | How you design your core offerings | The VW Beetle (in both its original and its newest form) took the market by storm, combining multiple dimensions of product performance. |
| | 6 Product system | How you link and/or provide a platform for multiple products. | Microsoft Office "bundles a variety of specific products (Word, Excel, PowerPoint, etc.) into a system designed to deliver productivity in the workplace. |
| | 7 Service | How you provide value to customers and consumers beyond and around your products | An international flight on any airlines will get you to your intended designation. A flight on Singapore Airlines, however, nearly makes you forget that you are flying at all, with the most attentive, respectful, and pampering pre-flight, in-flight and post-services you can imagine. |
| Delivery | 8 Channel | How you get your offerings to market | Legal problems aside, Martha Stewart has developed such a deep understanding of her customers that she knows just where to be (stores, TV shows, magazines, online, etc.) to drive huge sales volumes from a relatively small set of "home living" educational and product offerings. |
| | 9 Brand | How you communicate your offerings | Absolut conquered the vodka category on the strength of a brilliant "theme and variations" advertising concept, strong bottle and packaging design, and a whiff of Nordic authenticity. |

| | 10 Customer experience | How your customers feel when they interact with your company and its offerings | Harley Davidson has created a worldwide community of millions of customers, many of whom would describe "being a Harley Davidson owner" as a part of how they fundamentally see, think, and feel about themselves. |

## 2.3 Innovation Diffusion

Diffusion is the process through which an innovation spreads via communication channels over time among the members of a social system. An innovation has a more rapid rate of adoption when it is easy to "re-invent" (Rogers et al., 2005). Re-invention is defined as "the degree to which adopters can change a new idea, practice, or technology as it diffuses" (Rogers, 2003).

Rogers' (2003) definition contains four elements that are present in the diffusion of innovation process:

1. **Innovation:** Ideas, practices, or object that is perceived as new by an individual or other unit of adoption. The characteristics of an innovation, as discussed in section 2.1, determine its rate of adoption.

2. **Communication channels**: The means by which messages get from one individual to another. Most individuals assess innovation not on rational approach; they rely on individual feedback of near peers who recently adopted innovation. This peer-to-peer communication usually takes place between individuals who are homophilous, i.e. have similar beliefs, education, social status, etc. Heterophily, the opposite to homophily, exists in the diffusion of innovations; it is the extent to which two or more individuals communicating each other are different in certain attributes. Therefore, achieving effective communication may sometimes not be possible and lead to special problems.

3. **Time**: The three time factors are:
    a. Innovation-decision process
    b. Relative time with which an innovation is adopted by an individual or group
    c. Innovation's rate of adoption

An individual seeks information at various stages of innovation-decision process, as described in section 2.1.4 in order to reduce uncertainty.

4. **Social system:** A set of interrelated parts that take on mutual problem solving to accomplish a common goal. One aspect of a social system is norms, i.e. established behavior patterns for its members. A system has a structure as the patterned arrangements among its interrelated parts. The structure of a social system can smooth the progress of or slow down diffusion.

The roots of diffusion theory go back to beginning of 20$^{th}$ century when sociology and anthropology were coming forward as important social sciences. Tarde (1903, cited in Rogers, 2003), a French lawyer observed trends in his society and stated in his book "The Laws of Imitation", why only 10% of innovation is spread and the rest is forgotten. Tarde discovered the adoption or rejection of an innovation as an important variable in diffusion research and observed that a new idea's adoption rate followed an S-shaped curve over time (Rogers, 2003: 41). When opinion leaders in a social system use a new idea, adoption takes off along that S-curve. The term "diffusion" is used by early anthropologists in Britain and Germany-Austria. Their point of view is characterized as *diffusionism*, which regards social change is the consequences of innovations spreading from a single original source. Each academic discipline or sub discipline usually investigated diffusion of a single innovation. These research traditions are summarized in Table 4 (Rogers, 2003:44-45).

**Table 4** Major Diffusion Research Traditions (Rogers, 2003)

| Diffusion of Research Traditions | Typical Innovations Studied | Main Unit of Analysis | Major Types of Findings |
|---|---|---|---|
| Anthropology | Technological ideas (steel ax, water boiling) | Tribes or peasant villages | Consequences of innovations; relative success of change agents |
| Early Sociology | City manager government, postage stamps, ham radios | Communities or individuals | S-shaped adopter distribution; characteristics adopter categories |
| Rural Sociology | Agricultural ideas (weed sprays, hybrid seed fertilizers) | Individual farmers in rural communities | S-shaped adopter distribution; characteristics adopter categories; perceived attributes of innovations and their rate of adoption; communication channels by stages in the innovation-decision process; characteristics of opinion leaders |
| Education | Teaching/learning innovations (kindergartens, modern math programmed instruction, team teaching) | School systems, teachers or administrators | S-shaped adopter distribution; characteristics of adopter categories |
| Public health and medical sociology | Medical and health ideas (drugs, vaccinations, family-planning methods, AIDS prevention) | Individuals or organizations such as hospitals and health departments | Opinion leadership in diffusion; characteristics of adopter categories; communication channels by stages of innovation-decision process |
| Communication | News events, technological innovations, new communication technologies | Individuals or organizations | Communication channels by stages in the innovation-decision process |
| Marketing and management | New products (a coffee brand, a touch-tone telephone, clothing fashions, new communication technologies | Individual consumers | Characteristics of adopter categories; opinion leadership in diffusion |
| Geography | Technological innovations | Individuals and organizations | Role of spatial distance in diffusion |
| General Sociology | A wide variety of ideas | Individuals, other units | Characteristics of adopter categories |

The hybrid seed corn study, performed by Ryan and Gross (1943), made the term "diffusion" popular. They interviewed farmers in two Iowa communities and classified the segments of Iowa farmers in relation to the amount of time it took them to adopt the innovation. They found out that the rate of adoption of the agricultural innovation followed an S-shaped normal curve when plotted on a cumulative basis over time. The first farmers to adopt (the innovators) were more cosmopolite and of higher socioeconomic status than later adopters. One of the most important characteristics of the first segment of a population to adopt an innovation, the innovators, is that they require a shorter adoption period than any other category.

Although hybrid corn was an innovation with considerably high relative advantage, typical farmer proceeded slowly from awareness/knowledge stage to implementation stage, whose average is nine years. Neighbors were the most frequently mentioned communication channel leading to persuasion. The confirmation stage, took four years on average after planting first hybrid seed on till planting 100%.

A certain degree of uncertainty always characterizes an individual's or an organization's perceptions of a new idea, practice, or technology, which is one reason why the diffusion process occurs gradually (Rogers et al., 2005).

One of the most common approaches of the economic theory of innovation diffusion is that shifts from one technology or product to another follow a sigmoid curve (Zuscovitch, Heraud and Cohendet, 1988). This result has been obtained by various scholars in many different industries, for different countries and times (agriculture, U.S., Parker, 1978; chemicals, drugs electronics and machinery, U.S., Mansfield et al., 1977 and Mansfield, Schwartz and Wagner, 1981; high technology, U.S., Moore, 1999; information technology, UK, Swanepoel, 2005).

When firms adopt new technology, it does not necessarily mean that they fully utilize it, similar to the situation for farmers seeding hybrid corn. Therefore, one needs to distinguish between inter-firm diffusion and intra-firm diffusion. However, it is often assumed that inter-firm and intra-firm diffusion happens simultaneously (Geroski, 2000). Intra-firm diffusion of new technology means the replacement of a firm's old technology (Baptista, 1999) and rate of intra-firm diffusion can be occasionally be really slow. Nissan, for example, used industrial robots by 50% in production within 13 years after its first introduction, whereas it took General Motors and Ford more than twenty years to use industrial robots for 50% of their output (Mansfield, 1989).

There is much less research available on the degree of use of new technologies by firms. There have been empirical studies on numerically controlled (NC) machine tools that large firms were likely to be early adopters but their rate of intra-firm diffusion was relatively slow (Baptista, 1999). Similarly, Romeo (1975) contended that intra-firm diffusion of NC machine tools is negatively related to firm size. Battisti and Stoneman (2003) operationalized three diffusion indicators during their study about the use of Computerized Numerically Controlled Machine Tools (CNC) in the UK metalworking and engineering industry:

1. Inter-firm diffusion: the proportion of firms in the industry using the new technology;
2. Intra-firm diffusion: the proportion of each firm's output using the new technology;
3. Overall diffusion: Proportion of industry output produced via the new technology.

### 2.3.1 Adoption of Innovation

Some organizations are innovative and always aim to be technology leader in their industry. Some others are not such risk takers (or pioneers) and prefer to adopt the innovations after observing their validity. Different adopter categories are identified as (Rogers, 1962):

1. **Innovators:** Characteristics that are identified for the Innovators are as follows :
   a. Venturesome, desire for the rash, the daring, and the risky,
   b. Control of substantial financial resources to absorb possible loss from an unprofitable innovation,
   c. The ability to understand and apply complex technical knowledge,
   d. The ability to cope with a high degree of uncertainty about an innovation.
2. **Early Adopters:** Characteristics that are identified for the Early Adopters are as follows:
   a. Integrated part of the local social system,
   b. Greatest degree of opinion leadership in most systems,
   c. Serve as role model for other members or society,
   d. Respected by peers,
   e. Successful.
3. **Early Majority:** Characteristics that are identified for the Early Majority are as follows:

a. Interact frequently with peers,
   b. Seldom hold positions of opinion leadership,
   c. One-third of the members of a system, making the early majority the largest category.
   d. Deliberate before adopting a new idea.
4. **Late Majority:** Characteristics that are identified for the Late Majority are as follows:
   a. One-third of the members of a system,
   b. Pressure from peers,
   c. Economic necessity,
   d. Skeptical,
   e. Cautious.
5. **Laggards:** Characteristics that are identified for the Laggards are as follows:
   a. Possess no opinion leadership,
   b. Isolates,
   c. Point of reference in the past,
   d. Suspicious of innovations,
   e. Innovation-decision process is lengthy, and
   f. Resources are limited.

Rogers (1962) stated that adopters of any new innovation or idea could be categorized as innovators (2.5%), early adopters (13.5%), early majority (34%), late majority (34%) and laggards (16%), based on a bell curve. Each adopter's willingness and ability to adopt an innovation would depend on their awareness, interest, evaluation, trial, and adoption. This categorization is mainly developed for individuals however it is also applicable to organizations.

## 2.3.2 Technological Innovation Adoption

Different groups of organizational/institutional adopters have different characteristics concerning the adoption of innovations. Hence, factors explaining the adoption of innovations will change over time as the diffusion process continues. In the case of adoption of Enterprise Resource Planning Systems (ERP), adoption stimulating factors shift according to the level of diffusion. In the first stages of adoption of innovation by organizations, the most important stimulating factors are a combination of internal drives such as like the firm's attitude towards the innovation and the strategic importance of the innovation for the firm, together with external forces like the parent company, industry competitiveness and supplier activities. (Waarts et al., 2002).

Another important factor in elaborating innovation diffusion among organizations is the cluster effect. Various factors interact, hence consequences are not foreseeable. Industrial competitive advantage is affected via causal loops of manpower, money, technology and market (Lin, Tung and Huang, 2006). *Technology flows* are affected by government policy guidance besides the number of research institutions. Employee quality and quantity selection restricts technology flows. Further, entrepreneurial technological level is limited depending on a supportive environment maintaining technological progress. *Money flows* are strongly affected by the investment environment, because the investment environment affects investment attractiveness. *Market flows* are dependent upon economic use value of land and attractiveness of regional concentration. The completeness of related and supporting industries is difficult to achieve because of the trend of detailed specialized division and the industrial complication, variableness

## 2.4 Innovation Diffusion Models

As discussed in Section 2.3, diffusion of innovation, originally as a communications theory, focuses mainly on communication channels, which convey information about an innovation to or within a social system. Innovation diffusion theory started to appear in marketing literature in the 1960s (Mahajan, Muller and Bass, 1990),. Considerable research has been carried out among consumer behavior (Bass, 1969), marketing management (Arndt, 1967; Silk, 1966), marketing science (King, 1963) and management science (Frank, Massy and Morrison, 1964; Robertson, 1967) scholars. Researchers in management and marketing science foster innovation diffusion via various analytical models by forecasting diffusion of an innovation.

The most popular innovation diffusion model in marketing and management literature is the product growth model suggested by Bass (1969). Since the publication of Bass model, the model and its extensions have been applied for forecasting diffusion of innovations in various markets/industries:

1. Industrial technology (Mansfield, 1968; Sharif and Kabir, 1976; Jensen, 1982; Kalish and Lilien, 1986);
2. Cable Television (Dodds, 1973);
3. Agriculture (Hiebert, 1974; Feder and Omara, 1982; Akinola, 1986);
4. Education (Lawton and Lawton, 1979);
5. Consumer durable goods (Olshavsky, 1980; Gatignon, Eliashberg and Robertson, 1989);
6. Optical scanning equipment (Tigert and Farivar, 1981);
7. Video (Lancaster and Wright, 1983);
8. Pharmacy (Rao and Yamada, 1988).

The contributions of Bass model and its extensions through 1970s have been reviewed by Mahajan and Muller (1979). They argue that the objective of an innovation diffusion model is to present the level of spread of an innovation among a given set of potential adopters over time. During 1980s, a number of studies played significant role in understanding assumptions lying behind diffusion models. Hence Mahajan, Muller and Bass (1990) made a second critical review of innovation model and summarized these model developments over 1970s and 1980s in five areas as shown in Table 5.

Since Rogers (2003) provided extensive literature review on diffusion of innovations across various academic disciplines, this section will mainly focus on diffusion models in marketing, management and economics. As the above list reveals, there are different types of innovations. However, the main concern is about technological innovations, since their use by consumers and firms enable their diffusion.

**Table 5** Emergence of Diffusion Modelling Literature in Marketing (Mahajan, Muller and Bass, 1990)

| Research Areas | 1960s | 1970s | 1980s |
|---|---|---|---|
| Basic diffusion models | Formulation of relationship between imitators and innovators over time Saturation effect | | Unbundling of adopters Definition of innovators/imitators Development of models from individual-level adoption decisions |
| Parameter estimation considerations | Estimation when data are available: ordinary least squares estimation procedure | | Estimation when no prior data are available: - Algebraic estimation procedures - Product/market attribute-based analogical estimation procedures Estimation when data are available: - Time-invariant parameter estimation procedures (maximum likelihood, nonlinear least squares) - Time-varying parameter estimation procedures (Bayesian estimation, feedback filters) |
| Flexible diffusion models | | | Systematic (or random) variation in diffusion model parameters over time Flexible diffusion patterns in terms of timing and magnitude of peak of adoption curve |
| Refinements and extensions | | Dynamic diffusion models: Market saturation changes over time Multi-innovation diffusion models: Other innovation influence diffusion of an innovation Space/time diffusion models: Diffusion of an innovation occurs simultaneously in space and time Multistage diffusion models: Adopters pass through a series of stages in the innovation-decision process. | Multigeneration models: Timing and adoption of different generations of an innovation Multistage diffusion models: effect of negative word of mouth in the innovation decision process Diffusion models with marketing mix variables: effect of price (linkage with experience curves), advertising, personal selling, distribution, and timing of new product introduction, on diffusion patterns Controlled diffusion models: effect of supply restrictions on diffusion patterns Multiadoption diffusion models: incorporation of repeat sales and replacement sales in diffusion patterns Competitive diffusion models: effect of competitive actions in terms of pricing, advertising, and number of brands on diffusion patterns |
| Use of diffusion models | Forecasting | Forecasting: problems in use of diffusion models for forecasting | Forecasting: Problems in use of diffusion models for forecasting Descriptive: Testing of hypotheses related to diffusion of innovations across countries, effect of product/market attributes on diffusion patterns, relationship between innovation diffusion and market structure factors such as the experience curve phenomenon and proliferation of number of brands Normative: Derivation of optimal pricing, advertising, and timing strategies in monopoly and oligopoly markets |

## 2.4.1 Epidemic Diffusion Models

Edwin Mansfield is one of the main scholars who studied technical (or technological) change extensively over 40 years. Mansfield (1961) simply asked how soon other firms in the industry use a process innovation, when it is introduced by one firm (i.e. innovator). He investigated the spread of twelve innovations, displayed in Table 6. Mansfield's study has two main conclusions:

1. The diffusion of an innovation is a rather slow process. Many major industrial innovations had spread slowly in the U.S., which increased interests, while the U.S. was focusing on policies to accelerate economic growth in early 1990s.
2. The rate of imitation varies widely. As an example by-product oven is used only by half of firms in bituminous coal industry after 15 years since its first adoption, whereas it took only only three years that half of major coal producers use continuous mining machine.

Table 6 Innovations as Rate of Imitation in Mansfield (1961, 1993)

| Innovation | Industry | Rate of Imitation |
|---|---|---|
| Shuttle car | Bituminous coal | 50% by 5 years |
| Trackless mobile loader | Bituminous coal | |
| Continuous mining machine | Bituminous coal | 50% within 3 years |
| By-product oven | Iron and steel | 50% within 15 years |
| Continuous wide strip mill | Iron and steel | |
| Continuous annealing line for tin plate | Iron and steel | 50% by 13 years |
| Pallet-loading machine | Brewing | 50% by 5 years |
| Tin container | Brewing | 50% within 1 year |
| High-speed bottle filter | Brewing | |
| Diesel locomotive | Railroads | 50% by 9 years |
| Centralized traffic control | Railroads | 50% by 14 years |
| Car retarders | Railroads | 50% by 13 years |

From economics perspective, Mansfield stated that an innovation does not have full economic impact, until the imitation process progresses well. Therefore Mansfield's deterministic and stochastic models argued that the proportion of firms in an industry not using an innovation at time t, but introducing it at time t+1, is a function of

1. the proportion of firms who already use innovation at time t;
2. the profitability of implementing the innovation;
3. the size of investment in order to implement the innovation;
4. other variables.

This is why diffusion corresponds to the familiar S-shaped growth curve, since such epidemic model incorporates the assumption that lack of information about new technology and how to use new technology curb rate of imitation, i.e. diffusion speed (Geroski, 2000). Therefore, different industries react differently to a capital-embodied process innovation. Diffusion of numerically controlled (NC) machine tools in ten U.S. industries replacing conventional machine tools had different rates as shown Table 7, where those inter-industry differences were explained with Mansfield's model. Diffusion of NC machine tools was faster in less concentrated industries, and R&D has positive effect on rate of diffusion (Romeo, 1975).

Table 7 Period of adoption of NC until 25% of firms in that Industry use (Romeo, 1975)

| Industry | Number of Years |
|---|---|
| Aircraft engines | 12.7 |
| Airframe | 12.8 |
| Printing presses | 12.3 |
| Coal Mining Machinery | 10.3 |
| Digital Computers | 9,5 |
| Large Steam Turbines | 8.6 |
| Machine Tools | 9.4 |
| Farm Machinery | 15 |
| Tool and Die | 12.7 |
| Industrial Instruments | 5.9 |

Already at that time Mansfield acknowledged limitations such as changes in profitability over time, sales & promotion efforts by producers of innovations. However, as more information is available and experience accumulates about innovation, it is less risky to use that particular innovation, since uncertainty about profitability is perceived less due to competitive pressure and bandwagon effects. Mansfield's arguments are graphically displayed as cause and effect in Figure 3. Further, the rate of imitation tended to be faster for innovations that were more profitable and that required less investment, as expected.

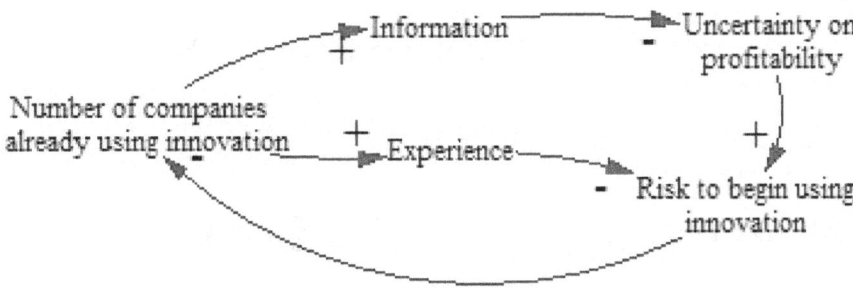

**Figure 3** Use of a Process Innovation (drawn from Mansfield, 1961)

Contrary to Mansfield's (1961) focus on manufacturing industries, Fourt and Woodlock (1960) investigated retail industry, studying early prediction of success or failure of new grocery products. Unlike Mansfield, where each firm can adopt single innovation, they consider both initial and repeat purchases. Hence four variables came into foreground.

1. Penetration: The proportion of households to make an initial purchase of an item.
2. First repeat ratio: The fraction of initial buyers who make a second purchase
3. Subsequent repeat ratios: Ratio of third purchase to second, etc.
4. Time interval between purchases

Their assumption is that price, promotion, distribution, product package, competitive activity are given (i.e. exogenous) and do not change over time. There are durable products that can only be sold one-time to the consumer, which makes penetration a critical success factor. Various empirical studies for grocery products show that there is maximum penetration ratio, which is below 100% of all households. In each time period, the increase in penetration ratio is the multiplication of a constant fraction with the difference between current penetration ratio and maximum possible penetration ratio. Mahajan, Muller and Wind (2000: 100) wrote this relationship in stochastic terms as follows, where p represents the constant fraction, f(t) probability density function, F(t) the proportion of buyers out of all households by time t, S(t) sales as first-time purchase during the unit time period at t, and m is total number of households:

$f(t) / (1-F(t)) = p$ ; $S(t) = me^{-pt}$ [3]

Within the context of grocery products, sales rate declines continuously such that number of households who buy a product for the first time is a negative exponential function of all households over time, whose sample pattern is displayed in Figure 4.

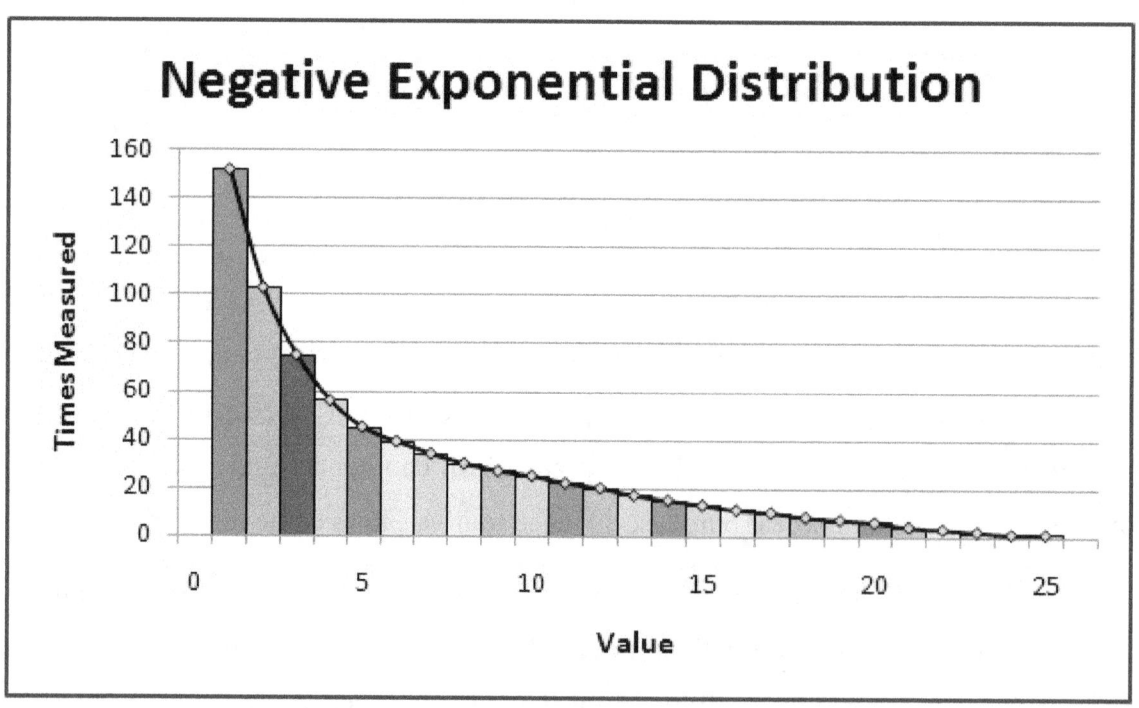

**Figure 4** Negative Exponential Distribution (Meier, et al., 2007)

Actually, this system is one of the common archetypes in system dynamics, called "Balancing Loop". Senge (1999) defines this archetype that balancing loop moves from some current state to a desired state through some action. In sales of grocery products, the penetration percentage via number of households who buy a product approaches to a desired maximum penetration percentage. This dynamics is displayed Figure 5.

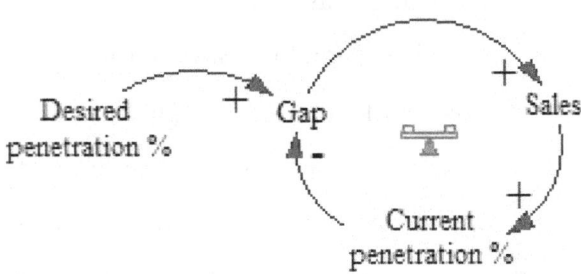

**Figure 5** Balancing Loop of Market Penetration (drawn from Fourt and Woodlock, 1960)

As explained in detail for Mansfield's (1961) model, epidemic models regard diffusion as a result of spread of information (Baptista, 1999). The most frequently criticisms on epidemic models are as follows:

1. Risk is only reduced as the number of users increases, not taking other sources of information, e.g. advertising into account. (Karshenas and Stoneman, 1995)
2. Potential adopters are regarded as passive recipients of information rather than seeking information actively. (Jensen, 1988)
3. Technology is assumed not to change over time, though it undergoes significant changes in terms of flexibility and performance. (Gold, 1981)
4. The population of potential adopters is assumed to be homogenous and constant. It does not change over time ignoring the dynamics of diffusion process. (Davies, 1979)

### 2.4.2 Bass Model

The Bass model comprises and includes the above mentioned models of Fourt & Woodlock and Mansfield as special cases (Mahajan, Muller and Bass, 1990). It is one of the influential models in marketing, where both analytical and empirical evidence is presented for the existence of S-shaped pattern (Mahajan, Muller and Wind, 2000). Bass

(1969) worked on timing of initial purchase of new consumer products for the purpose of model development.

As mentioned previously, Rogers (1962) classified adopters into five categories: Innovators, Early Adopters, Early Majority, Late Majority, Laggards. Bass termed the four categories apart from innovators as imitators. However, contrary to Rogers' definition of innovators as the 2.5% of adopters, Bass defines innovators as those people who adopt independent of decisions of other people in a social system. He argues that adoption pressures for innovators do not increase with the growth of adopters. Mahajan, Muller and Bass' (1990) literature review also state for Bass model that potential adopters are influenced either by mass media (external influence) or word of mouth (internal influence). As shown in Figure 6, innovators are influenced only by mass media communication, whereas imitators are influenced only by word of mouth communication. However, it points out a definition difference for *innovators* among scholars. As Mahajan, Muller and Srivastava (1990) contended, that Bass model's *innovators* are not the first adopters of an innovation, as defined by Rogers (1962).

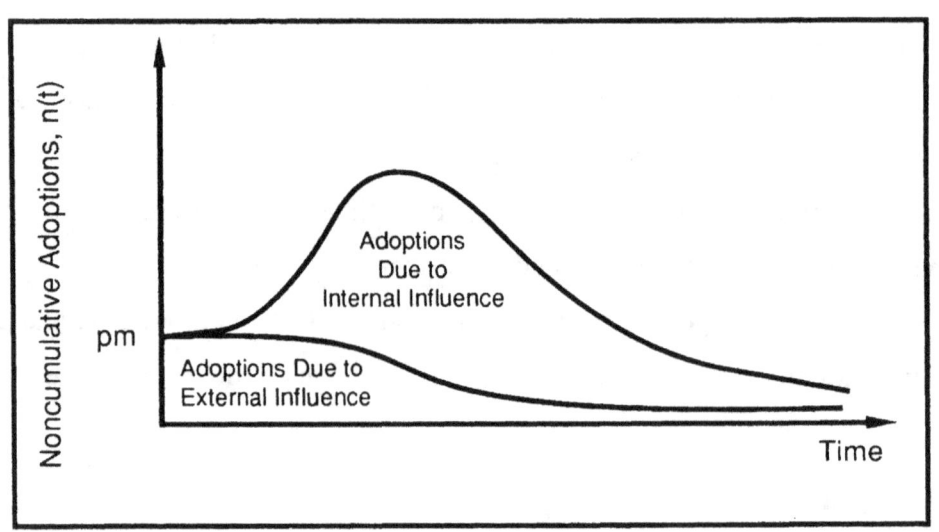

**Figure 6** Adoptions in Bass Model (Mahajan, Muller and Bass, 1990)

Since Bass formulated his assumption as "The probability that an initial purchase will be made at T given that no purchase has yet been made is a linear function of the number of previous buyers." Mahajan, Muller and Bass (1990) wrote the following mathematical expression for the Bass model:

$$n(t) = dN(t)/dt = p\,[m - N(t)] + q/m\,N(t)\,[m-N(t)] \qquad [4]$$

*m* is the market potential, i.e. number of potential adopters, where *n(t)* is number of adopters at time *t* only and *N(t)* is the cumulative number of adopters by time *t*. Bass (1969) referred to *p* as the "coefficient of innovation" and q as the "coefficient of imitation". The first term in equation 4 is indicates number of adopters due to external influence, whereas the second term *q/m N(t) [m-N(t)]* represents number of adopters who are influenced by the number of previous buyers. Equation 4 is graphically shown in Figure 6. Integrating equation 4 results in S-shaped cumulative adopter distribution, as analytically displayed in Figure 7, where the time T*, n(T*) denote the peak of noncumulative adoption curve, and the point of inflection on the cumulative adoption curve.

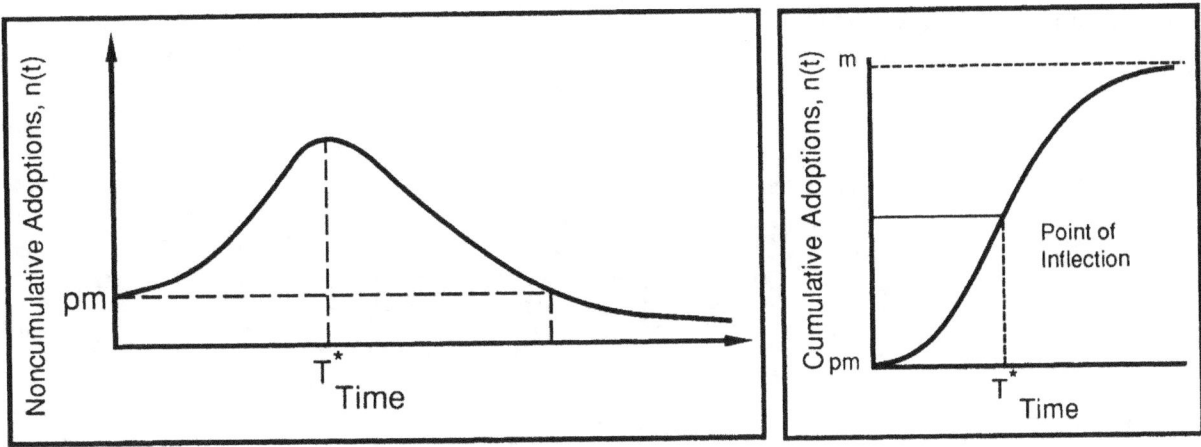

**Figure 7** Bass Model: Analytical Structure (Mahajan, Muller and Bass, 1990)

The use of Bass model for forecasting the diffusion of an innovation requires the estimation of three parameters: the coefficient of external influence (p), the coefficient of internal influence (q), and the market potential (m). To estimate diffusion parameters,

Bass (1969) proposed ordinary least squares (OLS) procedure by regressing adoption on cumulative adoption and cumulative adoption squared. Several estimation procedures for Bass model parameters are outlined in Table 5 within section 2.4. Market potential yields better forecasting results using exogenous sources of information such as management judgment (Heeler and Hustad, 1980), analytical models (e.g. Oliver, 1987). In empirical studies, parameters are usually estimated in cumulative adoption domain, but some utilize time varying estimation procedures (Bass, Krishnan and Jain, 1994). Sultan, Fahrley and Lehmann (1990) carried out a meta-analysis of 213 applications of diffusion models from fifteen articles state average value of 0.03 for coefficient of external influence and 0.38 for coefficient of internal influence. Further, the values of the coefficients are influenced by the type of estimation procedure. The most important application of diffusion models is early forecasting. Therefore, the main issue for a practitioner is why and which estimation procedure to use.

Considering cumulative number of adopters as a stock variable, equation 4 can be shown graphically as Figure 8. Although equation 4 does not foresee discontinuance of new product, the below graphical representation implies that total number of adopters can decline either. The dynamics of causal relationships will facilitate to explore the assumptions of Bass model.

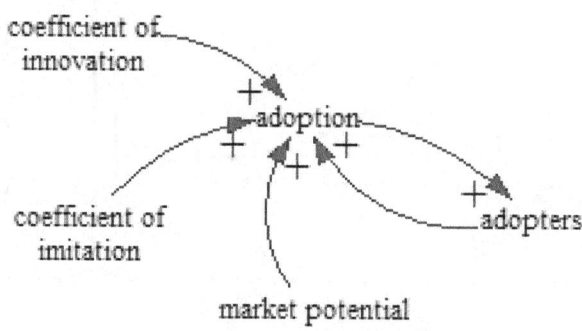

**Figure 8** Drawn from Bass (1969)

Mahajan, Muller and Bass (1990) state nine assumptions for the Bass model. The interpretation of these assumptions will be considered during the next sections when discussing other diffusion models.

1. Market potential remains constant over time.
2. Diffusion of an innovation does not depend on other innovations.
3. Characteristics of an innovation do not change over time.
4. Geographical boundaries of social system remain same during the diffusion process.
5. Potential adopters have only two choices: to adopt or not to adopt. Stages of adoption are not considered in the Bass model.
6. Marketing strategies do not influence diffusion of an innovation
7. Diffusion patterns are not affected by product and market characteristics.
8. Supply restrictions are ignored.
9. There are only first time buyers among adopters.

### 2.4.3 Diffusion Models with Marketing Mix Variables

A major limitation of early models of innovation diffusion such as the Bass model (1969) is that they do not include marketing-mix variables that can be controlled by managers. These models do not serve for policies about pricing and other variables under managerial control. (Mahajan, Muller and Wind, 2000:100)

The main models of innovation diffusion were established by 1970. There are eight different basic mathematical models as in depicted in Table 8, which are applied in modeling diffusion of innovations. Most of diffusion models tried to explain past behavior rather than forecasting future behavior (Meade and Islam, 2006). Because marketing literature places greater emphasis on forecasting performance of new products, a number of efforts are made to extend these basic models (Mahajan and Muller, 1979). Their literature review focused on the following questions:

1. What are the main assumptions for these models?
2. Where have the models been applied?
3. What are the differences among the models?
4. What are the limitations of these models?

5. What need to be done to make these models theoretically more reliable and practically more effective and realistic?

Table 8 Models for cumulative adoption (adapted from Meade and Islam, 2006)

| Literature | Model Name |
|---|---|
| Fourt and Woodlock (1960) | Modified exponential |
| Mansfield (1961) | Logistic |
| Bain (1963) | Cumulative lognormal |
| Rogers (1962) | Cumulative normal |
| Gregg, Hassell and Richardson (1964) | Gompertz |
| Bass (1969) | Bass Model |
| McCarthy and Ryan (1976) | Log reciprocal |
| Sharif and Islam (1980) | Weibull |

Robinson and Lakhani (1975) were the first to introduce decision variables into diffusion models. Their purpose was to examine the effects on profits of differences between optimal pricing policies contrary to myopic pricing policies. They concluded that classic marginal pricing is not optimum at all for a fast evolving business. If price is constant, their model reduces to Bass model. Bass (1980) included a constant-elasticity demand function, since firms choose prices to maximize profits myopically associating marginal revenue to marginal cost in each period. As in many technology products, since marginal costs follow experience curve, prices will be proportional to accumulated output raised to the power of a learning parameter. Under myopic behavior, today's price affects today's demand and does not carry through in the future; demand is a function of time only.

Another modified Bass model tests the impact of price on diffusion speed or market potential (Kamakura and Balasubramanian, 1980). Their empirical study on air conditioners, refrigerators and vacuum cleaners brought out that price significantly has an effect on adoption rate but not on market potential. However, price has no effect in relatively inexpensive product categories: toasters, blenders and mixers. A similar but methodologically different model (continuous time formulation of Bass model) is that price affects either market potential or "effective market potential", i.e. remaining sales potential after actual sales so far (Jain and Rao, 1990). Their model tests with air conditioners, clothes dryers and color televisions indicated that price influenced "effective market potential", which is equivalent to price affecting adoption rate.

### 2.4.4 Probit Models in Economics

In marketing, variations of epidemic diffusion models are based on influential contribution of Bass (1969), as discussed above, whereas they only played a role in earlier literature within economics (Geroski, 2000). Epidemic diffusion models considered that potential adopters would acquire new technology upon receiving information relating to its existence. Interpersonal contact between user and non-users of new technology leads to further use, which makes diffusion process self-propagating. Awareness and information spreading remained important factors in later empirical studies such as flexible manufacturing systems (Mansfield, 1993).

Diffusion models in economics literature are mainly **probit models**, which are alternative to epidemic diffusion models. It follows from the premise that different firms, with different goals, capabilities and actions, are likely to want to adopt the new technology at different times. In these models, diffusion occurs as firms of different types gradually adopt it (Geroski, 2000).

Assuming that all firms or consumers know about the existence of a technology, each individual/firm buying a technology gets different benefits than another. Therefore, an individual/firm will decide to acquire new technology when gross benefits are higher than the cost of acquisition. Since they have different characteristics, they have different gross returns from use of technology (Karshenas and Stoneman, 1993). Hence the rate of diffusion will depend on changes in both benefit and cost of new technology over time. Since technology gets cheaper and improves its performance over time, firms adopt new technology when cost of acquisition for new technology falls below their reservation acquisition cost. Therefore, probit models focus on heterogeneity among firms and are built on rational profit maximizing or utility maximizing behavior (David, 1969). The main categories of probit models are: rank, stock and order models (Karshenas and Stoneman, 1993).

**Rank models**, a category within probit models, assume that a firm's return from new technology does not depend upon its or other firms' use. Following factors influence diffusion path (Stoneman, 2002:44):

1. Firm characteristics: size, location, history, etc.;
2. Discount rates and attitudes towards risk;
3. Expectations about price, technology and market;
4. Number of product variants in the market;
5. Changes in all above.

Davies' (1979) model is an exemplified model for rank models. A firm will be a user of new technology, if firm size is greater than some critical level, assuming that each firm buys one unit of new technology irrespective of its size. The model compares a firm's expected pay-back period with some targeted pay-back period. As adoption of new technology proceeds, expected pay-back period declines, whereas targeted pay-back period increases, because perceived risks associated with new technology decline (Baptista, 1999). Considering that firm size of each potential user in an industry is normally distributed and firm size does not change with respect to time, total industry demand, i.e. diffusion, will follow a sigmoid path. Further, as cost of new technology decreases with respect to other inputs, smaller firms find it more desirable to buy it (Stoneman and Ireland, 1983).

In addition to the premise and empirical regularity that cost of new technology decreases over time, **stock models** assume that an adopter's benefit from new technology reduces as the number of previous adopters increases (Karshenas and Stoneman, 1993). When a firm implements a new process technology, it aims that its production costs decline. This cost reduction may lead a firm to change price it charges for its products. Therefore, it results in changes of the firm's output and in output levels of other firms in the industry. Further the firm's output level after implementing new technology will depend upon adoption behavior of other firms (Stoneman, 2002: 44). Therefore the gain from new technology is the comparison between the firm's profits after new technology and the firm's profits without new technology. Since industry output changes, industry prices are affected and profitability of using new technology changes. Therefore when other firms adopt new technology, a firm's profit, which is not using new technology, may well decline rather than remaining constant.

A major approach among stock models is game theory. In game-theoretic approach, even if firms in an industry have equal size and perfect information about new technology, each firm's adoption date differs due to their strategic behaviors (Reinganum, 1981b). The model showed that payoff from adoption of new technology depends on the stock of firms who are already using new technology. Unlike Reinganum (1981b), Quirmbach (1986) contended that firms choose adoption dates according to incremental benefits from new technology and sunk cost of new technology. Therefore patterns of incremental benefits and adoption costs are key factors for adoption decision whether or not to take firm's strategic behavior into account.

Another application of stock model is by Schumpeter (1934). As more firm use new technology, they generate excess, entrepreneurial profits. As other firms follow, industry output expands. However, demand increases prices for inputs with limited supply, too. Consequently, firms using or not using new technology lose profits. A further development of Schumpeterian analysis is termed as **evolutionary school** (Stoneman, 2002:48). Unlike rank and stock models, perfect information and competition assumptions are seriously questioned. There is more focus on limited information and bounded rationality. In particular, firm sizes are endogenous to the diffusion process as in standard stock models, and changes in firm size cause self-propagating dynamic behavior as seen in epidemic diffusion models. In evolutionary economics, diffusion can be regarded as a selection process among substitute technologies (Baptista, 1999). Firms that invest in good technologies will realize profit gains with respect to other firms and will grow at the expense of others. Therefore, when a non-adopter firm exits the industry, it increases the proportion of firms using that good technology in the industry, similar to the increase when that firm would become user of that technology (Stoneman, 2002:49).

**Order models** assume that a firm's return from adopting new technology depends on the order of adoption. High-order adopters, i.e. firms who adopted earlier, have greater return on their technology investment than low-order adopters, i.e. firms who adopted later (Karshenas and Stoneman, 1993). For a given cost of new technology, it will be profitable only for a certain number of firms who adopted new technology until that time. The net present value of adopting new technology by a firm is related to the number of other firms who already adopted new technology at that adoption date. Early adoption of new technology, being the first user, may cause higher profits for that firm over the whole ownership cycle of that technology (Fudenberg and Tirole, 1975). One reason is that firms who are early users of new technology are able to preempt certain inputs that are in limited supply such as scarce skilled labor. Another reason is that early users of new technology benefit from learning by doing (Stoneman, 2002:50). An adopter firm can also enjoy first mover advantages and affect adoption decisions of other firms.

The first difference of probit models is that adoption decision of individual/firm is considered in comparison to epidemic diffusion models. Further epidemic and evolutionary approaches fall into the category of *disequilibrium* models, where diffusion is self-perpetuating such that use of new technology causes further use tomorrow. The incremental benefit from adopting new technology is compared with the cost of new technology at that particular time such that net present value of adopting new technology is positive and postponing adoption decision is not profitable, when a firm adopts new technology. Therefore, probit models are *equilibrium* models, since diffusion depends on exogenous factors (they are endogenous when supply side of technology, i.e. process innovation is considered); it may stop when technology does not improve or becomes cheaper. Rank models highlight difference among firms and therefore different preferred adoption dates. Stock models point out that profitability of adopting new technology depends on number of other firms who already use new technology. Order approach underlines the position in the order of adoption such that a certain number of firms only will find adoption profitable for a given cost of new technology.

## 2.5 Causal Loops Regarding Innovation Diffusion

### 2.5.1 Technology

Technology is definitely one of the most important factors for economic and social growth (Betz, 1994). An increasing rate of technological change and increase in global competition are two major forces that push organizations to increase their ability to innovate and create value (Jones, 2004:425).

Most social, economic, environmental, etc. changes (shortly called SC, EC and EnC respectively) are either directly caused or related to the following (Drejer, 2002):

1. Development of new technology (DoT)
2. Perception of new technology (PoT)
3. Use of new technology (UoT)

Due to these complex relationships as illustrated in Figure 9, there have been different traditions and approaches to management of technology. From an organization perspective, management of technology not only involves R&D but also the management of product and process technologies.

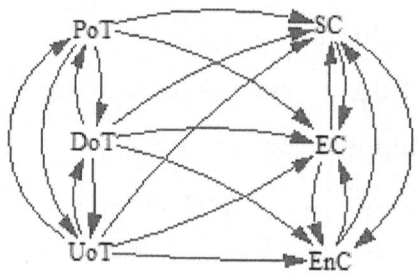

**Figure 9** Causal Relationships of Technology and Change (drawn from Drejer, 2002):

Technological change describes changes in knowledge that either increases output or enable a qualitatively superior output from a given amount of resources (Blackmon, 1996). The S-curve phenomena of technology lifecycle can be described in four stages: technological discontinuity, era o ferment, dominant design, era of incremental improvement (Tushman and Rosenkopf, 1992). Hence there is relationship of technology lifecycle to creative destruction of industries and firms as shown in Figure 10.

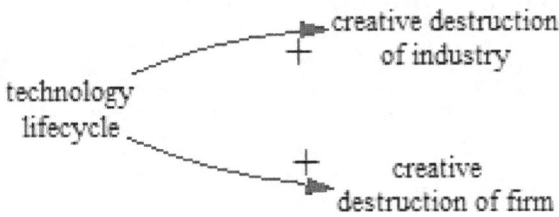

**Figure 10** Technology lifecycle (drawn from Drejer, 2002)

Social scientists have been interested in diffusion of technological and social innovations. An important research question has been which organizational characteristics promote adoption of an innovation (Baldridge and Burnham, 1975). Their empirical study contended that large complex organizations in heterogeneous environments are more probable to adopt innovations than simple organizations in homogenous environments. Since technological change in the environment of firms lead to organizational changes as depicted in Figure 11, management of technology becomes a considerable part of managing a firm (Drejer, 2002).

**Figure 11** Technological innovation (drawn from Drejer, 2002)

A firm has to manage technological knowledge as a resource to gain competitive advantage. Firms want to use technology (Garcia, Kalantone and Levin, 2003). Diffusion of technological innovations, whose empirical studies in industries originate from Edwin Mansfield, is primarily a knowledge transfer and the issue of imitability is central to the analysis of competitive advantage (Spender and Grant, 1996). Since firms innovate for profit, they develop skills and tacit knowledge (Metcalfe, 1994). Evolutionary economists regard innovation as a learning process such that firms acquire and enhance their core competences (Bessant and Rush, 1993), whereas firms need to reengineer their internal operations in order to gain to full benefits of technology such that they can obtain competitive advantage, if any (Ramamurthy and Premkumar, 1995). Since there is market pull for new technology due to decreasing technology life cycles, knowledge workers and new organizational forms form the base for competitive advantage, as graphically shown in Figure 12.

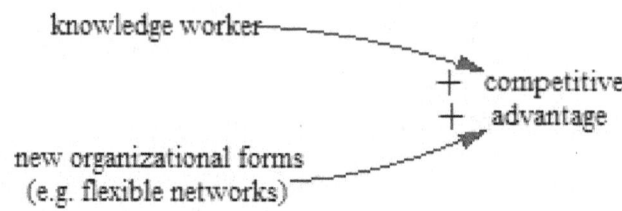

**Figure 12** Competitive advantage (drawn from Drejer, 2002)

A contingency is an event which might take place and must be planned for such as changing technology, to which organizations have to respond (Jones, 2004:13). According to contingency approach in organization theory, an organization designs its structure to fit the environment. Within strategic management and management of technology, contingency models incorporate historical view on contingency factors separating different schools of thought as depicted in Figure 13. However, dividing management of technology into four schools of thought is similar to Henry Mintzberg's five organizational schools who later proposed more schools of thought (Drejer, 2002). A technological change from one S-curve to another, as discussed in section 2.1.2, can have different implications to different firms. Further, evolution of firms over time requires varieties of technology management at different time periods.

**Figure 13** Management of Technology Theory (drawn from Drejer, 2002)

Network externalities occur when the value of a product/service to users increases, as the number of users rises (Gowrisankaran and Stavins, 1994). Technologies such as fax, e-mail possess market externalities, i.e. until users reach critical mass, their relative advantage is not clear at the beginning (Markus, 1987). Each user increases his/her own utility, as more people/organizations use that technology (Teng, Grover and Güttler, 2002). As externality increases, the desire for compatibility increases as well. (Lange, McDade, and Oliva, 2004)

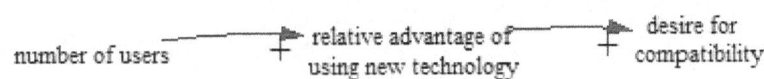

**Figure 14** Network externalities (drawn from Mahajan, Muller and Wind, 2000)

Although government and industry associations are important actors in determining standards, usually market forces shape up technology choices. Dominant firms achieve standardization either individually or by collaborating with other firms. (Mahajan, Muller and Wind, 2000)

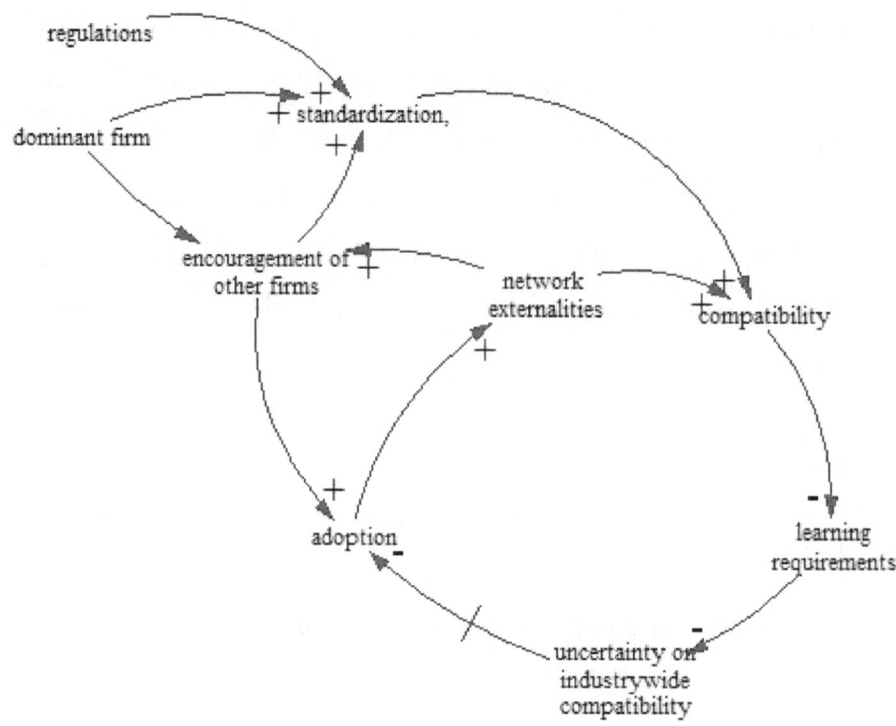

**Figure 15** Product compatibility (drawn from Mahajan, 2000)

Technology is a key resource of profound importance for corporate profitability and growth. When a company considers investing in technology in order to realize process innovation, it certainly experiences risk and uncertainty due to several aspects. Taking all companies in a particular industry into account, when a company uses that technology, other companies perceive less uncertainty. Hence they start to use technology. This self-propagating nature of diffusion is shown in Figure 16. Regarding expected profitability, price of technology and its maintenance costs may not be clear. In addition to cost of technology, its performance can be uncertain such that additional profitability by the means of adopting new technology can be ambiguous. (Stoneman, 2002: 55)

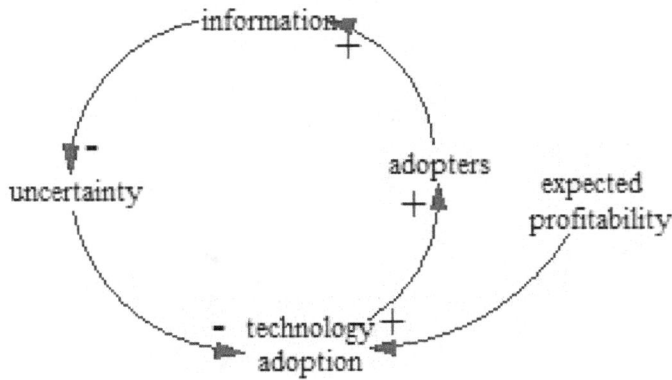

**Figure 16** Diffusion of process technologies (drawn from Stoneman, 2002:56)

### 2.5.2 Industry

The probability that a given firm will adopt a product or process is thought to be an increasing function of the proportion of firms in the industry already using it and of the profitability of doing so, but a decreasing function of the size of the investment required (Mansfield, 1968). Such epidemic theories have been criticized due to primitive choice theory (Stoneman and Ireland, 1983).

There are several industry (or market) related constructs that might influence the diffusion of a new technology in a particular industry. Firm size for example is one of the most common constructs in innovation diffusion literature. Some papers provide approaches incorporating explicit theories of technique choice. Thus David (1969) and Davies (1979) build a probit, or threshold firm size, model. Their models indicate that the probability is higher that larger firms become users of a new technology. David's model states that smaller firms tend to buy new technology, when price of new technology decreases relative to other costs. When firms are ranked with respect to their expected returns of using new technology from highest to lowest, each firm has its threshold cost to justify the cost for adopting new technology. According to Baptista (1999), since adoption of new technology is costly, only larger firms are able to take risks of adoption, because their expected profitability is higher due to scale economies. As technology gets cheaper and quality improves, when the adoption cost of new technology becomes lower than the threshold costs of more firms (Karshenas and Stoneman, 1993; Popp, 2005). This relationship among firm size, price and adoption is shown in Figure 17.

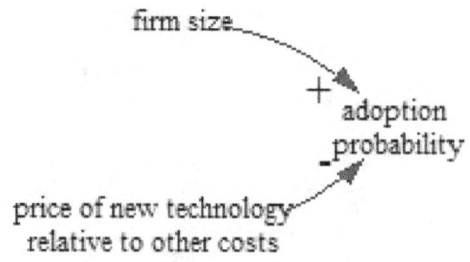

**Figure 17** Firm size and price on adoption (drawn from Stoneman and Ireland, 1983)

Unlike epidemic theories, where adoption rate depends on the number of firms, who already use technology, rank effects consider the beginning of diffusion with the adoption decision of the individual firm. Since firms want to increase their profits and adoption cost of new technology is presumed to fall over time, diffusion is a sequential adoption by individual firms instead of simultaneous one (Götz, 1999). Rank effects indicate that firms differ about expected returns from adoption due to differences in firm size, market shares, R&D expenditures, and expected profitability of a new technology. Götz (1999) states a positive relationship between firm size and speed of adoption assuming that adoption cost of new technology is indivisible, similar many other studies on innovation diffusion (rank models, Karshenas and Stoneman, 1993; higher expected profitability due to scale economies, Davies, 1979). Decreasing firm size delays adoption, if adoption cost of new technology is independent of size. However, there may be a linear relationship between adoption costs and firm size, which throws away the indivisibility assumption of new technology, i.e. smaller firms can buy new technology in lower cost due to smaller scale and scope (Colombo and Mosconi, 1995). This reciprocal relationship of firm size and adoption cost is demonstrated in Figure 18.

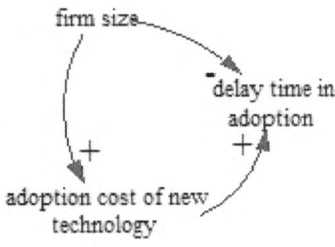

**Figure 18** Firm size and adoption cost (drawn from Götz, 1999)

Further, stock effects assume that a firm's expected return from adoption decreases, as the number of previous adopters increases. Therefore for a certain adoption cost of new technology, a certain amount of firms becomes adopters. As the adoption cost of new technology declines, other firms become further adopters. Since previous adopters lead to changes in industry output, expected profitability, i.e. return from adoption is affected (Karshenas and Stoneman, 1993). Such situations are characterized as game-theoretic. There is mathematical proof that an industry comprising identical firms producing same good with no imperfect information yield different adoption dates due to their strategic behavior (Reinganum, 1981b) The incremental profit of a firm due to adoption of new technology becomes less, as previous adopters increase until the adoption of that firm. The assumption that adoption cost of new technology falls over time is also displayed in indicating closed loop relationships among firm profitability and use of new technology changing over time. The models discussed so far in this section consider the diffusion process as a demand phenomenon.

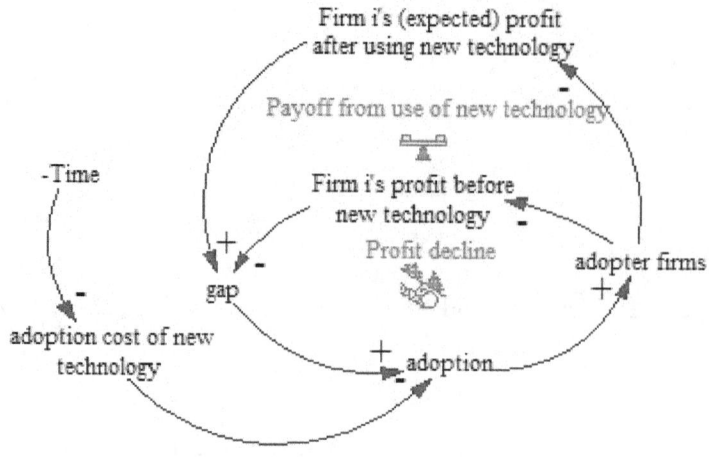

**Figure 19** Stock effects of adoption (drawn from Reinganum, 1981)

Without distinguishing epidemic, rank or stock effects of technology diffusion, firm size is an important factor. Larger firms have usually more experience and better resources for absorbing new and complex technology. Lack of awareness, resources, and experience in innovation might be some reasons that some firms are late adopters. These are smaller firms or firms in less technologically advanced industries. (Bessant and Rush, 1993)

### 2.5.3 Technology Suppliers

The most important management question for technology suppliers is how they make suitable and timely decisions in order to diffuse new technology to adopters. As discussed in Section 2.4, most of diffusion models are deterministic, binomial (i.e. adoption or no adoption) and result in a typical S-shaped diffusion curve. Regarding the diffusion process, the probability of adoption by a new user depends on the quality of experience by existing users. Hence satisfied users lead to subsequent diffusion (Yeon et al., 2006). This causal relationship is shown in Figure 20.

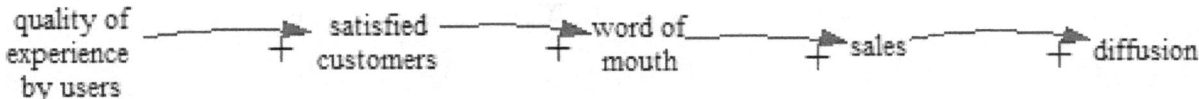

**Figure 20** Causal relationship between User Experience and Diffusion (drawn from Yeon et al., 2006)

However, suppliers tend to disseminate technology hypes, in order to improve sales in the short-term, which increase customer expectations. However, those customers are often dissatisfied due to exaggerated expectations, which impede diffusion in the longer term (Swann, 2001). This causal relationship is depicted in Figure 21.

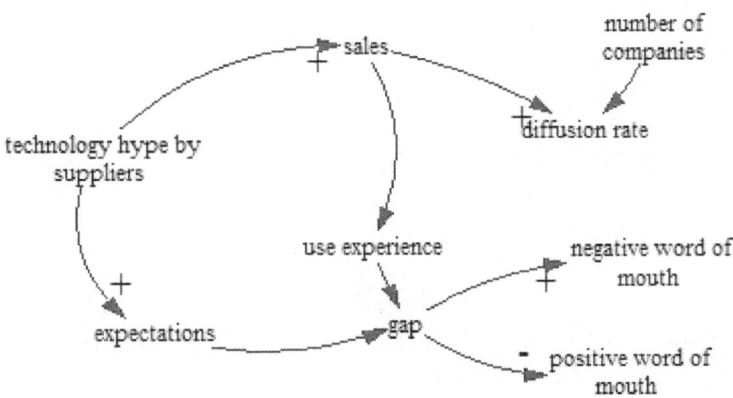

**Figure 21** Impact of Technology Hype on Diffusion (drawn from Swann, 2001)

The diffusion process should clearly define behaviors due to causal relationships and feedbacks among variables. Further, the dominance of which feedback mechanism may alter the behavior of diffusion. Wind and Mahajan (1987) argue that marketing hype programs to influence adoption of a new product may have side effects such as cost, increased expectations and legal consequences. The causal relationships in addition to the ones in the above paragraphs are displayed in Figure 22.

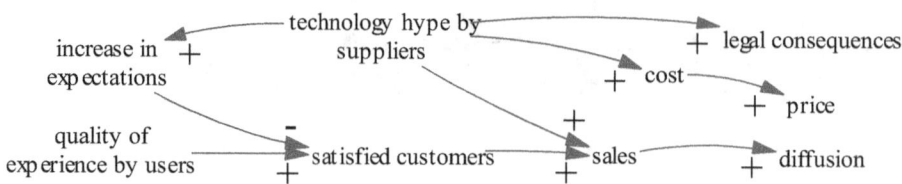

**Figure 22** Customer Satisfaction andDiffusion
(drawn from Mahajan, Muller and Wind, 2000 and Yeon et al., 2006)

Mathematical models in the diffusion literature are usually in logistic functional form. The underlying hypothesis is that the number of firms who use technology and the potential number of firms who do not use technology yet, determine the speed of adoption for new technology (Yeon et al., 2006). This relationship is illustrated in Figure 23.

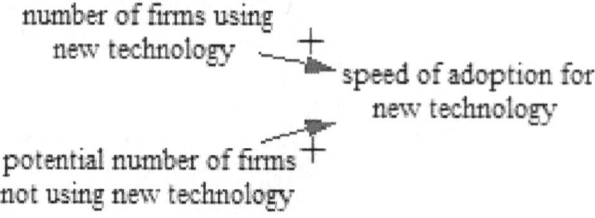

**Figure 23** Diffusion models' assumption drawn from Yeon et al. (2006)

As also shown in Figure 22, technology adoption is related to user satisfaction. Technology Acceptance Model (TAM) states that internal beliefs, attitudes and intentions influence are influenced by external factors. For information technologies, Davis (1989) formulated that perceived usefulness (PEOU) and perceived ease of use (PU) are the main determinants whether a firm decides to use technology. Same argument is valid for consumers as well, which is shown in Figure 24 as a generic causal relationship.

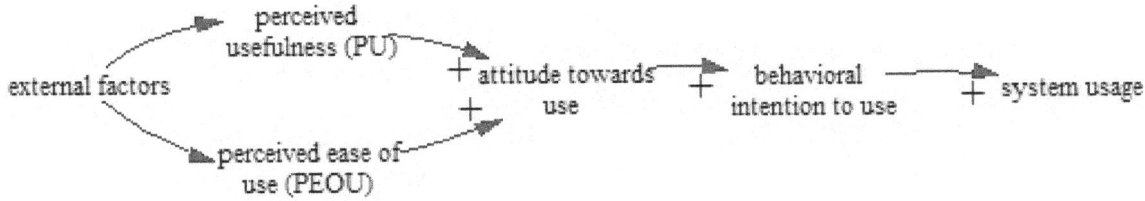

**Figure 24** Technology Acceptance Model (drawn from Davis, 1989)

Diffusion models are actually customer satisfaction models (Yeon et al., 2006). Philip Kotler, the marketing guru, defines customer satisfaction as post-consumption evaluation of product quality with respect to expectations prior to purchase. An extensive literature review on customer satisfaction based on various consumer studies indicate that expectations, perceived quality, disconfirmation are the forerunners of customer satisfaction (Oliver, 1980; Yi, 1991).

Anderson and Sullivan (1993) introduce an analytical framework for customer satisfaction based on expectation-disconfirmation paradigm. The degree that perceived quality does not correspond to expectations prior to purchase is labeled as disconfirmation. Buyers have expectations prior to purchase. After they have bought, they regard a perceived quality level influenced by the difference between expectation and actual product quality. Since perceived quality can increase or decline, it can confirm or disconfirm those expectations prior to purchase. This analytical model, as shown in Figure 25, categorizes disconfirmation as negative and positive disconfirmation. Expectations are presumed to affect perceived quality in positive way. Ease of evaluating disconfirmation will increase magnitude of disconfirmation construct in positive or negative direction.

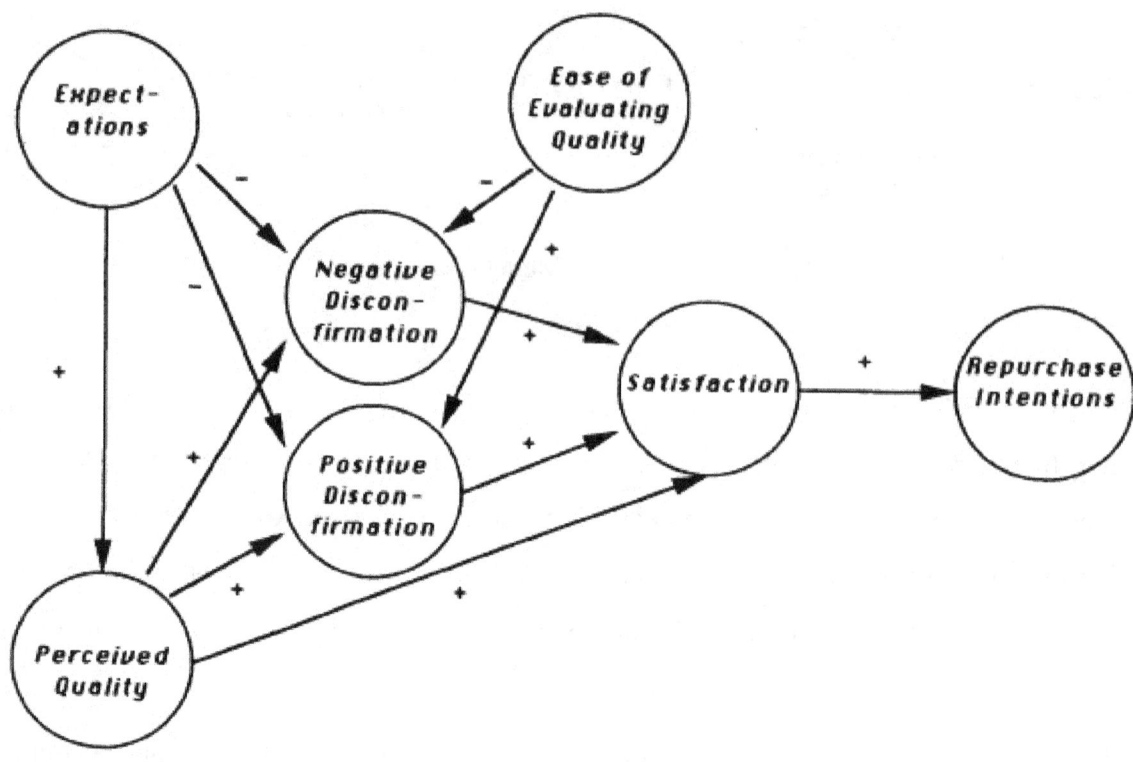

**Figure 25** Analytical framework for customer Satisfaction (Anderson and Sullivan, 1993)

Empirical studies, mentioned in Anderson, Fornell and Lehmann (1994), indicate that quality affects customer satisfaction positively, and customer satisfaction (0.4) leads to profitability. Customer satisfaction requires experience with a product/service and is an overall indicator based on past, current and future performance of the firm. Customer satisfaction can be regarded as value as a ratio of perceived quality with respect to benefits and price (cost to the consumer). Although increased expectation has negative effect on customer satisfaction in the short-term, customer satisfaction is affected positively in the long term, because expectations capture knowledge about past quality information and experience from the market. These dynamic relationships can be viewed in Figure 26.

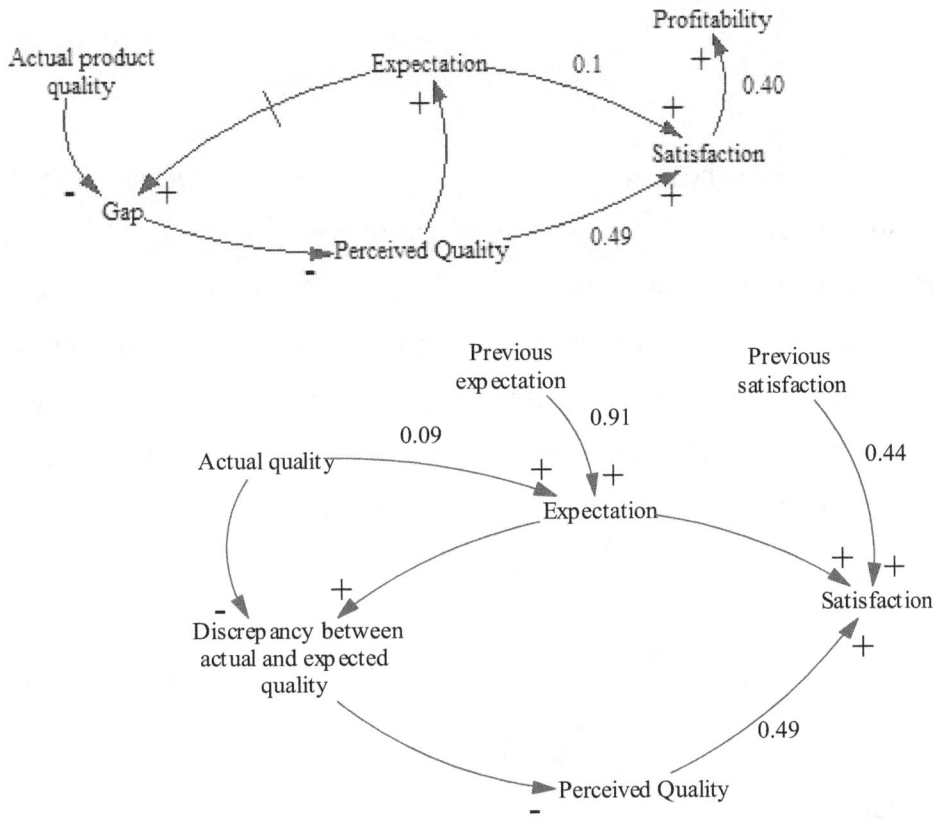

**Figure 26** Customer Satisfaction (drawn from Anderson, Fornell and Lehmann, 1994)

### 2.5.3.1 Technology Market

Various studies find out a negative relationship between price of technology and adoption probability. They claim that price expectations influence adoption positively (Karshenas and Stoneman, 1993). The causal relationship is shown in Figure 27. Further, there are other relationships between technology and price. Increase in fuel prices trigger development and use of fuel saving technologies, whereas increase in wages lead companies to invest in labor saving technologies (Rose and Joskov, 1994; Hannan and McDowell, 1984)

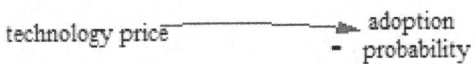

**Figure 27** Price and adoption (drawn from Karshenas and Stoneman, 2003)

Consumers buy new products, when the actual price is below the consumer's reservation price s/he would buy and vice versa. Though, since there is uncertainty about the new product's performance, the reservation price is the expected value of the two outcomes, which is clearly lower than the value under full information. Once consumers are informed about the product, the individual's reservation price increases, since there is no more uncertainty (Kalish, 1985). Further he argues that price is increasing, if advertising is decreasing. These causal relationships are displayed in Figure 28.

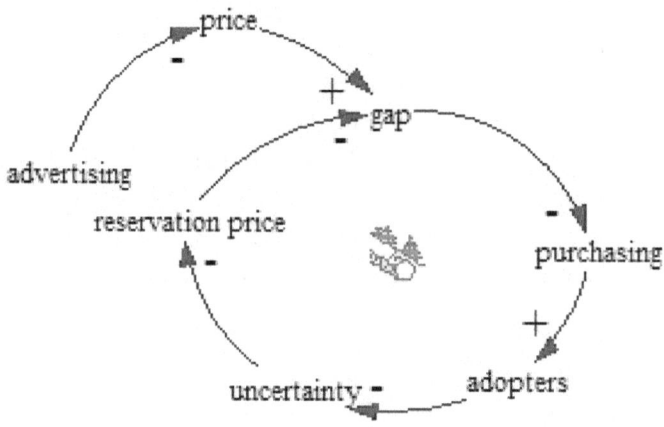

**Figure 28** Reservation price (drawn from Kalish, 1985)

Demand for a new product does not depend on current price, but also on consumer expectations about future price of that product. Kamakura and Balasubramanian (1988) examined two ways in which price may affect the diffusion of new products, one in which price affects the market potential and the other in which price affects the rate of diffusion. There are two problems with incorporating price in the Bass diffusion model using their approach.

1. They used the discrete-time formulation of the Bass model to incorporate the effects of price;

2. It is not obvious that the way price is modeled to impact the rate of adoption is appropriate, since the rate of adoption is independent of price.

OECD studies indicate that price is key factor when U.S. companies spend for information systems. Therefore technology suppliers influence the diffusion pattern of an IT innovation (Green and Hevner, 2000). Expectations of new generations of products will reduce the rate of diffusion by setting the price level before the launch. Sales will decline as potential adopters expect new products to be available soon and restrain from adopting existing ones. The accumulated sales will release after the launch, raising the adoption level considerably in a very short time. This causal relationship added to Figure 28, is shown in Figure 29.

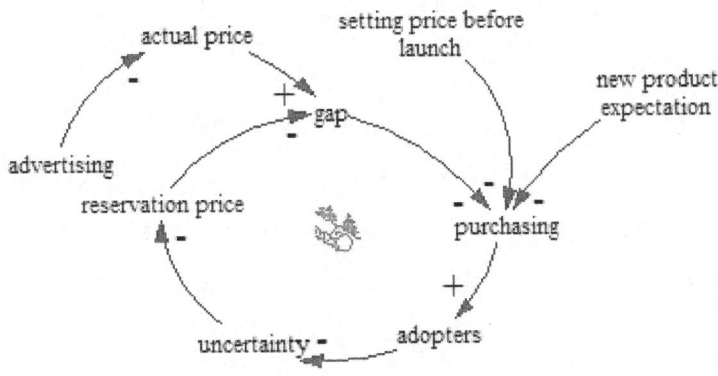

**Figure 29** Price and new product (drawn from Kalish, 1985; Tam and Hui, 1999)

Kim and Srivastava (2005) indicate that price of one product category can influence market size of related product categories. As argued by Robinson and Lakhani (1975), conventional price theory is based on market demand corresponding to sales volume, which is related to unit price and cost structure based on unit cost and production volume. Profit is maximized, when marginal revenue is equal to marginal cost. The causal relationships in price models have been displayed in Figure 30 as follows:

**Figure 30** Dynamic price model (drawn from Robinson and Lakhani, 1975)

Sales growth pattern of an innovation, whether it is new product or service, and factors bringing about the diffusion process have been an important study area in marketing from theoretical, behavioral perspective, and also quantitative modeling perspectives. The diffusion modeling tradition in marketing (Bass 1969) owes its conceptual foundation to mathematical models of contagion in such applications as the diffusion of news and rumors (Bartholomew 1967). The modeling approach takes an aggregate perspective and formulates a differential equation (or a-'set of equations) to specify the flow(s) between mutually exclusive and collectively exhaustive subgroups (e.g., adopters and nonadopters in a two-state model). This modeling paradigm has produced a rich stream of literature. According to the study of thirty-two products, there is positive relationship between incubation time and time to peak sales and a negative association with the coefficient of innovation as shown in Figure 31. They found no evidence that the incubation time was changing over time; this led them to comment that innate innovativeness is not increasing (Kohli, Lehmann and Pae, 1999). Though findings of a study, which examined diffusion speed of innovations over the period 1923-1996, showed that diffusion speed increased with respect to the past due to increased purchasing power, demographic changes, and characteristics of products in the study (Van den Bulte, 2000).

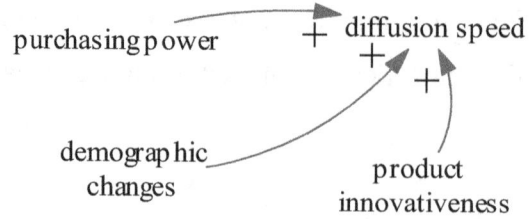

**Figure 31** Innate innovativeness

(drawn from Meade and Islam, 2006)

As Meade and Islam (2006) indicated from innovation diffusion literature, it may not be possible to classify first-time purchase of a product (i.e. adoption) and replacement purchases. As a product/technology becomes mature, the proportion of repeat purchase out of total sales increases. A different but similar example is from Norton and Bass (1987), which studied high technology products analyzing dynamic sales behavior of successive generations, where sales data of computer processors have been analyzed in terms of both diffusion and substitution. The causal relationships in their mathematical equations are displayed in Figure 32.

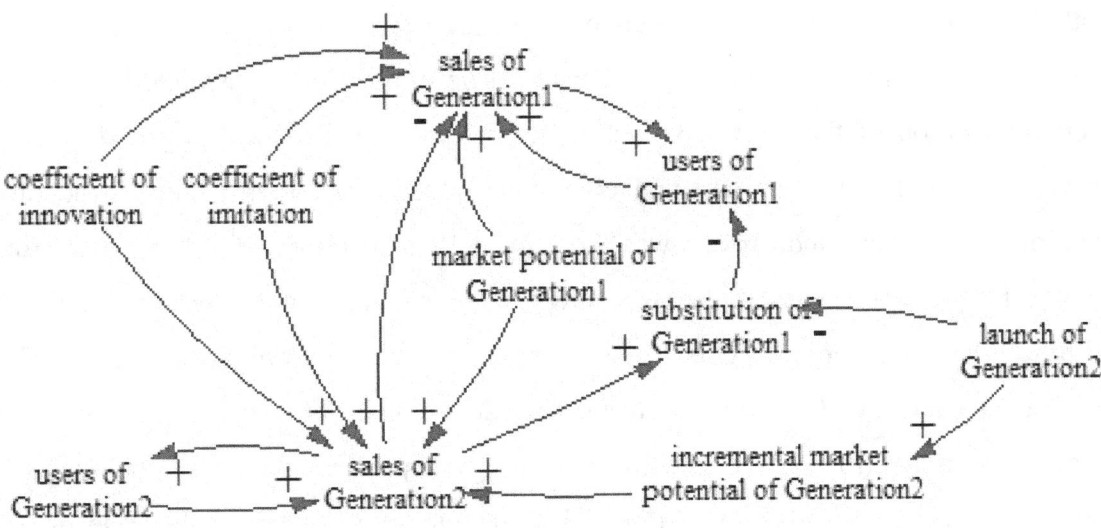

**Figure 32** Sales of successive generations (drawn from Norton and Bass, 1987)

Technology suppliers do not only need sales, but also want to make profit when selling technologies as process innovations. Quirmbach (1986) points out market structure differences among both technology suppliers as the seller's side of the capital equipment market and firms as buyers of capital equipment. When market power is on the side of technology suppliers, adoption is faster than is socially optimal. When market power is on the buyer's side, firms want to protect their existing investment, which slows down diffusion. When there is no market power, on either side, diffusion of capital equipment is still faster than socially optimal. This relationship between diffusion and market power is indicated in Figure 33.

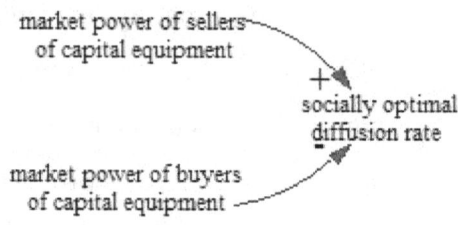

**Figure 33** Market Power (drawn from Quirmbach, 1986)

Another important determinant of revenue for technology suppliers is possible change in price of a new product/technology. When a new product is invented, even the commercialization of that particular innovation takes time. Bayus, Kang and Agarwal (2005) gave the example of personal computer industry that there is an introductory period of low sales and industry growth. Prices usually start high and decrease over time. They refer to some previous studies that new firm entry (Agarwal and Bayus, 2002) and declining prices (Golder and Tellis, 1993) increase the likelihood of sales take-off. Their empirical analysis of 30 markets indicate that declining prices slow down new firm, though firms may still want to become technology suppliers as well, if they regard a revenue-cost differential due to relatively low development costs. In the case of high development costs, new-entry firms still occur, when they expect price stability to compensate additional costs. These multiple relationships are displayed in Figure 34.

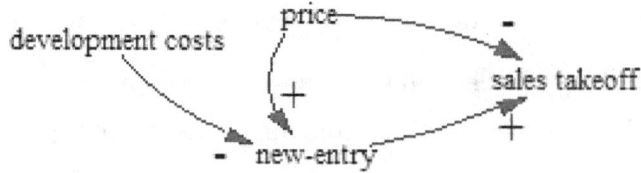

**Figure 34** Price and Firm Entry (drawn from Bayus, Kang and Agarwal, 2005)

### 2.5.4 Social Networks

Learning through social networks is a common phenomenon (Borgatti and Cross, 2003) and there are several studies which aim to reveal how the properties of social networks can help businesses (e.g. business power and corporate elite, Scott, 1991; network power, Barabasi, 2002; collaboration and value creation, Dawson, 2003). This individual based interaction increases the (technology) awareness. As summarized in Figure 35, the probability of someone seeking information from another person is a function of several variables such as communication (Krackhardt and Hanson, 2003) and interaction (Borgatti and Cross, 2003).

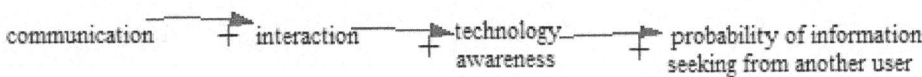

**Figure 35** Information flow (drawn from Krackhardt and Hanson, 2003; Borgatti and Cross, 2003)

There are even some (government or private) companies which are kind of knowledge brokers in that they don't actually produce anything themselves, but are more in the business of spreading information to those who need it (Hargadon, 1998). These efforts will definitely increase the level of innovation diffusion as shown in Figure 36.

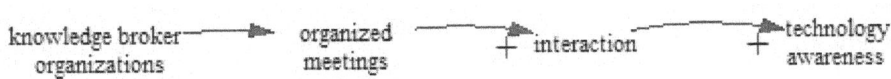

**Figure 36** Information spread (drawn from Hargadaon, 1998)

Social network is a significant field for the analysis of innovation diffusion. Some major variables need to be comprehensively evaluated to understand the correlation between social network and the diffusion of a technology.

Communication may be considered as the most critical variable. Two types of communication structures exist in any social system: formal and informal. A formal structure is designed to promote goal fulfillment, process control, and predictability. This structure gives regularity and stability to the system and tries to reduce the uncertainty of human behavior within the system. Informal structures include mechanisms like friendships, leisure activities, and gossip that are not designed consciously or explicitly. They usually come into existence because of the members' social needs. (Raghavan and Chand, 1989)

Internal influence, on the other hand, is the influence that the members of a social system exert on one another as a result of their social interaction (Lekvall and Wahlbin, 1973). The active use of friendship relationships in information seeking concerning the innovation not only reinforces the societal findings but makes real the concept of diffusion as a social process in the industry (Czepiel, 1974).

Similarly, research on innovation diffusion has social science research in its foundation and is inspired by the early works of Tarde (1903, cited in Rogers, 2003). Many of the early works in innovation diffusion have taken the factor model approach. The aggregate findings suggest that change agent and opinion leadership, interaction patterns among members of the social system, communication channels, and effects of diffused innovation are important factors in innovation diffusion. (Higa et al., 1997)

The entity of innovators can affect such factors as the type of innovation selected for adoption, the nature of interactions between the source of an innovation and an adopter, the importance of strong vs. weak social ties in adoption, and the macro vs. micro character of adoption outcomes. Individual actors adopt innovations with mainly private personal, individual consequences. Such innovations depend on interactions through strong ties, such as the community ties and face-to-face interactions critical and the network connectedness that facilitates interpersonal interactions in the adoption of scientific methods in professional specialties (Wejnert, 2002) as shown Figure 37.

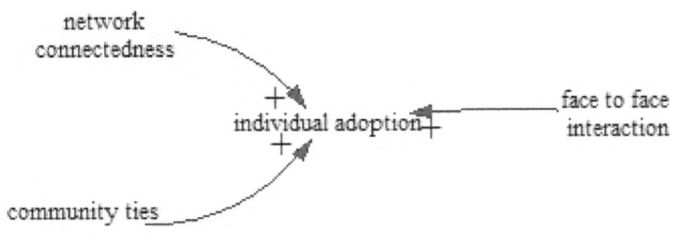

**Figure 37** Interaction on adoption (drawn from Wejnert, 2002)

Since timing of adoption typically depends on the interaction of social units in a process of communication (Rogers, 2003), a major focus in diffusion research has been on variables that mediate communication processes—including both the transmission and absorption of information—between members of societal microstructures. Interactions can occur between individuals, between individuals and the media, or via business/professional organizations. Thus, research has examined an actor's position in social networks in relation to their interactions within four major spheres: (a) interpersonal networks for individual actors, (b) organizational networks for collective actors, (c) structural equivalence of individual and collective actors, and (d) social density. (Wejnert, 2002)

National innovation systems are generally recognized as comprising complex functions and interactions among various institutions involved in the generation, diffusion, and utilization of innovations (Chang and Shih, 2005). An important aspect of the process of innovation diffusion is the network of interpersonal communication that links potential adopters to each other. A perfect network structure is one where there is perfect mixing in the population, that is, every person has an equal chance of communicating with every other person. (Frenzen and Nakamoto, 1993)

Many economists acknowledge that technological innovation and progress result from numerous interactions between industries and technologies (Lin, Tung and Huang, 2006). This study, therefore, includes the effect of external pressure, such as government pressure and industry pressure on the adoption decision, which is shown in Figure 38.

Government pressure relates to the efforts of the governmental agencies to encourage e-Government services adoption.

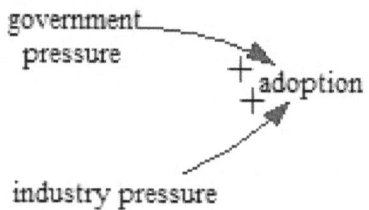

Figure 38 External pressure on adoption (drawn from Tung and Rieck, 2005)

Industry pressure relates to the efforts of industry associations or lobby groups to encourage adoption (Chwelos et al., 2001). Finally, a third external pressure may arise when organizations presume that competitors may gain comparative advantages as a result of using e-Government services. Hence, we also considered the impact of competitive pressure in our study, referring to the ability to maintain or increase competitiveness within the industry (Tung and Rieck, 2005)

### 2.5.5 Public Policies

Since both economists and policy makers agree that technical change is essential to economic growth, generating and sustaining growth is a major target of public policy (Greenaway, 1994). Public policy is necessarily variable and as a result it changes with changing conditions (Husserl, 1938). As discussed in section 1.1, Schumpeter's distinction between invention, innovation, diffusion lets policy makers realize that invention of products/services and their commercialization does not provide major benefits, if there is no widespread use. This argument is particularly valid for process innovations (Greenaway, 1994). Hence one of the main interests of this study is to analyze the variability of public policy from the perspective of innovation diffusion.

Policy debates concerns three main topics: rationale, instrument and impact. Corresponding to each topic, governments face following questions for their following policy making. (Stoneman, 2000:175)

1. Rationale – Why should government intervene?
2. Instruments – How should government intervene?
3. Impact – What is the impact of previous interventions?

In particular government policies are subject to study. Although there are various levels of government policies such as regional, national or supra national (e.g. European Union), the instruments for analysis are regarded as same. Public policies in most developed economies focused until recently on invention and innovation such that science and R&D have been targets of government policies, not technology diffusion. Though public authorities realize that it is diffusion of process innovations and use of technology that create productive potential and competitiveness, public authorities direct their policy efforts towards technology diffusion. (Stoneman and Diederen, 1994)

Stoneman and Diederen (1994) provide both the rationale for intervention and to look close at past diffusion policies and impacts. Use of new technology is the interaction of supply and demand factors. Demand depends on pattern of costs of acquiring technology along time, whereas supply is concerned with cost of producing technology and pricing strategy changing over time. These factors are shown as cause-effect relationships in Figure 39.

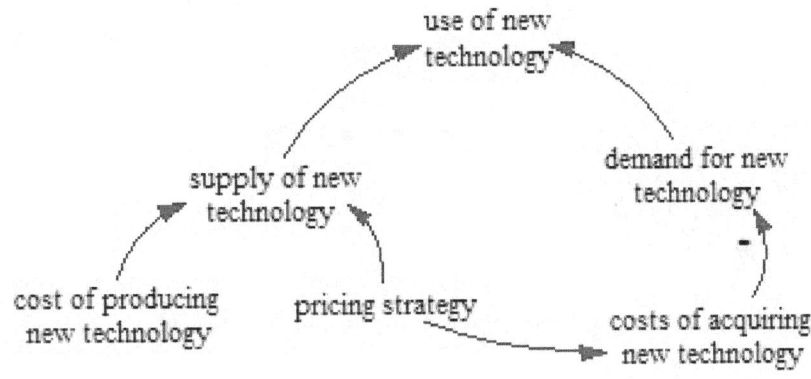

**Figure 39** Supply and Demand Interaction (drawn from Stoneman and Diederen, 1994)

Effectiveness of public policies is considered as the net present value of social benefits and costs. The benchmark is the welfare optimal diffusion path, where the social benefit of adoption of technology by an additional user (e.g. firm) is equal to additional social cost for producing that technology. Though defining a welfare optimal diffusion path for new technology is complex, since there are both improvements in new technology and in use of new technology. There is a feedback mechanism, since technology suppliers allocate more resources into research and development, because they make more profits during earlier stages of innovation diffusion process. That firms adopt new technology as fast as possible may not be desirable, since a less developed technology with higher price can be purchased today instead of better or cheaper technology in the future. Due to market failure, actual diffusion can differ from optimal diffusion path. These relationships in addition to supply and demand interaction are exhibited in Figure 40.

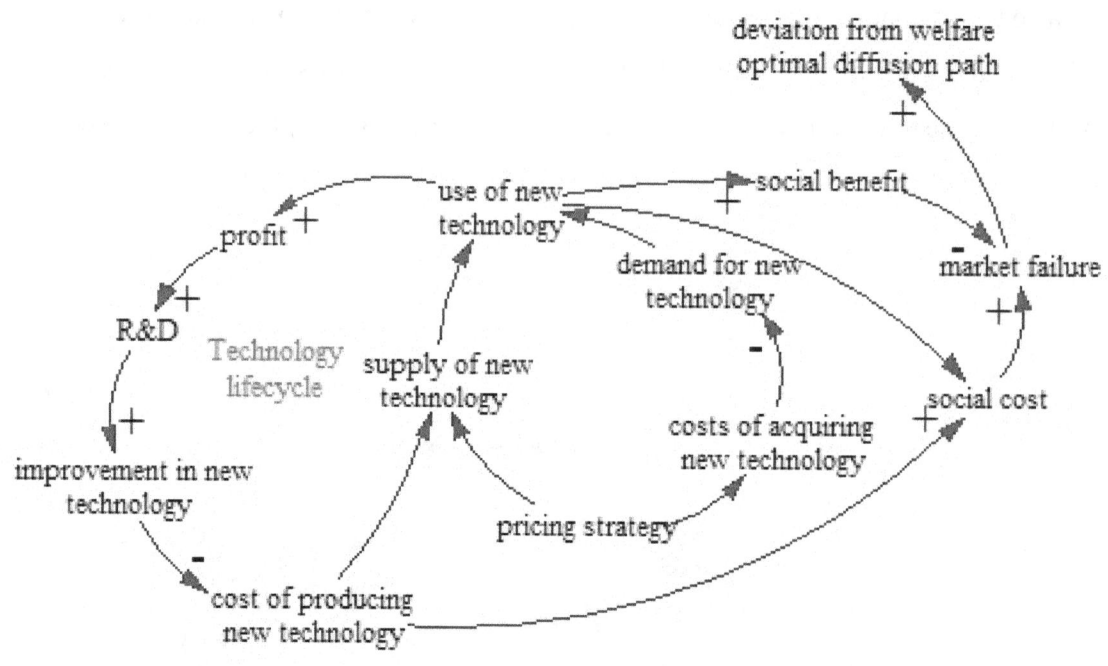

**Figure 40** Diffusion Path (drawn from Stoneman and Diederen, 1994)

### 2.5.5.1 Imperfect Information

There are three sources of market failure that relate to diffusion of innovation: imperfect information, market power, and externalities (Stoneman and Diederen, 1994). Both theory and empirical studies reveal that technological change in terms of both change and direction is influenced by market and regulatory incentives (Jaffe, Newell and Stavins, 2005). Their research about environmentally beneficial technologies confirms that properly designed regulations create such incentives. Hence, environmental policies can incorporate two approaches: one that promotes payoff from new technologies and one that that encourages development and diffusion of new technologies. Governments should try various ways to minimize policy problems. Therefore governments should have systematic policy evaluation, such that policy initiatives can be terminated or improved without becoming failure of policy experimentation. These policy associations are displayed as causal loop in Figure 41.

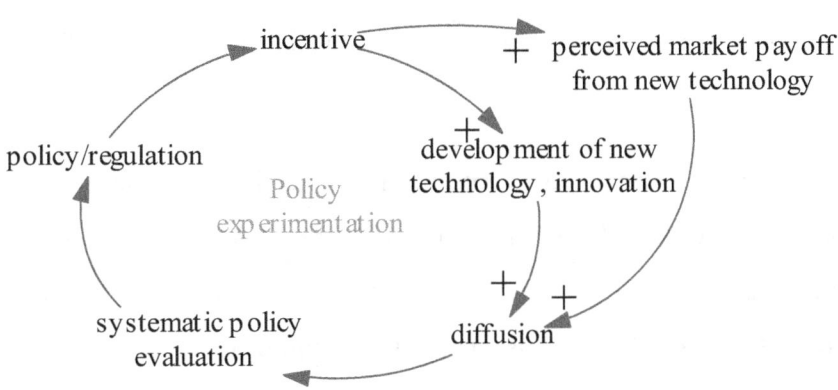

**Figure 41** Public policies (drawn from Jaffe, Newell and Stavins, 2005)

Jaffe, Newell and Stavins (2005) argue that imperfect information can slow down the diffusion of new technology. Information has public good attributes. Therefore, once it is becomes available, many other people can use it at little or no additional cost. Apart from imperfect information about characteristics of new technology, expectations about future improvement and acquisition cost of new technology can be unclear. Since imperfect information is one of the main categories in market failure for diffusion of new technology, a good policy instrument is information provision, since a better informed economy is presumed to be a better functioning economy (Stoneman and Diederen, 1994). However, information provision may not speed up diffusion, although information leads to earlier adoption of new technology by risk averse people/firms, since information can lead to increased expectations for improvements in new technology. The relation of imperfect information to diffusion is displayed in Figure 42.

**Figure 42** Imperfect information and diffusion (drawn from Stoneman and Diederen, 1994)

Another public policy instrument to overcome imperfect information is that public sector takes over risks associated with imperfect information. Governments create information in order to reduce uncertainty as third public policy instrument. For example, they can impose technical standards. Variations of a new technology cannot be cross compatible. When an industry standard is established under free market circumstances, earlier adopters of new technology may have opted for wrong standard. This uncertainty slows down diffusion (Stoneman and Diederen, 1994). Therefore, governments have track record being involved in standard setting, which is demonstrated in Figure 43.

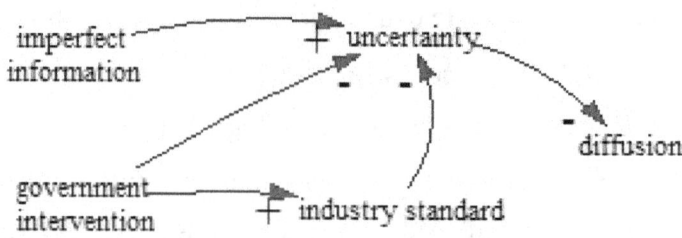

**Figure 43** Imperfect information and government (drawn from Stoneman and Diederen, 1994)

Even if there were perfect information and the industry comprised identical firms, one can talk about "diffusion" of new technology rather than simultaneous adoption (Reinganum, 1981a). As the number of firms who already adopted new technology increases, the value of adopting cost reducing process innovation declines, as shown in Figure 44. Stoneman (1986) simplifies Reinganum's (1981a,b) models such that as other firms start to adopt new technology. Both the profitability of using new technology and the profitability of using existing technology decline, since output will increase and prices will decline. Each firm in that industry can behave myopically that the profitability difference is above the cost of new technology or may have other strategic reasons when deciding upon the time of adoption. Hence identical firms with perfect information adopt new technology in different time periods, such that the S-shaped pattern of diffusion arises, whereas the speed of adoption depends on market structure (Baptista, 1999). This situation is termed by economists as the Nash equilibrium structure of adoption dates (Reinganum, 1981b).

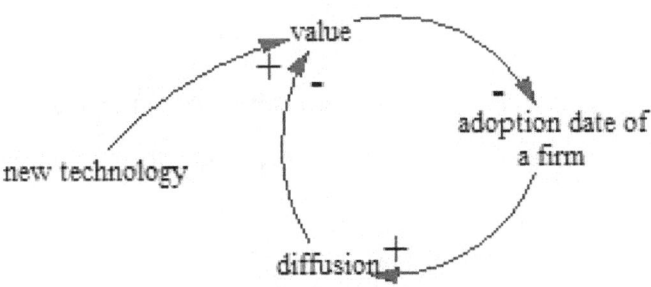

**Figure 44** Diffusion of new technology (drawn from Reinganum, 1981a)

Assuming that each identical firm in that particular industry has perfect information about new technology, as more firms adopt new technology with respect to each adoption date as foreseen by the Nash equilibrium, two conflicting effects arise. Competitive pressures in the industry accelerate adoption. However, a firm who adopts new technology later will capture less increase in profit than another firm who adopts earlier. Consequently, as time passes, firms have less incentive to adopt. However, as more firms adopt new technology, firms not using new technology may cease production, since they may not profit using current technology. These statements are expressed as causal relationships in Figure 45.

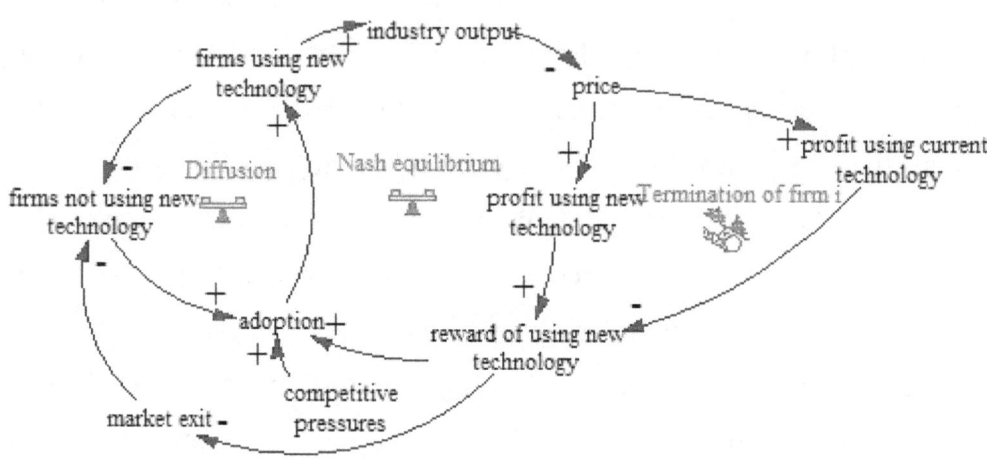

**Figure 45** Adoption under perfect information (drawn from Reinganum, 1981b; Quirmbach, 1986)

Reinganum's game theoretic model (1981b) states that for each firm, the difference between profit using current technology prior to adoption and profit using new technology immediately after adoption together with market structure determines the timing of adoption, whereas new technology changes market structure such that firms not using new technology stop their activities and those firms can reenter their industry using new technology. Despite assuming linear demand, i.e. whatever the output is converted into sales, it is quite complex process. The increase in the number of firms in an industry delays adoption of new technology, though late adopters are not unaffected. The causal relationships of Reinganum's (1981b) game theoretic model are displayed in Figure 46.

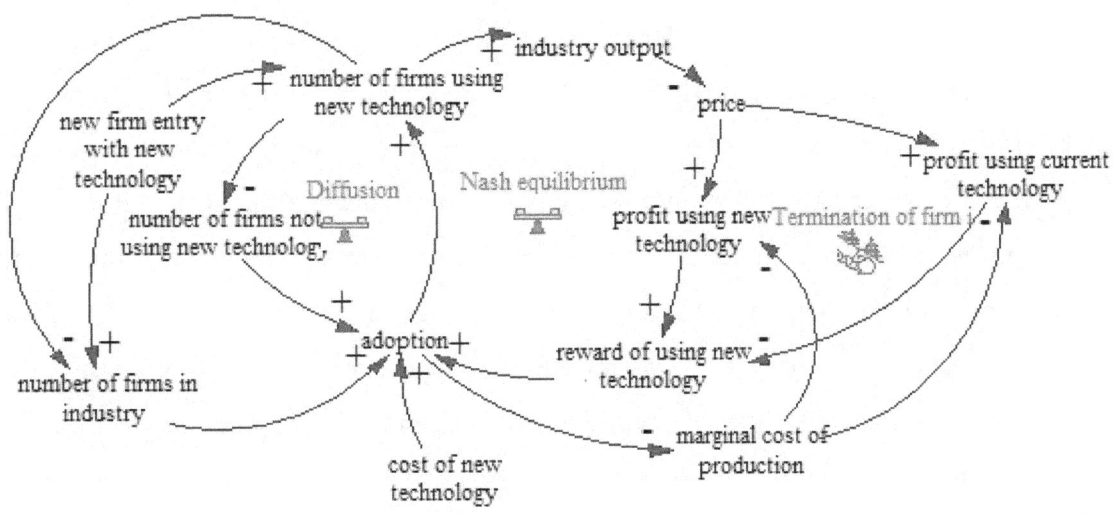

**Figure 46** Market Structure and Diffusion of New Technology (drawn from Reinganum, 1981b)

Quirmbach (1986) compares various market structures for new capital equipment (i.e. industry structure, comprising firms using or not using new technology) that later adoptions decrease incremental benefits of new capital equipment and cost of new capital equipment decline for later adoptions. This pattern leads to diffusion, as shown in Figure 47. Contrary to Reinganum (1981b), he argued that strategic behavior of firms does not have affect on diffusion. There are signs of a positive relationship between the degree of competitiveness and the rate of diffusion. But with respect to the effect of the market structure, ambiguity remains (Götz, 1999).

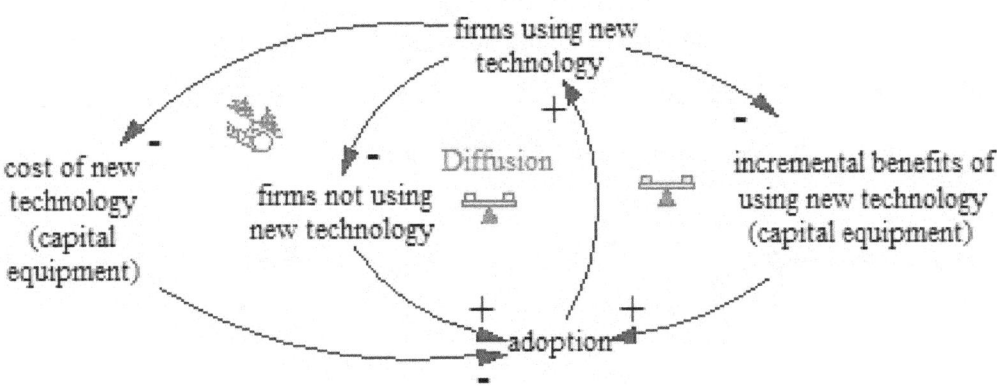

**Figure 47** Diffusion capital equipment as process innovation (drawn from Quirmbach, 1986)

Quirmbach (1986) compares diffusion rates of new capital equipment for different market structures such as market power on capital equipment suppliers, market power on firms as users of capital equipment, no market power and welfare optimal case. If a certain number of firms implemented new capital equipment and if the incremental benefits are larger under market structure A than under market structure B, the immediately next firm adopts new capital equipment earlier within market structure A with respect to market structure B. Quirmbach (1986) modified Reinganum's framework by varying market structure on both the supply and demand (adoption) sides for new technology. When the market power is on firms buying new technology, a joint-venture among firms slows down the rate of diffusion, since firms are interested in protecting their investments in existing equipment. As long as the existing capital equipment employed remains operable, new capital equipment as process innovation will be introduced first until its average total cost of production is lower than the average cost of production for the older process. Since the joint venture of firms does not take consumer surplus into account, diffusion will be slower than socially optimal.

In the case that monopoly technology supplier has market power, the rate of diffusion among firms is likely to be faster than the social optimum. As Baptista (1999) summarized, this diffusion pattern arises because monopoly technology supplier is not concerned with existing investments of firms, whereas each firm not adopting new technology yet, has to worry about preemption by adopter firms. The case of no market power has been discussed in the previous paragraphs according to Reinganum (1981b). The diffusion rate as a consequence of individual adoption by firms (i.e noncooperative behavior) is faster than socially optimal (Quirmbach, 1986). Effect of different market structures on rate of diffusion are summarized in Figure 48.

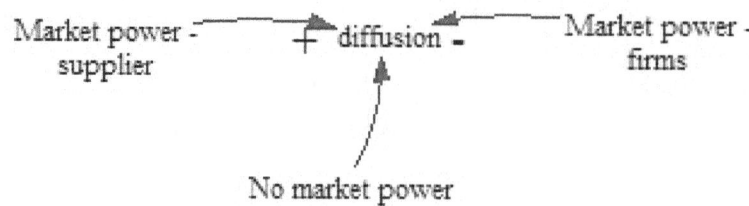

**Figure 48** Market power and diffusion (drawn from Quirmbach, 1986)

More recent studies in this stream have highlighted the interplay between two types of effects on the rate of diffusion. On one end, uncertainty connected to the rapid introduction of incremental innovations has slowed the diffusion process, due to expectations of continuing incremental change. On the other hand, increased profitability resulting from early adoption (effects associated with market structure and pre-emption) might reinforce the rate of diffusion. (Baptista, 1999)

### 2.5.5.2 Government Support

Government support for diffusion of new technology incorporates various practices. One major practice is providing subsidies, i.e. financial funds to various entities. Another category is that governments are users of new technology. Wejnert (2002) points out that collective actors with high status, controlling either political power or economic resources, (e.g. governments, large corporations, etc.) usually impose adoption of the innovation on lower status actors, after they have adopted the innovation.

Bessant and Rush (1993) classify government support for manufacturing innovations according to firm size. Larger and well-established firms, in order to exploit the opportunities in advanced manufacturing technologies, have had to acquire new skills, develop new ways of working, explore new markets, etc. Such strategic leaps in technology need extra help, particularly at the front end, and active government policies can play an important role in extending the learning capacity.

Smaller enterprises on the other hand have to face different challenges. Small firms, which are skillful, utilize networks and operate as extended firms knowing where to get resources and owning few ones. However, strategic technologies may challenge them. Some firms, while large in employee numbers or turnover, are still small- or medium-sized enterprises according to their behavior, since they are technology-inexperienced and lack key resources. (Bessant and Rush, 1993)

Vickery and Blau (1999) state four main reasons, why government support is enforced:

1. to overcome shortcomings in economic and industrial environments;

2. to facilitate transfer of new technology from developers or technology suppliers to users of new technology;
3. to undertake firm-specific obstacles to diffusion of new technology (e.g. lack of skill, awareness);
4. to increase availability of technical and managerial workforce.

Until mid-1970s, government support for innovation functions according to nature of each project and focused mainly on supply of innovation. That government policies need to focus on use of innovation as well as its supply, led government policies during 1980s promoting adoption and diffusion (Bessant and Rush, 1993). Examples are stimulating technology awareness, consultancy support and articulating needs for specific applications.

Technology-transfer policies for advanced manufacturing technologies now contain some or all of the following elements. The supportive elements related to technology transfer are illustrated as causal relationships in Figure 49.

1. Direct financial support-loans or grants-for capital expenditure and for development costs;
2. Information support, through subsidized consultancy schemes. Here the intention is to provide expert opinion and advice on advanced manufacturing technology opportunities and some measure of short-term-skills support to firms lacking such in-house capability;
3. Consultancy support for project management, strategy formulation, and areas where managerial competence is lacking, especially in SMEs;
4. Skills and training to improve the supply side;
5. Awareness raising at a general level through to more specific measures targeted at sectors or individual firms;
6. Infrastructure building, through strengthening R & D capability (e.g., within universities and polytechnics) and building better networks (e.g., through academic/industry or industry/industry liaison schemes).

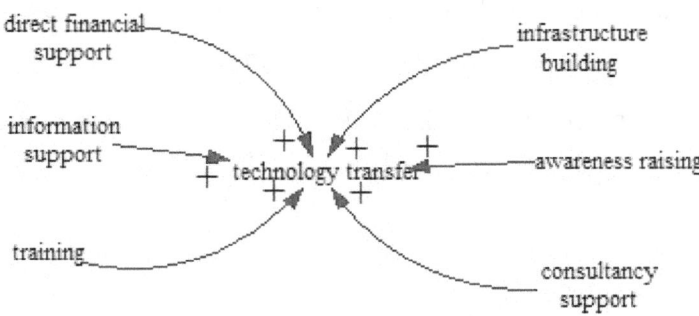

**Figure 49** Technology transfer (drawn from Bessant and Rush, 1993)

The role that suppliers of advanced manufacturing technologies play in successful implementation: degree the supplier understands the user's need and the context into which the innovation is to fit, the extent of support and service (hand-holding) offered during the transfer process, the nature of the relationship (arm's length or close partnership), the time spent on the user's site, etc. The main policy implication here concerns setting a basic standard for good supplier performance. (Bessant and Rush, 1993)

Several economists have intensively debated the merits of governmental interventions and support on the enactment of industrial and technological policies (e.g. cooperation of industry, labor and government - Thurow, 1984; government intervention in agriculture - Stiglitz, 1987; forms of government intervention - Porter, 1990). The role of government in economic and technological innovation is one of the extensively discussed topics especially for the last couple of decades. These discussions are fostered by the growing international economic competition. Some studies demonstrated the importance of government policies in determining national competitiveness (Porter, 1990) while others warn of the dangers if the government goes beyond its core roles of maintaining law and order, protecting property rights and providing the basic infrastructure and public services (Krueger, 1990). It is crucial for a well functioning economy that the government and the market are appropriately positioned and act effectively.

South Korea, Taiwan, Hong Kong and Singapore learned to innovate in electronics. Subcontracting and original equipment manufacture (OEM) mechanisms acted as a training school for latecomers, enabling them to overcome entry barriers and to assimilate manufacturing and design technology (Hobday, 1995). Innovative activity increases the barriers to entry due to patenting and the protection of intellectual property (Bayus, Kang and Agarwal, 2007) as shown in Figure 50.

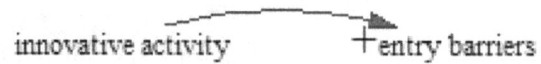

**Figure 50** Relationship between innovation and entry barriers (drawn from Bayus, Kang, Agarwal, 2007)

Industrial clusters facilitate ease of obtaining market information. Since market information is easily accessible in clusters and the disadvantages of products, services and supply chain can be identified and adopt correct action immediately. Industrial clusters also provide low entry barriers: it is easier to obtain outstanding professional personnel and components, as well as technical and fundamental base construction support, and consequently diminish the investment risks for investors and banking institutions. (Lin, Tung and Huang, 2006)

Industry-attractiveness criteria are derived from three sources as shown in Figure 51 (Thacker and Handscombe, 2003):

1. The objectives and characteristics of the firm (for example, size, growth, profitability and social role);
2. The demands or constraints placed on the firm by outside influences (for example energy and environmental considerations);
3. The economic and technological characteristics of the industry (for example pricing, market diversity and structure, customer financial strength).

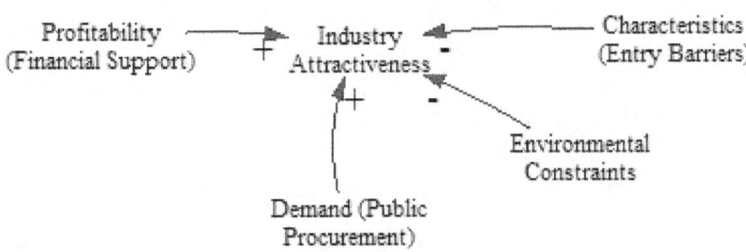

**Figure 51** Industry Attractiveness (drawn from Thacker and Handscombe, 2003)

Porter (1980) also evaluates 'industry attractiveness' by exploring the impact of relationships with suppliers and customers on profitability as well as considering concentration, firm conduct, barriers to entry and exit, and the strength of substitutes. Porter's five competitive forces, as shown in Figure 52, is a model originally from an economist and actually indicates why public policies play a critical role in the diffusion process of the innovations.

**Figure 52** Five Forces of Competition (Porter, 1980)

# 3 METHODOLOGY

## 3.1 System Theories of Organization

A system is a group of interrelated or interdependent parts which develop a complex and unified whole that has a specific purpose. The following characteristics are defining systems (Kim, 1999):

1. **Systems have purpose.** Every system has some purpose that provides a kind of integrity which holds it together. Nevertheless, purpose is a property of the system as a whole and not any of the parts. The purpose of an automobile is to provide a means to take people, whereas engine as a part does not incorporate that purpose.
2. **All parts must be present for a system to carry out its purpose optimally.** If you take a piece away without affecting the functioning of a system, it is then not a system, merely a collection of parts.
3. **The order in which the parts are arranged affects the performance of a system.**
4. **Systems attempt to maintain stability through feedback.** Feedback is the transmission and return of information. In a car example, driving into a curve too sharply results in feedback as visual cues and internal sensations such that you adjust the degree of your turn and/or change your speed.

*General systems theory*, originating from the biologist Ludwig von Bertalanffy, is the name to describe a level of theoretical model building. Its objective is to point out similarities in theoretical constructions of different disciplines and to develop theoretical models which can be applied to at least two fields of study. General systems theory incorporates two complimentary approaches (Boulding, 1956):

1. To look over empirical universe and pick certain general phenomena which are found in many different disciplines such that general theoretical models are built up relevant to these phenomena.
2. To arrange empirical field of behavior investigating them in a hierarchy of complexity and to make abstraction with respect to that hierarchy of complexity.

Organizations are cooperative systems (Barnard, 1938:65), and Chester Barnard was influenced by systems views of Vilfredo Pareto and Talcott Parsons (Kast and Rosenzweig, 1972). Systems approach became influential in management and organization theory during 1950s. Organizations are regarded as open systems and consist of patterned activities (by a number of individuals) which are complementary and interdependent (Katz and Kahn, 1966). The stability and recurrence of activities can be examined in relation to energic input, transformation of energies within the system and the resulting product or energic output such that energic return from the output reactivates the system. The application of general systems theory to organization theory can be summarized that an organization should be regarded as integrated whole (Scott, 2002).

Unlike traditional organizational theories, *systems school* regards organizations as a complex set of dynamically intertwined and interconnected elements involving inputs, process, outputs and feedback loops, and environment which an organization operates in and interacts with (Scott, 2002). Whereas classic organization theory considered organizations as static structures, system theories tended to be multidimensional and complex in their assumptions about cause-and-effect relationships. Organization as a main system consists of several parts (subsystems) such as marketing, finance, production that gets input from its environment, a larger suprasystem, and then transforms the input into output and sends the output back to the environment.

Hence, systems theory has been utilized in the investigation of relationships between subsystems in organizations and in studying environmental interfaces, though scholars of management and organization theory are not sophisticated enough to use it (Kast and Rosenzweig, 1972). Major reason is that systems approach does not provide quick-fix methods for solving problems in organizations. Management practitioners tended to contingency approach which aimed at fit between the organization and its environment (Jones, 2004:118). One argument is that organizations should achieve a balance between differentiation and integration with respect to contingency approach (Lawrence and Lorsch, 1967), though mainly relationships between organization and environment are considered in a static context. Therefore systems approach requires fundamentally new ways of thinking and acting such that "everything is connected to everything else" and "you can't just do one thing" need to be understood to see the world as a complex system (Sterman, 2000:4).

## 3.2 Systems Thinking

Often, well-intentioned efforts to solve pressing organizational problems create unanticipated side effects. People's attempts to solve a problem often make it worse, which is termed as "counterintuitive behavior of social systems" (Forrester, 1971). People's event oriented view of the world brings about an event-oriented approach to problem solving, as depicted Figure 53. Management decisions cause unforeseen consequences which result in policy resistance, the tendency of the interventions to be overcome by the response of the system (Sterman, 2001).

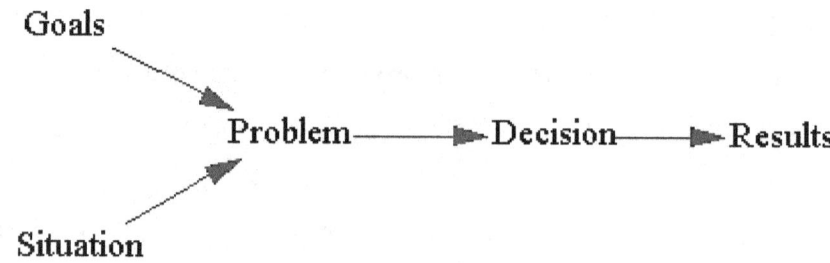

**Figure 53** Event-oriented view of the world (Sterman, 2000)

However, the results of an individual/organization's actions change that environment. S/he reassesses the new situation and makes tomorrow's decisions accordingly. There is feedback as shown in Figure 54. Other people/organizations also react to restore the balance that has been disturbed. Policy resistance arises, because the full range of feedbacks operating in a system is often not understood. Unanticipated side effects arise, because they often assume that cause and effect are closely linked in time and space, though in complex systems such as business, economy, ecosystems, cause and effect are distant in time and space. (Sterman, 2000:11)

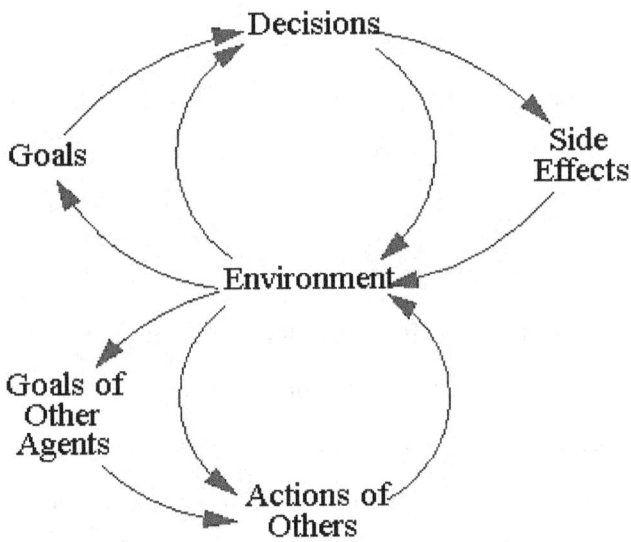

**Figure 54** Feedback view (Sterman, 2000)

Some management questions have been as follows (Sterman, 2001):

1. How can one understand a whole system?
2. How does policy resistance arise?
3. How can one learn to avoid it and find high leverage policies which can produce sustainable benefit?

Most scholars argue that answer to those questions lie in the ability to regard the world as a complex system. The term *systems thinking* does not have clear definition and usage. Although some scholars mean that systems thinking is equivalent to *system dynamics*, it is rather a general and shallow awareness of systems (Forrester, 1994). Systems thinking became popular, because the essence of systems thinking requires a shift of mind to look at the interrelatedness of factors and understanding them as part of a common process (Senge, 1990).

Systems thinking is especially useful for defining problems, formulating and testing potential solutions and implementing effective solutions that endure (Goodman et al, 1997). It helps to understand to realize things on three levels (Richmond, 1993):

- Events,
- Patterns of behavior,

- System structure.

However, systems thinking does not exclude traditional reductionist, analytic view, because some problems can be solved by analytic thinking and others through a systemic perspective (Kim, 1999). If a problem does not have all of the following characteristics, it may not be suitable for systems thinking analysis (Goodman, 1992):

4. The problem is important to the individual and the business,
5. The problem is chronic, rather than a one-time event,
6. The problem has a known history that one can describe.
7. Others have tried to solve the problem with little or no success.

Systems thinking requires intensive practice and patience, and serves as a language for communicating complexities and interdependencies (Goodman, 1991). It highlights wholes, rather than parts focusing on the role of interconnections. Systems thinking emphasizes closed interdependencies and brings in special terminology describing system behavior such as (Kim, 1994):

1. Balancing processes: a feedback flow that controls change and maintains system stability,
2. Reinforcing processes: a feedback flow that generates exponential growth or collapse.

Applying systems thinking requires seven different but mutually dependent skills (Richmond, 1993). These systems thinking skills are briefly explained in

Table 9 contrary to traditional thinking skills.

**Table 9** Systems Thinking Skills

| Systems Thinking skill | Contrasts with... |
|---|---|
| *Dynamic Thinking* – Focusing on patterns of behavior (trends) over time | *Static Thinking* – Focusing on specific events |
| *System-as-Cause Thinking* – Choosing to focus on the system within the organization's control as responsible for performance issues | *System-as-Effect Thinking* – Choosing to focus on forces outside the organization's control as generating the performance issues (creating "victimitis") |
| *Forest Thinking* – Taking the 30,000 foot view of the system | *Tree-by-tree Thinking* – Focusing on the details, often getting lost in spreadsheets! |
| *Operational Thinking* – Looking for causality (How is this behavior generated?) | *Factors Thinking* – Developing a list of factors associated/correlated with the behavior |
| *Closed-loop (Feedback) Thinking* – Understanding the feedback and ongoing process responsible for behavior | *Straight-line Thinking* – Believing causality is a one-way, linear relationship |
| *Quantitative Thinking* – Understanding how to represent non-physical, immeasurable variables in analysis | *Qualitative Thinking* – Including only those variables believed measurable |
| *Scientific Thinking* – Building the most useful, entertainable theory of causality | *Proving Truth Thinking* – Looking for "The Answer" |

Systems thinking refers to a set of tools such as causal loop diagrams, stock and flow diagrams, systems archetypes and simulation models (Richmond, 2000). Tools for systems thinking enable to understand and explore dynamic complexity of systems and helps communicate about one's understanding of a system's structure and behavior to other people. There at least ten distinct types of systems thinking tools, which are categorized in four broad areas (Kim, 1994):

1. Brainstorming Tools

- Fishbone Diagram,
- The Double-Q (QQ) Diagram,
2. Dynamic Thinking Tools
    - Behavior Over Time (BOT) diagrams,
    - Causal Loop Diagrams (CLDs),
    - Systems Archetypes,
3. Structural Thinking Tools
    - Graphical Function Diagrams,
    - Structure-Behavior Pairs,
    - Policy Structure Diagrams,
4. Computer Based Tools
    - Computer Models,
    - Management Flight Simulators,
    - Learning Laboratories.

Systems thinking can be a door opener to system dynamics but it can only be a first step in order to have dynamic understanding of complex problems (Forrester, 2007). Systems thinking enables to organize processes and obtain information from people in real systems such that it provides useful insight to system dynamics, whereas model building and simulation stages of system dynamics provide thoroughness and clearness to systems thinking, which can be drawn from Figure 55 (Forrester, 1994). Much of systems thinking uses causal loop. However, causal loops create a general overall impression of a problem or subject. Systems thinking has probably a share of 5% along the way of understanding systems, whereas 95% lies in structuring system dynamics models and simulating them (Forrester, 1994).

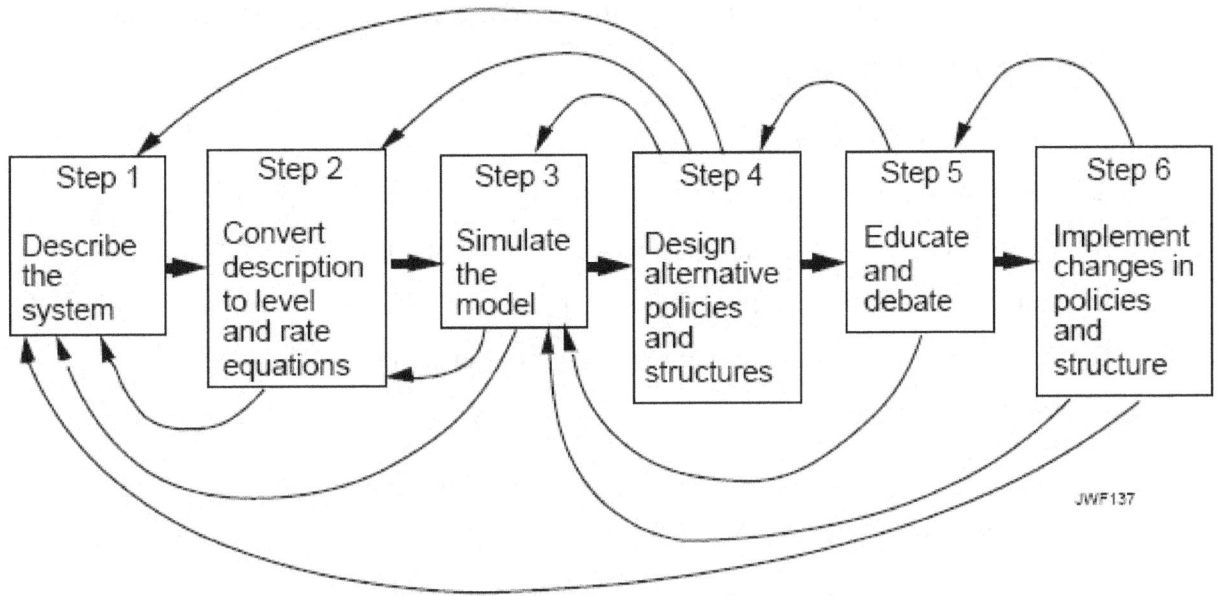

**Figure 55** System dynamics steps from problem symptoms to improvement (Forrester, 1994)

## 3.3 System Dynamics

Systems Dynamics was founded in the early 1960s by Jay W. Forrester of the MIT Sloan School of Management with the establishment of the MIT System Dynamics Group (Sterman, 2001). It is a methodology for studying and managing complex feedback systems, such as one finds in business and other social systems like population, ecological and economic systems (Forrester, 1961). In fact it has been used to address practically every sort of feedback system. It is for sure that the word system has been applied to all sorts of situations; feedback is the differentiating descriptor here. The definition for feedback is given with an explanation: It refers to the situation of X affecting Y and Y in turn affecting X perhaps through a chain of causes and effects. One cannot study independently the link between X and Y and Y and X, and predict how the system will behave. Only way to do so is to study the whole system as a feedback system, which will lead to correct results.

What makes using system dynamics different from other approaches to studying complex systems is the use of feedback loops with mutual or recursive causality. Stocks and flows help describe how a system is connected by feedback loops which create the nonlinearity found so frequently in modern day problems. The methodology of system dynamics is as follows (Sterman, 2000:86):

1. identifies a problem,
2. develops a dynamic hypothesis explaining the cause of the problem,
3. builds a computer simulation model of the system at the root of the problem,
4. tests the model to be certain that it reproduces the behavior seen in the real world,
5. devises and tests in the model alternative policies that alleviate the problem, and
6. implements this solution.

System dynamics comprises set of techniques for thinking and computer modeling such that its practitioners begin to understand complex systems such as human body, national economy or the earth's climate. Systems tools help us keep track of multiple interconnections; they help us see things whole. Because much of conventional wisdom comes from seeing things in parts and focusing on one small part at a time, system dynamicists tend to have surprising points of view. They generate a lot of controversy. (Meadows, 1989)

System dynamics consists of four components: system, feedback, level, and rate. (Meadows, Meadows and Randers, 1992) A system is a set of elements sharing a particular purpose within a boundary. Depending on its boundary, a system can be a corporation, an environment, an economic entity, a country, an inventory system, etc.

The causal relationship indicates one element affecting another element. In order to model the causality, a causal-loop diagram (CLD) has been used. CLD has been used to formulate a cognitive model and to hypothesize the dynamic interactions between elements. Representing the feedback of related elements requires additional positive and negative polarity to the CLD diagram. The dynamic movement of the system can be caused by a feedback loop, and there are two types of feedback: reinforcing (R) and balancing (B). As illustrated in Figure 56, increases in population increases the numbers of birth, which again increases the overall population: 'reinforcing loop'. To the contrary, the greater the population, the higher the number of deaths, and then the population decrease: 'balancing loop'.

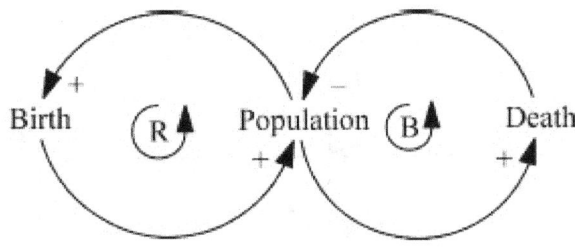

**Figure 56** The diagram of causal relationship

Whilst the simplicity of CLD has improved communication and comprehensiveness among its users, it does not reflect all elements for sensitivity testing a target system There are two variables required for simulating all elements inside a system: level and rate. The 'level' refers to a given element within a specific time interval. Meanwhile, the rate reflects the extent of behavior of a system,. Specifically, the differences between the level and the rate depend on whether the element contains a time factor.

The level and the rate can be formulated using the stock-flow diagram (SFD) for a simulation test. The level can be represented with a stock level; the rate is described as a variable on the flow. 'Stock' is represented as a rectangle; 'Flow' can be expressed as a double-direction arrow. In the example shown in Figure 56, the variable entitled 'population', is only depicted as the stock (unit: person), whilst both 'birth' and 'death' (unit: person/year) are presented as the flow. As shown in Figure 57, additional variables for the simulation are also added to SFD. Here, the birth increases the population, and it also proportionally increases the death. This will lead to the decrease in population, which in turn, decreases birth. Consequently, a non-liner relationship exists among variables, and then the population cannot be calculated through linear equations.

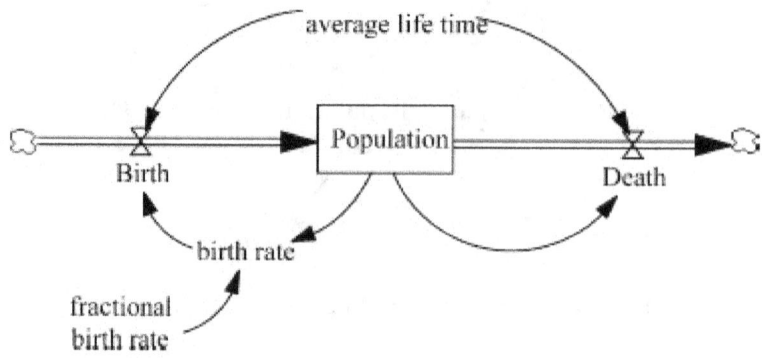

**Figure 57** Stock-flow diagram;

Comparison of system dynamics with other methods as a research method, the system dynamics approach can be compared to Management Science. However, the research on system dynamics starts with a different assumption from the traditional assumptions of Management Science (Richardson, 1983, cited in Yim et. al, 2004):

1. Developing models based on numerical figures,
2. Analyzing most problems by linear relationship,
3. Reflecting a limited number of variables which are influenced by results in a static condition,
4. Accuracy of model parameters is more important than the overall problem structure,
5. Pursuing optimal support decision making.

As system dynamics attempts to understand the basic structure of a system, and thus understand the behavior it can produce, computers are used to simulate such models. Running "what if" simulations to test certain policies on such a model can greatly aid in understanding how the system changes over time (Sterman, 2000).

# 4 PROPOSED MODEL

## 4.1 Introduction

Technological change is considered as the main factor of economic growth. Although existing literature provides comprehensive understanding to the concepts such as research & development, innovation, imitation, diffusion reaches certain levels, prediction of success or failure of new technologies has not been achieved so far by firms and government agencies. (Mansfield, 1996) Innovation diffusion, as one major category within technological change, has been elaborated by agriculture, marketing, management, economics and other scholars. Like this study, it continues to require researchers who have interest in both basic and applied work, and enrich previous studies. (Mansfield, 1995, p. xxi) Accordingly, this study will analyze all major areas of innovation diffusion in holistic way.

Regarding any process innovation, that is going to be adopted within an industry, the framework has been outlined in Figure 58. *Market* is the particular industry (in this case: Turkish automotive supplier industry). There are *technology suppliers* who make those process innovations available to the market. Further, *customers* are those people or entities who buy from the companies in the particular industry. The characteristics of process innovation (i.e. technology) influence decision processes of the companies in the particular industry. In addition to technology suppliers and customers on the market, there are governments and other public authorities making laws, regulations and allocating resources, which are shortly defined as *policies*. Policies have affect on both demand and supply for technologies. Finally there are *social networks*, which do not necessarily perform economic activities of buy & sell, however enable factor endowment for technology diffusion, such that both advanced and specialized factors such as knowledge and human resources are available to the market. (Porter, 1990: 75)

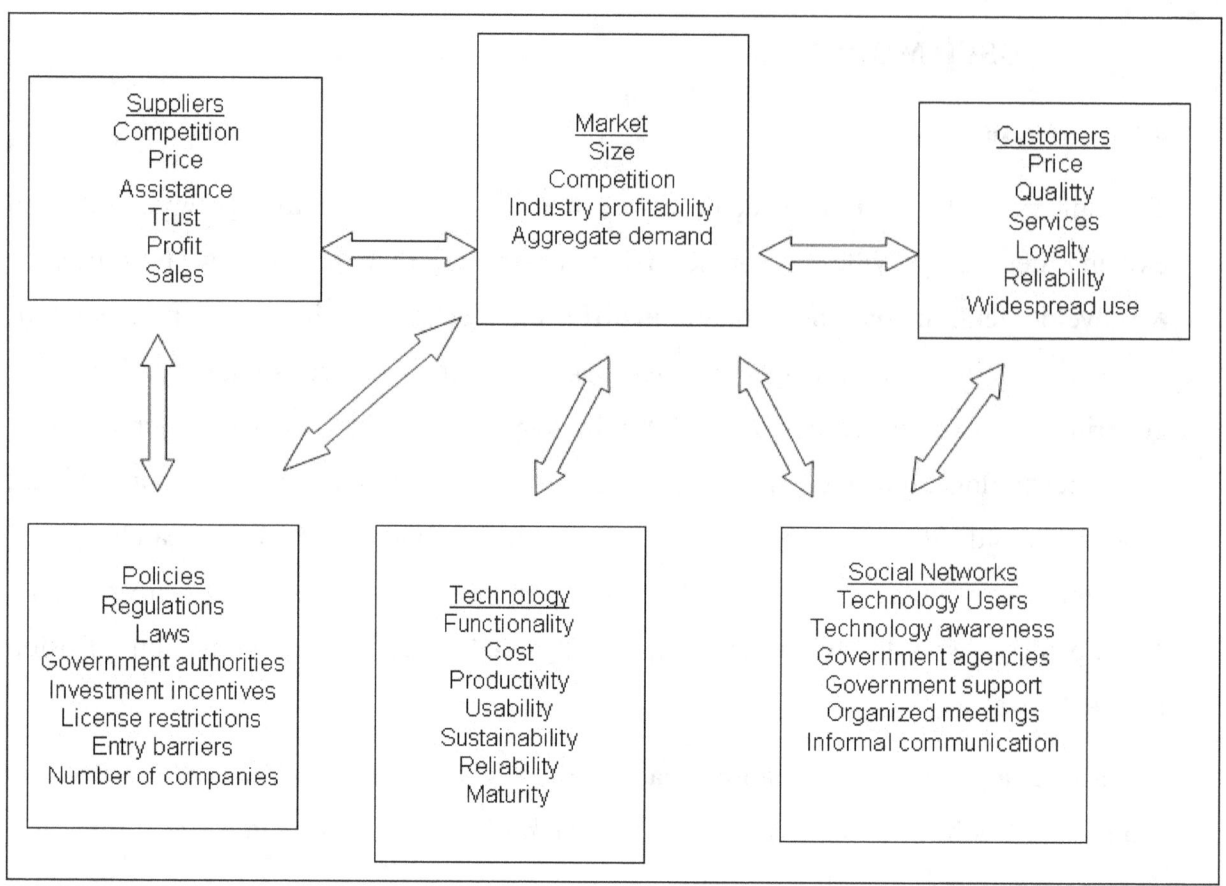

**Figure 58** General configuration on innovation diffusion

In this section four, system dynamics models are going to be constructed, sensitivity analysis is carried out, and the time behavior graphs of variables will be analyzed. The six areas that are outlined in the framework are not mutually exclusive as shown in Figure 59. Social networks cover the broad area of relationships not necessarily related to buying and selling. It is about individuals' relationships whether they are professional and/or personal, and incorporates all other areas. Technology is a process innovation for firms to be adopted and implemented by firms in the market. During each technology lifecycle, there are different interactions among suppliers and firms in the market, whereas public policies can have significant role in influencing behavior towards technology of both suppliers and market.

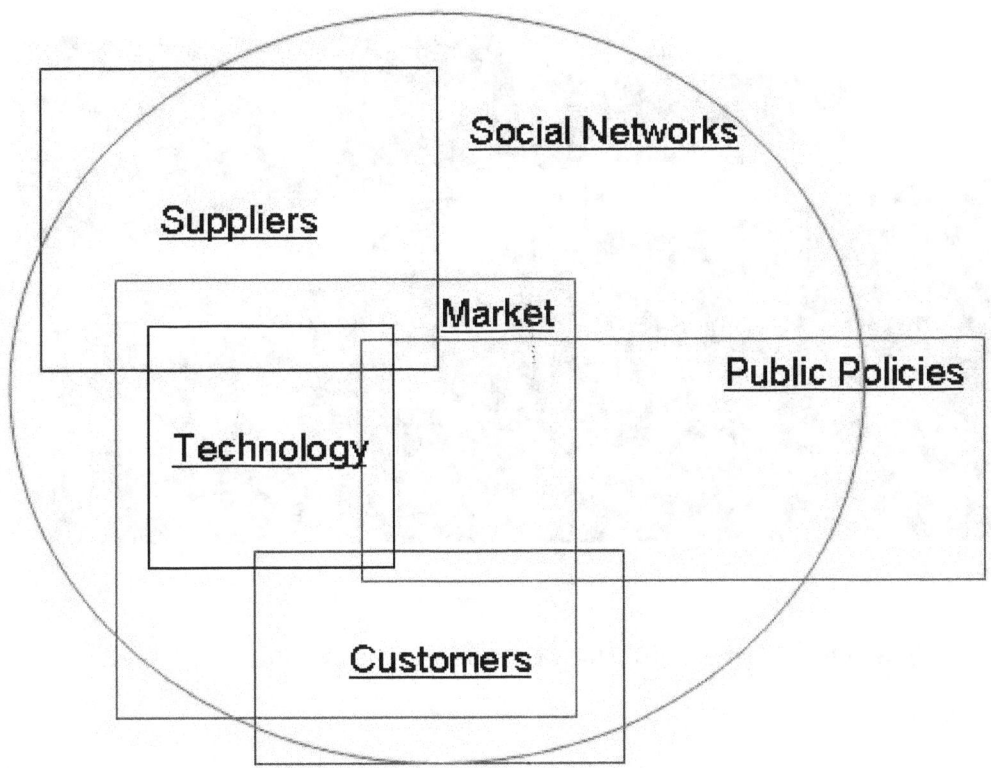

**Figure 59** General configuration on innovation diffusion

According to the literature review we identified six main areas related to the diffusion of process innovations as illustrated in Figure 60. Process innovations are those innovations that are adopted and implemented by firms in their business processes.

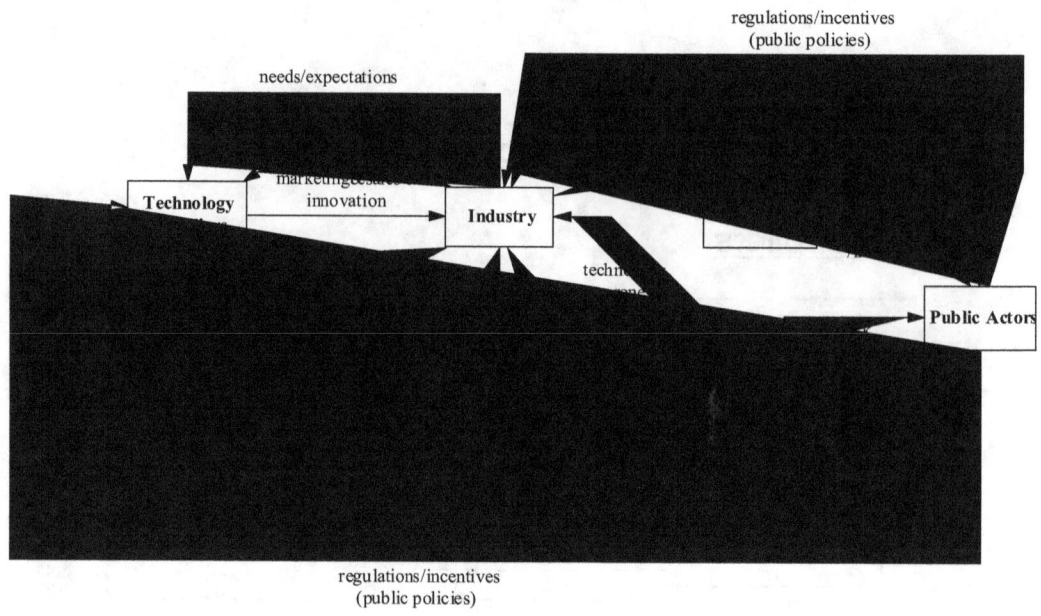

**Figure 60** Innovation Diffusion Structure and Material/Information Flows

From the aspect of systems thinking, marketing and management scholars are intensively focused on the product innovations whereas economists are interested in process innovations and economics of technological change.

In this study our primary goal is to combine the aspects of process and product innovations. We will consider process innovation as investment for new technology from the perspective of buyer firm, whereas the same technology is product innovation from the perspective of a selling firm. In this study, a firm that sells a particular innovation/technology is addressed as technology supplier.

Automotive parts industry is selected as the sample field for application, data collection, and model building. However most of the concepts and relationships developed or proposed in this study are generically characterized and applicable also in other manufacturing industries.

## 4.2 Expert Executive Interviews

To understand use of technology and supply of innovation, interviews were conducted in order to understand implications of investment for new technology. The first interview was conducted with the boss of an automotive parts manufacturer in Turkey, which is a small-medium enterprise manufacturing gears and other similar products. The latter interview involved the supply side of technology, a machine tool supplier. They shared their experience of sales of CNC machine tools to both automotive industry and other industries, whereas a representative from an automotive supplier industry association contributed with his views about manufacturing firms' use of new technology.

### 4.2.1 Executive Interview with Automotive Parts Manufacturer

This automotive parts manufacturer is located in an organized industrial zone in Istanbul who produces gears and mills. Its main customer is Türk Traktör, which is a subsidiary manufacturer of New Holland agriculture and farming equipment. The company has currently eighty employees and was founded in 1982 as a workshop in Bayrampasa, where most part manufacturers were located in Istanbul.

During 1980s, automotive supplier industry was utilizing conventional machine tools. Toward the end of 1980s, computerized numerically controlled (CNC) machine tools were introduced as new technology. CNC machine tools were new technology for automotive parts manufacturers in 1990. The Turkish distributor of Okuma Corporation, one of the world's leading machine tool manufacturers in the world, had an office in the same industrial estate as the company.

The company was owned by two male siblings at that time. In 1990 Okuma Corporation had sent this Turkish distributor a CNC turning machine for display in Turkey. Meanwhile, the sales manager of the Turkish distributor of Okuma Corporation was carrying out his sales activities. Knowing each other personally, he approached the elder brother as the company owner. After several contacts and investigation by the two brothers about CNC turning machine, the sales manager offered a price of equivalent to more than 110,000 EURO. The amount was extremely high for a relatively small automotive parts manufacturer running in a workshop. Certainly, the two brothers declined the offer. However, the sales director provided a counterargument to their rejection by asking how much cash they have. They told that they can only afford an equivalent amount 15,000 EURO. The sales director argued for the sales CNC turning machine that they pay the remaining of 110,000 EURO after they have earned money.

The sales director's final offer was very surprising for the elder brother; he could not sleep at that night asking himself, why the sales director was making that favor.

On the morning of next day, the two brothers went to visit the sales director in his office. They directly asked why he was making such goodwill. They emphasized that he did not ask any guarantee letter, contractual commitment, etc. The sales director made his case as follows:

1. He does saving in the showroom space for the CNC turning machine.
2. His arguments for sales might be nice, but he did not have clear sales indicator for CNC machine tools to automotive supplier industry. Since the elder brother is known as "tough buyer", use of his CNC turning machine will cause a word of mouth effect and would provide prestige to Okuma brand. Other automotive parts manufacturers would think that CNC machine must have really sophisticated capabilities, since the company uses it.
3. Potential buyer firms for CNC machine tools would trust him to a certain extent, since he is a seller. However, those firms' executives would believe their views and opinions as a user of that CNC turning machine.
4. Regarding finance and terms of payment, he does have faith in the company, since it owned by the two brothers. Even if either of the brothers would disappear for any reason, he is confident that the payment will be received, since the other brother would anyway continue the business.

Return on investment for CNC machine tools, has usually been around three and four years, according to the elder brother as owner of the company. After sales support availability had been a critical factor, while CNC machines were new technology in Turkey at the beginning of 1990s. But around 2000, service & support for CNC machines are already available by various machine tool companies.

When they were going to buy new CNC machines for production capacity, the distributor of Okuma Corporation offered a high technology CNC machine. However, since the company is producing tractor spare parts, they do not need such strict tolerance limits. Therefore such sophisticated CNC technology was a luxury for them.

Until end of 2008, the company bought fourteen CNC machine tools in total. Only one is the replacement of previous universal machine tool, whereas all the rest is about purchase of new machinery. There are two main drivers for investing in CNC machine tools:

1. To manufacture a new part;
2. To increase capacity in order to meet rising demand for existing product.

On the average, CNC machine tools have a useful life of ten years; after that period performance tends to decline and maintenance costs increase. There is a considerable market for sales & purchase of second hand CNC machines. When buying a new CNC machine, a payback period of five to six years is assumed with an available leasing plan of three to four years. Out of those fourteen CNC machine tools, ten were decided for the above former purpose, whereas only four were implemented for the latter purpose. The company invested in CNC machine tools mainly for turning and vertical/horizontal machining processes discontinuously as its turnover increases, as shown in Table 10. Except the initially bought CNC machine tool, all CNC machine tools are in operation.

**Table 10** Year of CNC purchase and Company Turnover

| CNC Machine | Purchase Year | Turnover (KEUR) |
|---|---|---|
| $1^{st}$ | 1991 (until 2006) | 500 |
| $2^{nd}$, $3^{rd}$ | 1996 | 1.000 |
| $4^{th}$, $5^{th}$ | 1998 | 1.200 |
| $6^{th}$, $7^{th}$, $8^{th}$ | 2004 | 1.600 |
| $9^{th}$, $10^{th}$, $11^{th}$ | 2007 | 2.000 |
| $12^{th}$, $13^{th}$, $14^{th}$ | 2008 | 2.500 |

Unlike the company, many firms in automotive supplier industry create imitative demand, which often results in "unconscious use" of new technology. The owner siblings of the company were evaluating characteristics and performance of CNC machines and then decided upon procurement. However, the so called "Konya" approach is that a boss of a manufacturing small-medium enterprise sees a new machine either in his neighbor firm or nearby competitor. That boss can also see a new CNC machine at a trade fair or industry exhibition and may quickly decide to buy the technology without investigating about the features and functionality of that CNC machine in detail.

The main problem of automotive supplier is "conscious" buyer and user of new technology. After having in invested in new machines, they cannot entirely generate performance enabled by new technology. Pareto principle works on the opposite. 80% of automotive supplier firms have staff that does not have formal education, whereas only 20% of automotive supplier firms incorporate personnel with relevant formal education and experience.

### 4.2.2 Executive Interview with Machine Tool Supplier

DMG Gildemeister is among the major machine tool suppliers in the world. Its headquarters is based in Germany. Its Turkish subsidiary was officially established in 2004. They have a diverse customer base in the world from different industries including but not limited to:

- Automotive and automotive parts;
- Aerospace and defense;
- Medical technologies;
- Clock.

In Turkey, DMG Gildemeister sells its CNC machines to both automotive and automotive supplier industries. Investment in new technology CNC machines requires considerable amount of money from 50 KEUR till 500 KEUR depending on the complexity, capacity and size of the machine. Fatih Girit, General Manager of DMG Gildemeister Turkey, states that critical success factor in sales is the requirements of user (Consciously, it is not termed as buyer). His customer firm(s) from aerospace & defense industry provide detailed requirements, since engineers in that firm know what they need to produce and put acceptance criteria accordingly with respect to 70% payment of that CNC machine price. Consequently, appropriate choice of new technology appears to be crucial in aerospace and defense industry therefore they are relatively insensitive to marketing hypes by machine tool suppliers, since they work on longer term commitments as briefly described in Figure 61.

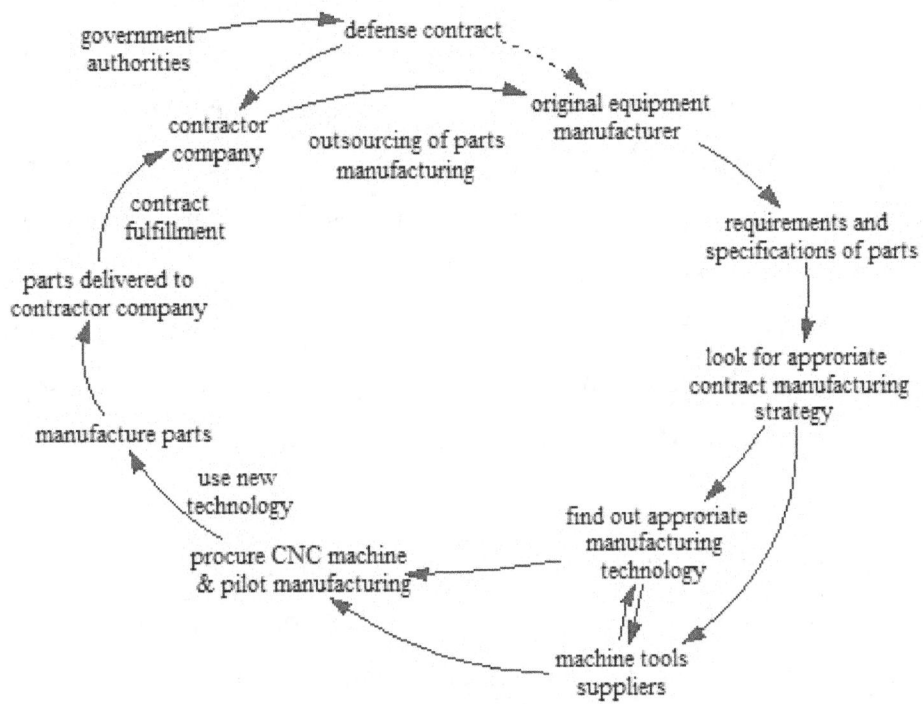

**Figure 61** Manufacturing cycle of aerospace and defense industry (drawn from executive interview)

Hence for "conscious" users, price as a factor is not an entry barrier. The total cost of ownership and incremental benefits play the major role. For example, a Turkish mold company who supplies to Boeing and Airbus scrutinized DMG Gildemeister's offer. They already were using CNC machines from a Japanese machine tools supplier for nearly 100,000 USD, whereas CNC machine price of DMG was around 250,000 EUR. Fatih Girit gave that machine for use by that company to be paid later on. They realized that DMG's performance and capabilities were superior to that of Japanese competitor such that maintenance and personnel costs over the planned lifecycle were considerably lower. There this Turkish mold company decided to buy additional three CNC machine tools from DMG replacing existing Japanese machine tools supplier's, even though they actually did not have an urgent need for lower tolerance limits such as four micrometers instead of fifty five micrometers.

Also from the perspective of machine tools supplier, lack of efficient and effective use of new technology is a major problem. "Unconscious" buyer, mentioned as "Konya" approach among automotive parts manufacturers, leads to unintended sales of high technology. A supportive example of the "Konya" approach is given from a yoghurt mold manufacturing company located in Konya. Although the nature of yoghurt mold work requires only loose tolerance limits around 2%, the boss of this manufacturing company found out the best CNC machine tool, which he looked for, is from DMG Gildemeister. Despite the statements that the company does not need that particular CNC machine, they paid 380,000 EUR for it. Hence this boss became proud of owning that sophisticated CNC machine apart from Boeing, Airbus, Rolls Royce and Renault Formula One Division.

Mehmet Dudaroglu, Vice President for Association of Parts and Components Manufacturers (TAYSAD), is in the point of view that "Konya" approach cannot only be considered as a word of mouth demand or imitation effect only. Owners of such manufacturing companies have psychological motives due to jealousy towards other people that they must have better and bigger stuff. Hence it is not about diffusion of a particular technology due to imitation, which can be categorized as mimetic isomorphism (Jones, 2004:349). However, such non-rational behavior to have better stuff does not necessarily coincide with normative isomorphism, since norms and values corresponding to better use of new technology are not adopted. Another such example is from Fatih Girit that his neighbor as owner of an automotive parts manufacturing firm, watched the functioning CNC machine tool for two months while drinking coffee every day. The owner was just stating that he bought a very good and nice machine.

Conventional machine tools for turning, milling, drilling, etc. have been the usual equipment of automotive parts manufacturers. Numerically controlled machine tools have been a milestone in automotive and automotive parts industries. Each year, there have been incremental upgrades and improvements in machine tools. First commercial numerically controlled machine tool was deployed to the world market in 1955 (Romeo, 1975).

CNC machine tools are available technology for more than twenty years. According to Mehmet Dudaroglu, CNC technology will still be in use for another twenty-thirty years. From technology lifecycle aspect, it can be regarded as mature technology. However, CNC technology S-curve can still have a way to go in terms of technology improvement according to both Mehmet Dudaroglu and Fatih Girit. Therefore, new models of CNC technology can be regarded as upgrades, i.e. incremental innovations rather than radical innovations.

## 4.3 Causal Loop Modules

This study proposes six causal loop modules for six areas of innovation diffusion, as displayed in Figure 59 of section 4.1. For each area, these causal relationships are presented and explained in terms of causal loop diagrams (CLDs) as briefly explained in section 3.3. Based on the discussions in section 2.5 of literature review, CLDs are a powerful tool to map the complex relationships and feedback structure among variables with regard to innovation diffusion.

They are helpful in presenting results of modeling work in a nontechnical manner. However, CLDs are never final. As the researcher's understanding improves, CLDs evolve either. CLDs are drawn indicating the relationships in Vensim software (developed by Ventana Systems). Since simulation is essential for systems thinking (Sterman, 2002), the next section 4.4 will utilize stock and flow diagrams focusing on the area of technology suppliers in order to build a model for running simulations in Vensim software.

### 4.3.1 Technology Causal Loop Module

Technology in a company is the knowledge of the productive capabilities of the company's business. Formulation of a technology strategy is necessary in order to anticipate, create, and use technology for economic advantage. Managing strategic technologies-rapidly changing core technologies is essential to the future competitive position of a company (Betz, 1993).

Technological change is a major factor in long-term commercial failure or success. New technologies create new markets or substitute in existing markets by making the affected current technologies obsolete and any of the products, services, or production processes in which these technologies are embedded. In a company there are two principal economic goals for managing strategic technologies:

1. to innovate new markets or
2. to dominate and keep existing markets.

Therefore, companies need to manage innovation and technology to effectively solve the problems of anticipating, planning, and implementing technological change for commercial advantage (Betz, 1993). Due to the increased competition and accelerated product development cycles, innovation and the management of technology is becoming crucial to corporate success (Wheelen & Hunger, 2004:278).

Technology is a key resource of profound importance for corporate profitability and growth. When a company considers investing in technology in order to realize process innovation, it certainly experiences risk and uncertainty due to several aspects. As summarized in Figure 62, first price of technology and its maintenance costs may not be clear. In addition to cost of technology, its performance can be uncertain such that additional profitability by the means of adopting new technology can be ambiguous. (Stoneman, 2002: 55)

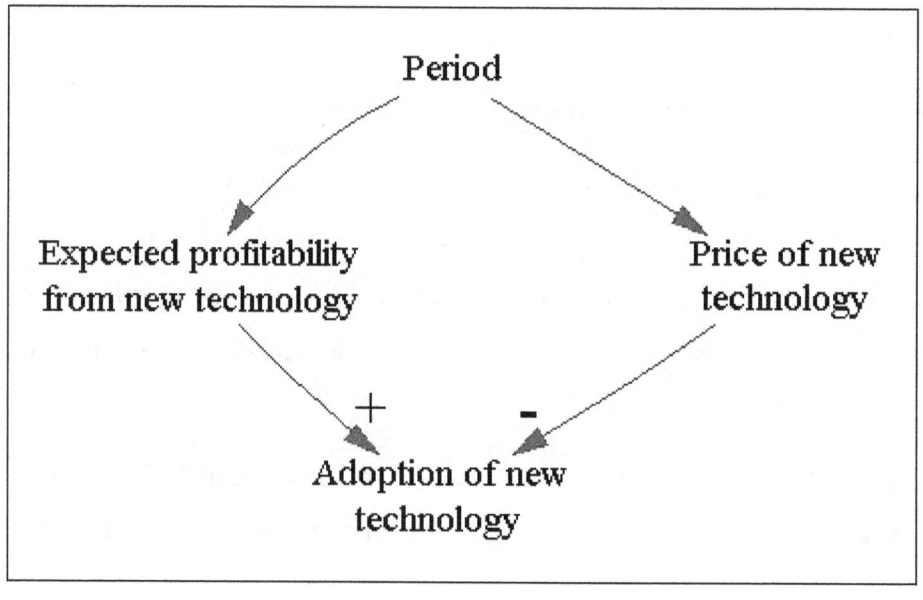

**Figure 62** Adoption of technology

Although there have been epidemic models for innovation diffusion, risk and uncertainty are first pointed out in the influential work on the diffusion of new process technologies by companies (Mansfield, 1968). In the inter-firm level, that a company becomes adopter of new technology depends on both expected profitability of adoption and on the uncertainty attached to the adoption. Though adoption by another company in that particular industry reduces uncertainty, such that the self-propagating nature drives diffusion process to the asymptote, where all companies would have adopted. On the intra-firm level, contrary to the expected profitability by a company there is uncertainty about the use of technology. As the company starts to learn about the technology, corresponding uncertainty declines, and the company produces more output utilizing new technology.

From technology lifecycle aspect, usually the price of a new process technology is relatively higher, when they are first introduced into the market. As displayed in Figure 62, price of a technology is one major factor having effect on the level of uncertainty, when companies decide to adopt (or not to adopt). The cost loop, which elaborates these relationships, is shown in Figure 63. Accordingly, when technology suppliers are able to present that relative cost of new process technology is lower than those companies in the market perceive. As this new process technology is adopted by more companies in the market, technology diffusion takes place as desired by technology supplier(s). That process technology is regarded as more mature in the market. Hence reliability of the process technology is perceived higher across the market, since risk and uncertainty decrease due to both experiences in actual performance and in more effective use of technology, as adopter companies progress along their learning curve. That technology proves its reliability triggers demand by non-adopter companies, since they do not want to stay behind their competitors, which have adopted this process technology and achieved better performance so far. As that process technology moves forward towards later stages in its lifecycle, reduced cost of technology will not have any marginal effect on reliability, hence demand for this particular process technology will decline.

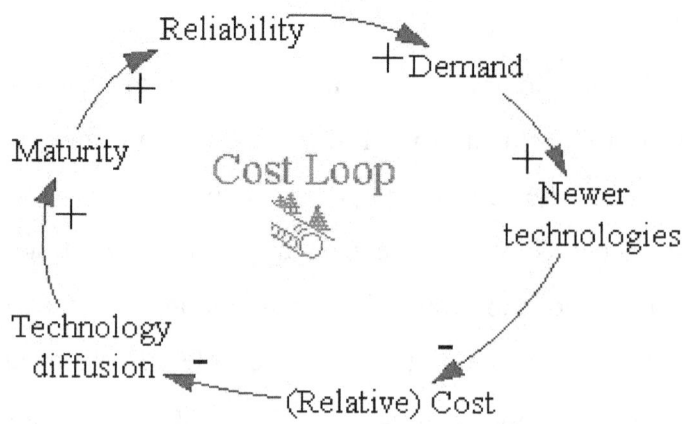

**Figure 63** Cost Loop

As displayed in Figure 64, second aspect of a process technology lifecycle is the productivity loop, which elaborates the other major factor for adoption of technology: expected profitability, which is actually the origin of risk and uncertainty. In any process innovation, a company seeks additional profitability via improving its productivity by increasing its output and/or by reducing cost via efficiency and effectiveness of new technology. When companies in the market start to adopt technology due to its perceived superiority, they undergo the experience of technology lifecycle as described for cost loop.

Adding the usability loop to causal loop diagram in Figure 64 puts forward Figure 65, which provides a holistic view on technology lifecycle from diffusion perspective, taking process innovations into account. When a company deploys new technology as process innovation, it faces uncertainty in using new technology resulting as variable output. Therefore companies do not replace their existing process technology immediately. As companies accumulate experience in use of technology, the variability in output declines to inherent variance (Stoneman, 2002:57). Variability, i.e. uncertainty, reduction leads to increased use of new technology. As discussed in previous paragraphs, uncertainty reduction has both intra-firm and inter-firm aspects. Along technology lifecycle, the interaction of three major loops takes place: productivity loop, cost loop and usability loop.

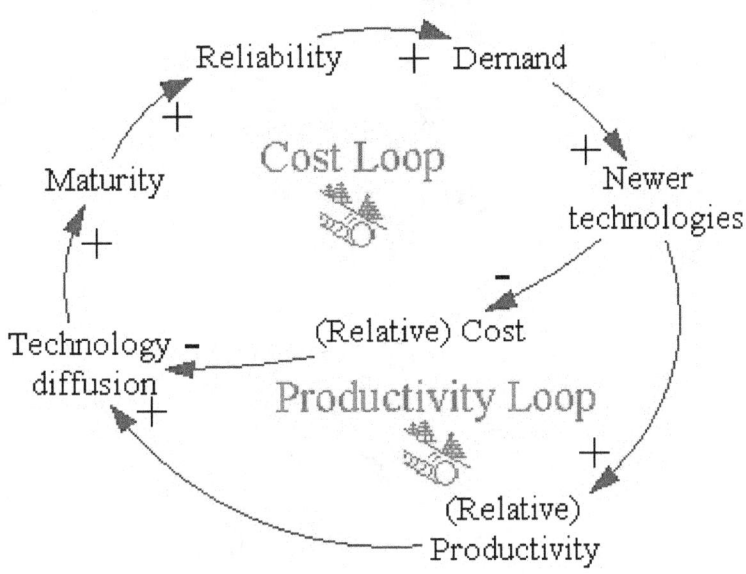

**Figure 64** Productivity Loop

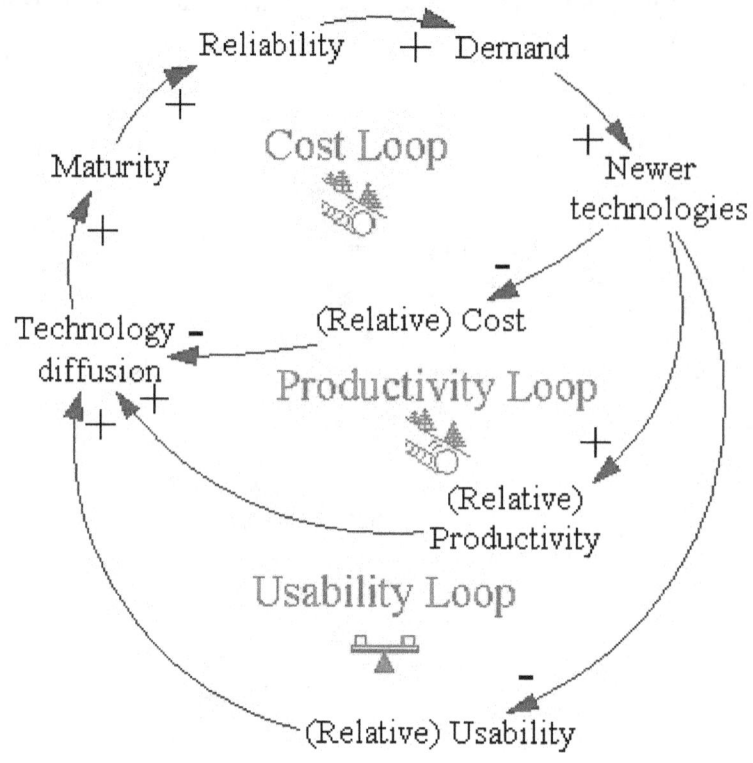

**Figure 65** Technology Lifecycle

Although technology lifecycle has been elaborated in the above paragraphs having technology diffusion of a single process innovation in the foreground, the variable *Newer technologies* does not appear to explain the lifecycle stage of a particular technology. Causal loops for technology lifecycle, which are summarized in Figure 65, actually indicate the movement from one technology S-curve (current technology, which companies use) to another technology S-curve (new technology, which companies adopt as process innovation). S-curve analysis had been developed to address challenges associated with technological discontinuities such that companies integrate technology into strategy. (Foster, 1986) Since the existence of more effective or more efficient technologies leads to multiple S-curves, the strategic challenge facing a company is choosing correct technology at the right time (Fleisher and Bensoussan, 2003: 388). The above mentioned causal loop clearly display that how economics of innovation is endogenous to the firm, though the level of analysis, both company and industry, cannot be clearly distinguished among variables in the above causal loop diagrams. Further, demand without considering other factors, does not have any particular effect on technology itself, contrary to the relationships in the above diagrams. Since demand by a person means that s/he ends up in buying product/service, that companies demand for new technology should results in procurement and use of it. Hence the relationships among technology as process innovation, demand for technology and adoption of technology should be reconsidered.

Each firm decides whether to adopt new technology, however the aggregate number of firms who use new technology determines diffusion. Systems thinking enables both firm-level and industry-level analysis simultaneously since causal loop diagrams provide to look through multiple cause and effect relationships among different variables regarding technology diffusion as shown in Figure 66. Although demand is an industry-specific aggregate variable, adoption is a firm's individual decision, which results in purchase of new technology by comparing its relative cost with respect to existing technologies. As time passes and more firms learn to use new technology, technology reliability increases as discussed above. Although diffusion of technology is an industry-specific indicator, investment in new technology happens as each firm's individual adoption decision with respect to factors changing over time.

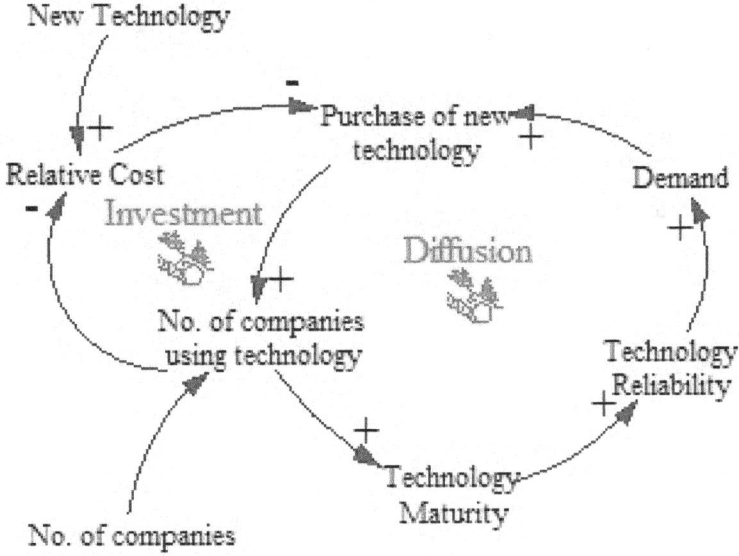

**Figure 66** Technology Diffusion

Bass (1969) model as discussed in literature review is one of the most popular diffusion models extensively utilized for consumer market. Similarly, diffusion of technology as process innovation can be expressed as stock-flow diagram corresponding to Bass model such as Figure 67. **Relative cost** is the cost of new technology with respect to existing technologies. Since **cost of new technology** depends on pricing policies of technology suppliers, relative cost can be considered as factor of external influence. **Technology maturity** increases as more firms learn to use new technology, though it is measure related to technology itself. **Technology reliability** is more about predictable performance of new technology as process innovation in the manufacturing environment. Increase in technology reliability strengthens **demand for new technology**, though purchase of new technology results upon evaluation of relative cost.

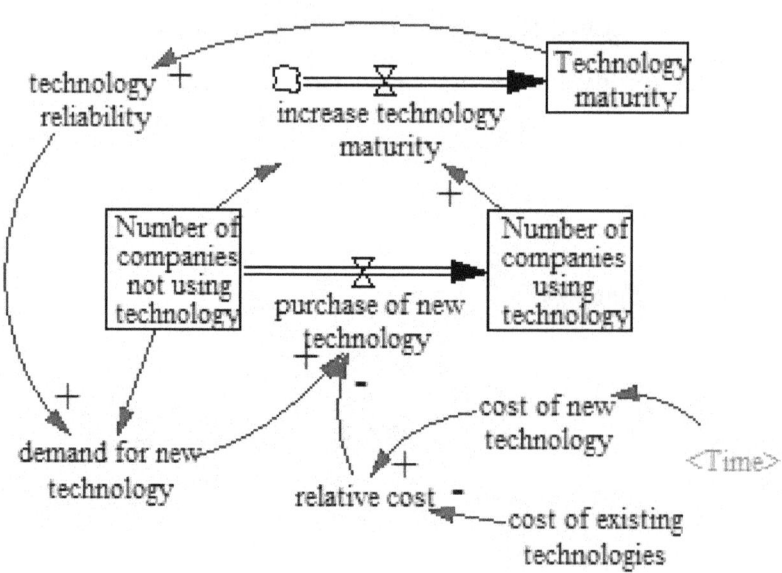

**Figure 67** Stock Flow Diagram – Technology Diffusion

### 4.3.2 Market Causal Loop Module

In this study, market is regarded as a specific industry, which comprises various companies in that industry. Those companies can be adopter or non-adopter of a particular new technology. As Mansfield (1961) argued, once a process innovation has been adopted by one company, the important question in the market arises: How later do other companies follow? As discussed in literature review, adopter categories of innovators, early adopters, early majority, late majority and laggards are not only used for consumers also for companies as well. There are various categories for companies, which are related to their approach towards innovation.

Similar to Rogers' (1962) adopter categories, Figure 68 categorizes companies with respect to their orientation towards innovation. If a company is relatively small within its industry though regarded as innovative due its characteristics, then that company possesses high innovation orientation but low market orientation (innovator). When a major company adopts new technology, it both displays relatively high innovation orientation and high market orientation due its characteristics influencing its industry (early adopters). As time passes, other companies will realize the change in their industry and follow those companies who already adopted technology (late adopters). There are always some companies in the industry, who do not adapt to the changing conditions in their task environment (laggards). They remain isolated from their industry by not investing in technology, which their competitors already deployed. A company which had previously been regarded as shaping the industry in terms of market and innovation orientation can miss the emergence of a new disruptive innovation, such that they remain isolated from their task environment. Consequently they face difficulties not being able to adapt to their environment. They either terminate or are exposed to mandatory change. Adopter categories and mapping companies' approaches to those adopter companies illustrates the overall picture of a process innovation within the industry, or the market as called in the proposed model terminology. This study will not consider multiple generations of technologies.

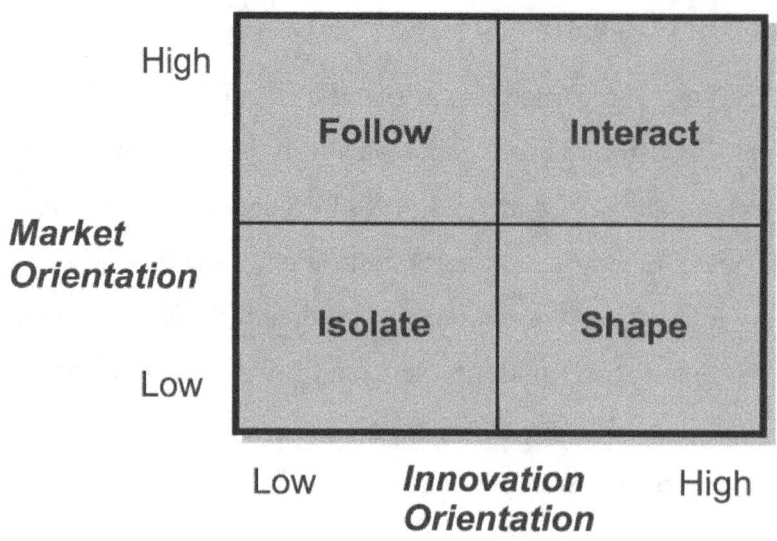

**Figure 68** Market vs.Innovation Orientation (Source: Berthon, Hulbert and Pitt, 1999)

The system dynamics model as depicted in Figure 69 is based on the assumptions by Mansfield (1961) such that factors affecting innovation diffusion such as cost of technology, competition, expected profitability are regarded as exogenous. Further, companies are presumed that they learn from their previous experience and other companies' experience, though Mansfield's logistic diffusion model does not take into account that also companies search for information. The advantage of system dynamics methodology is that various factor affecting innovation diffusion can be included as endogenous variables interacting among each other.

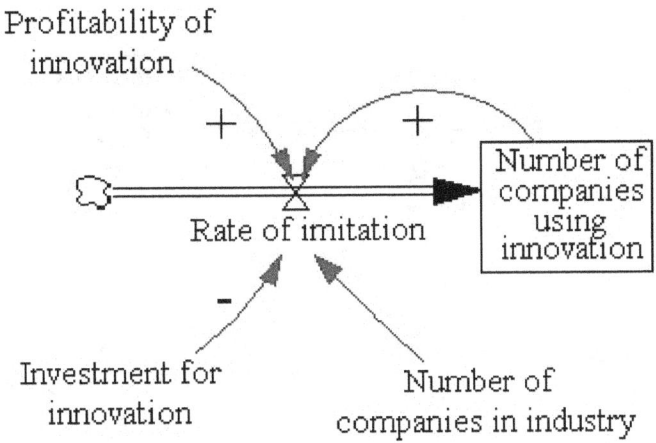

**Figure 69** Diffusion of an Industrial Innovation (drawn from Mansfield, 1961)

Although the Bass (1969) model, used for diffusion of new products does not distinguish among the personal differences of each consumer, the model can be adapted to technology adoption by companies instead of consumers as well. The original Bass model assumes that potential adopters are influenced by mass-media communication (external influence) and word of mouth communication (internal influence). Bass grouped those adopters that are exposed to mass media as innovators, and those that are exposed to word of mouth as imitators. (Mahajan, Muller and Bass, 1990) Though, the term "innovator" does not correspond to the adopter category of "innovator" mentioned in the above paragraphs. Therefore, in order to avoid confusion of terms when elaborating the diffusion of process innovations, Maier's (2002) mixed influence model, which is based on the Bass model, is utilized, where they label external and internal influence as innovative demand and imitative demand respectively. Within the context of diffusion of process innovation, Bass system dynamics model is displayed in Figure 70. Adopters and non-adopters of technology are stock variables of innovation diffusion, whereas purchase/use of the particular technology corresponds to the rate of diffusion. When the Bass model is reviewed from system dynamics point of view, it represents the overall diffusion process that companies within a particular market adopt technology over time such that the number of adopters will follow a logistics path due to the effects of both innovative demand and imitative demand.

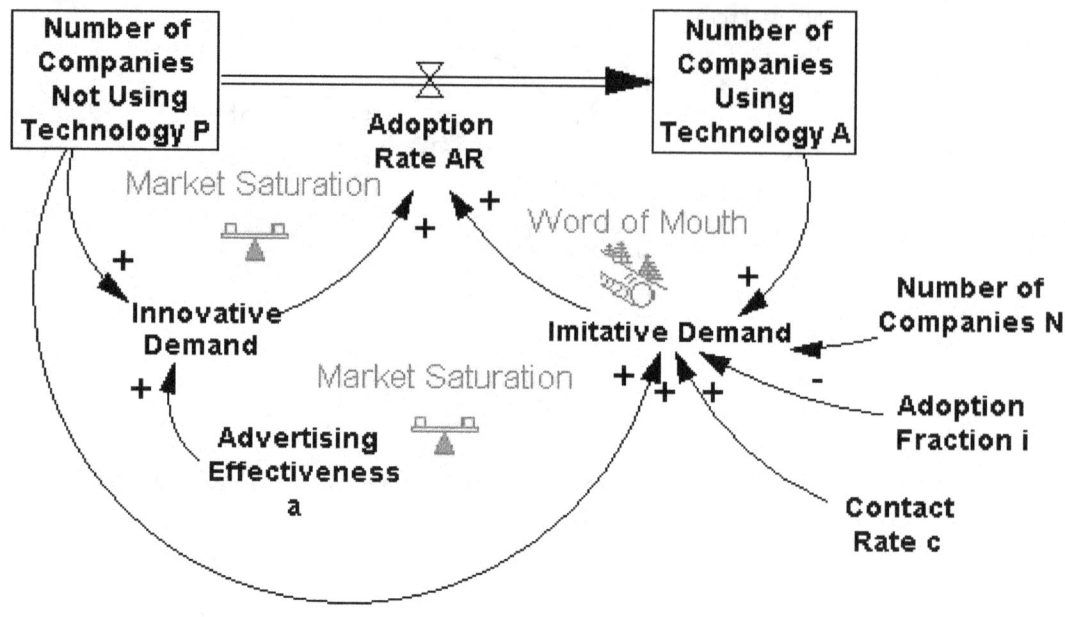

**Figure 70** Bass Mixed Influence Model (modified from Sterman, 2000 and Maier, 2002)

According to the Bass mixed influence model, an industry, which incorporates 1000 firms as **Number of Companies**, is going to adopt new technology as process innovation. Model parameters and initial values of stock variables are shown in Table 11. Except for **Number of Companies**, values for model parameters are inherited from Sterman (2000:325). Since **Number of Companies Using Technology** is initially zero, **Adoption Rate** will initially be determined by **Innovative Demand** such that **Number of Companies Not Using Technology** is multiplied by **Advertising Effectiveness**. As **Adoption Rate** starts to increase **Number of Companies Using Technology**, Imitative Demand accelerates Adoption Rate. Market saturation loop decreases **Innovative Demand** since the pool of **Number of Companies Not Using Technology** declines. The inclusion of advertising effect solves the startup problem of logistics innovation diffusion model.

**Table 11** Model Parameters and Stock Variables

| Model Parameter | Value | Stock Variable | Initial Value |
|---|---|---|---|
| Number of Companies | 1000 | Number of Companies Using Technology | 1000 |
| Advertising Effectiveness | 1.1% | Number of Companies Not Using Technology | 0 |
| Adoption Fraction | 1.5% | | |
| Contact Rate | 100 | | |

**Adoption Rate** is the number of companies who adopt new technology due to factors related to both innovative demand and/or imitative demand. Since **Adoption Rate** is a whole number, the model converts rational numbers as the sum of effects for innovative demand and imitative demand into integer values. Using the terminology in Figure 70, model equations are as follows and simulation results are displayed Figure 71:

$$P + A = N$$
$$A = INTEGRAL\ (AR, A_0)$$
$$P = INTEGRAL\ (-AR, N-A_0)$$
$$AR = INTEGER\ (aP + ciPA/N)$$

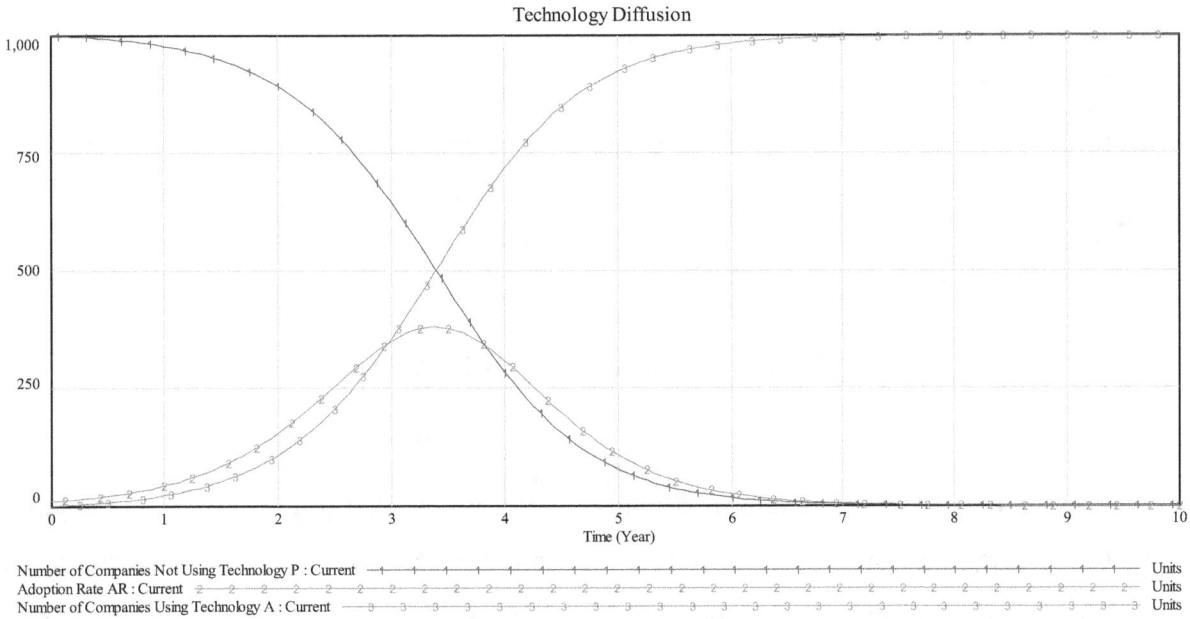

**Figure 71** Simulation Results for Bass Mixed Influence Model

When the model is simulated in Vensim, **Adoption Rate** becomes zero at 8.375 years, i.e. all companies become users of new technology after nine years. As shown in Figure 71, **Number of Companies Not Using Technology** is completely migrated to **Number of Companies Using Technology**. **Adoption Rate** reaches its maximum of 380 firms during the fourth year. As discussed in literature review for Bass Model, since Adoption Rate has a normal distribution over time, diffusion of technology follows an S-curve. When **Imitative Demand** and **Innovative Demand** are displayed together with **Adoption Rate**, results shown in Figure 72, are equivalent to Figure 6 in literature review, since innovative demand corresponds adoptions due to external influence, whereas imitative demand corresponds to adoptions due to internal influence.

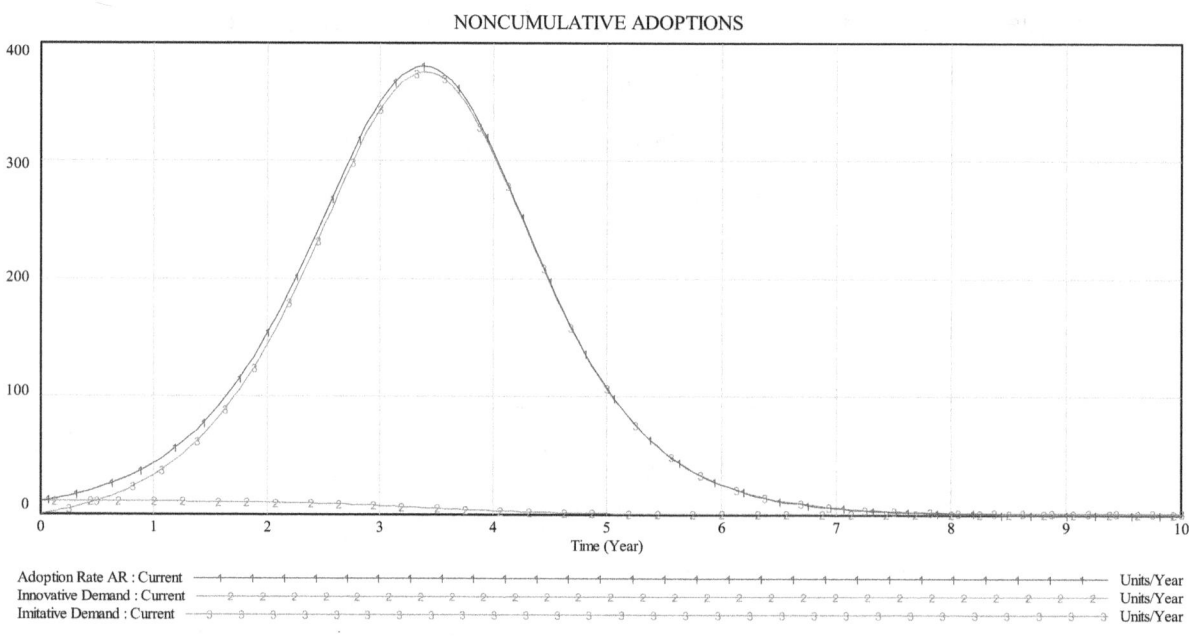

**Figure 72** Simulation Results for Adoption

According to system dynamics methodology described in section 3.3, this modeling process passed the four stages of problem articulation, dynamic hypothesis formulation and formulation of simulation model and testing, since it is an application of a known system dynamics model (Sterman, 2001). Policy design and formulation as the fifth step provides better insight to managers and decision makers about the diffusion path of an industrial innovation such as carrying out simulations with different values for model parameters and sensitivity analysis to analyze change under different scenarios. The rate at which active **Number of Companies Using Technology** is **Number of Companies Not Using Technology** is **Contact Rate**. **Adoption fraction** is the probability that a contact between a technology user firm and a non-user firm results in adoption of new technology by that non-user firm. A firm in an industry who uses technology may have contacts with other companies in that industry. However, both firm characteristics and industry characteristics make **Contact Rate** variable according to circumstances. Therefore changing **Contact Rate** will yield different **Adoption Rate** as displayed in Figure 73. When the model is simulated for different Contact Rates of 100, 50 and 20, the diffusion rate that 50% of **Number of Companies** becomes **Number of Companies Using Technology** is four years, six years and eleven years respectively. Different parameter values for **Contact Rate** also provide evidence that an industrial innovation may not necessarily diffuse across all firms in parallel to the discussion in the literature review of diffusion models.

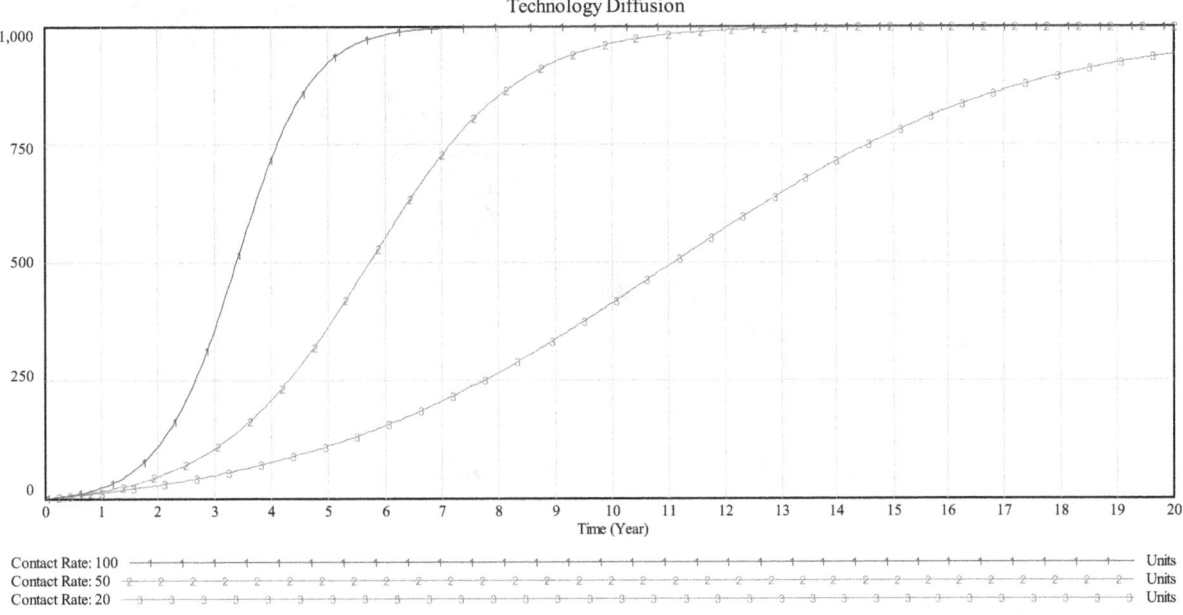

**Figure 73** Technology Diffusion and Contact Rate

Hence decision makers may test their assumptions with respect to different circumstances such that they can both formulate and evaluate their policies. Sensitivity analysis enables to understand whether conclusions change with respect to varying assumptions based on a range of uncertainty. As an example, probability of adoption may not be same for each individual firm, as discussed for probit models in section 2.4.4. When **Adoption Fraction** is simulated between the symmetric range of 0.5% and 2.5% (i.e. base run as 1.5% indicated in blue line of Figure 73.), diffusion rate that 50% of **Number of Companies** becomes **Number of Companies Using Technology** has an interval from three to eight years instead of four years. If firms would not imitate other firms using new technology, i.e. Adoption Fraction would be zero, diffusion rate that 50% of firms in a particular industry would be become users of industrial innovation after 68 years.

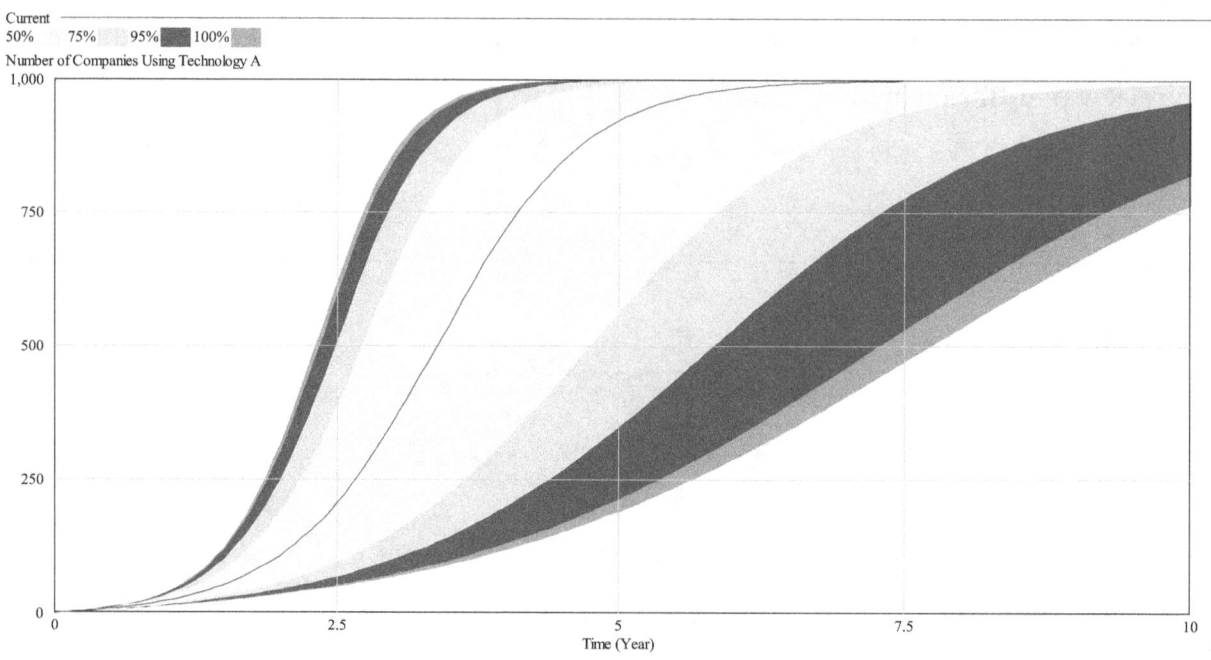

**Figure 74** Sensitivity Analysis – Technology Diffusion and Adoption Fraction

From an industry perspective using technology, both task environment and macroeconomic conditions can induce a particular industry in general to look for improving competitive edge. Accordingly, companies in that industry will actively seek improvement in their processes. Consequently, they tend to deploy process innovations within their organizations. Within the context of process innovations, they investigate investment alternatives for new technology such that they consider purchase of a single technology as discussed in technology causal loop module. The causal loop diagram under perfect information in Figure 46 is revised taking the above Bass mixed influence model into account and going away from perfect information assumption. When each firms adopts new technology due to innovative demand and/or imitative demand in an industry, number of firms using new technology increases. Due to new technology, both cost of production increases and firm output increases due to new technology's relatively higher performance with respect to existing technologies, whose causal relationships are comprehensively shown in Figure 75. Hence industry output increases. However supply-demand equilibrium from economics clearly indicates that increase in output results decline in prices. Consequently incremental benefits of using new technology narrow down such that firms who are not profitable enough may exit that particular industry. Even without considering new firm entry into industry and influence of public policies, causal relationships regarding adoption of new technology among firms are quite complex and dynamic.

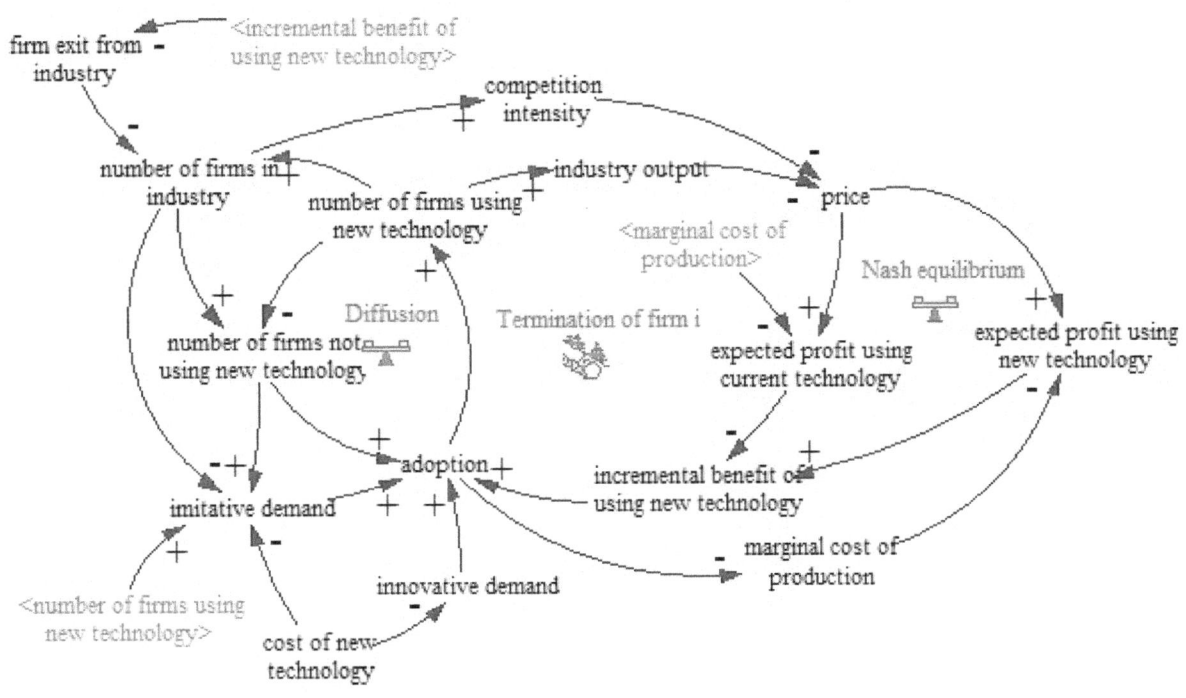

**Figure 75** A causal loop of technology diffusion in any industry

### 4.3.3 Customers Causal Loop Module

The process of innovation begins with identifying the outcomes customers want to achieve; it ends in the creation of items they will buy. When desired outcomes become the focus of customer research, innovation is no longer a matter of wish fulfillment or serendipity; it is instead a manageable, predictable discipline (Ulwick, 2002).

Positive business performance effects of customer orientation and innovation orientation are widely recognized. However, these two are, to some extent, conflicting and mutually exclusive. Many scholars have warned that too much innovation orientation results in forgetting customer needs. This, in turn, results in unprofitable business performance. Respectively, other scholars have argued that following customer needs may augment inertia and inhibit radical innovation. (Kauppila, 2008).

The traditional approach of asking customers for solutions tends to undermine the innovation process. That's because most customers have a very limited frame of reference. In other words customers should not be trusted to come up with solutions; they aren't expert or informed enough for that part of the innovation process. What customers value is a far more fruitful exercise than merely asking them to submit their own solutions (Ulwick, 2002).

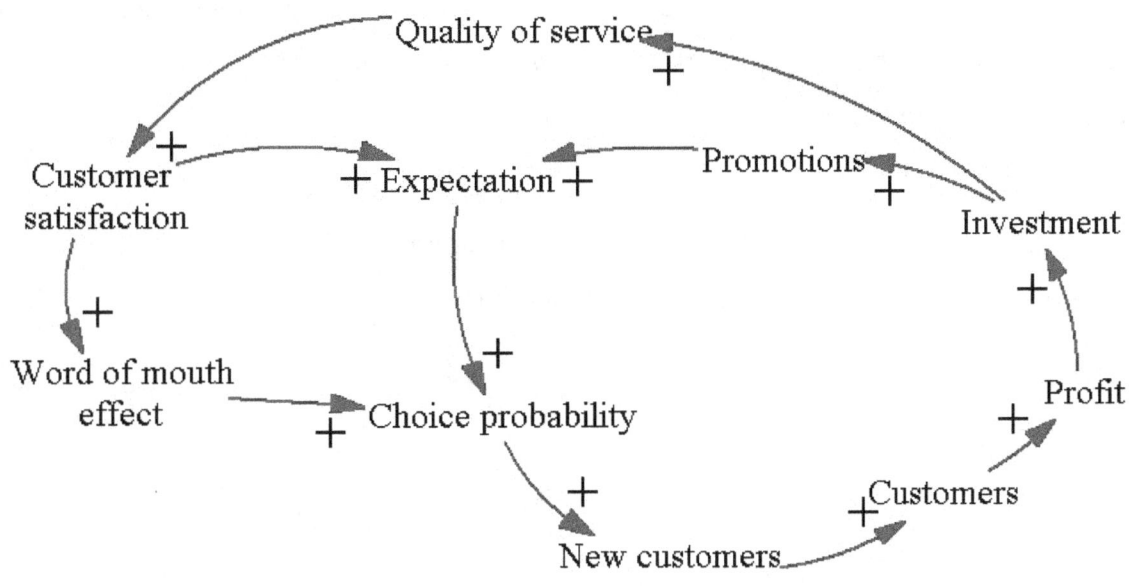

**Figure 76** Customers

### 4.3.4 Technology Suppliers Causal Loop Module

A supplier is defined as the organization or person that provides a product, material or service to another business. The supplier may be internal and dependent to the organization or external and independent from the organization. A supplier which provides a constant stream of incremental innovations is a potential source of competitive advantage (Wolter and Veloso, 2008).

If organizations are tied to a single internal supplier they may miss out on innovations (Langlois & Robertson, 1989). In order to continuously expand their customer base and in contrast to internal suppliers, independent external suppliers have greater incentives to expand their knowledge and skill bases, keeping abreast of new technological developments (Nooteboom, 1999; Poppo & Zenger, 1998). Consequently, intermediate markets including independent suppliers may offer a pluralism of technological alternatives in the form of capabilities and resources that any firm can access at any time (Wolter and Veloso, 2008).

Empirical studies showed that industries where modular innovations occur exhibit a relatively high stability of players at the systems integrator level, with entry and exit occurring at the supplier level (Hobday, 1998).

This study mainly focuses on technology suppliers who make particular innovation(s) available to the market. The causal loop diagram in Figure 77 summarizes the relationships between technology suppliers and innovations.

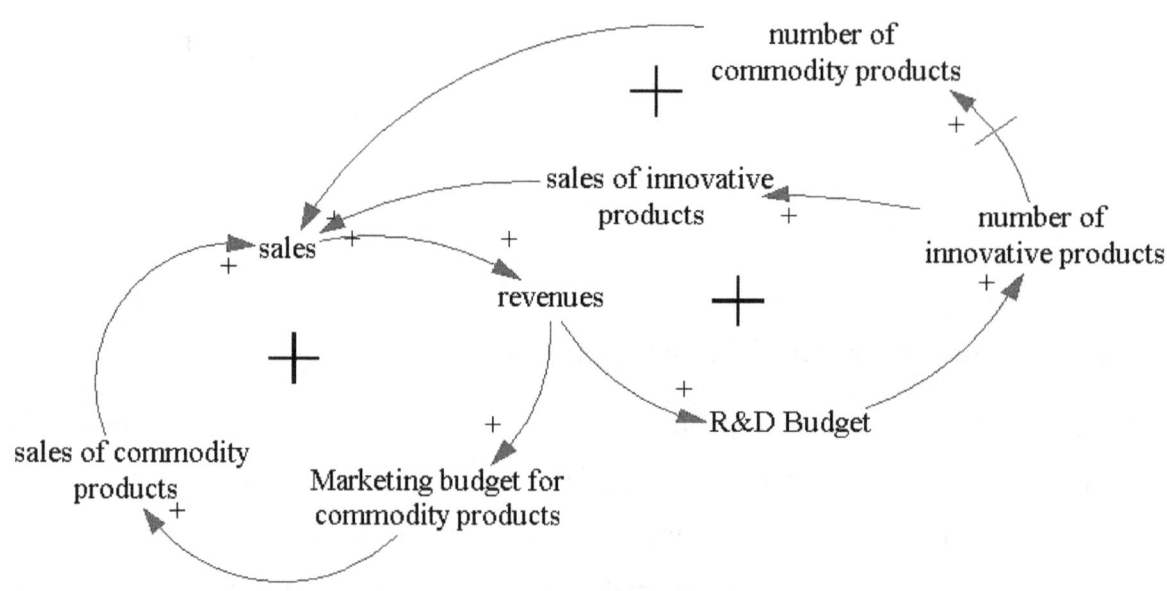

Figure 77 Technology suppliers

The causal loop diagram, which explains the effect of innovation on technology suppliers' performance, comprises three major loops. The first loop might be addressed as *research and development (R&D) loop* and is displayed in Figure 78. The second loop as shown in Figure 79 is called as *revenue growth loop*, because sales is achieved over the lifecycle of that particular product (i.e. technology), such that innovative products become mature and obsolete over time. Finally the third loop, which is displayed as Figure 80, is labeled as *marketing loop*.

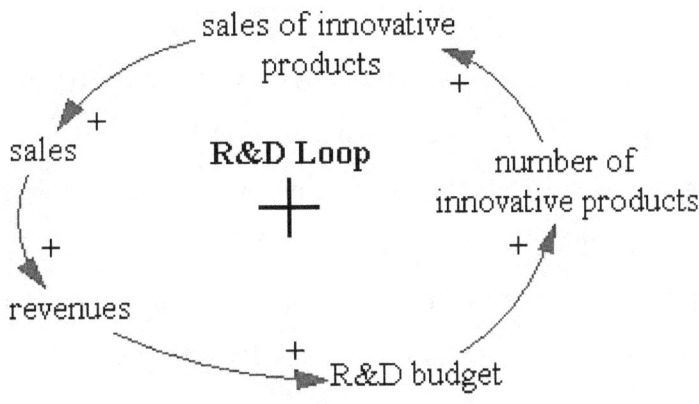

**Figure 78** R&D Loop

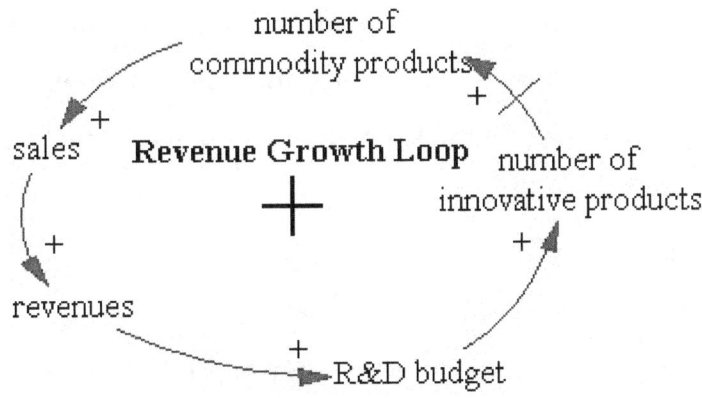

**Figure 79** Revenue Growth Loop

**Figure 80** Marketing Loop

When a technology supplier makes an innovation available to the market, i.e. particular industry(ies), it desires that companies in that market buy that particular innovation as their investment in new technology. As this technology supplier increases its revenues by increasing sales, it can deploy more resources in R&D, such that R&D budget becomes larger due to belief in future growth prospects. As a consequence of increased R&D efforts, more innovations (i.e. new products) will be introduced to the market. Such innovations, i.e. new products, will create new demand in the market and hence increase sales of the supplier.

Similar to the R&D loop, revenue growth loop investigates the consequences of new innovation as a consequence of increased R&D budget of a technology supplier. As displayed in Figure 79, technologies, i.e. innovations become mature and obsolete, as time passes. However, later stages of technology lifecycle, i.e. growth, maturity, decline, have overall positive effect on sales. Consequently, revenues of technology suppliers increase.

Marketing loop, as shown in Figure 80, indicates that increase in revenues results in more budget allocation for marketing of current technologies, which technology supplier possesses. As technology becomes mature and obsolete, increased marketing efforts will cause growth in sales of existing technologies towards the market. Both R&D and marketing loops are clear examples of the trade-off between R&D and marketing, which is elaborated in management science literature for many years. Technology suppliers need to decide on marketing and R&D budget fractions each and every year. They need to have new technologies, i.e. innovative products, in order to attract companies. They also need to market both their new products and existing products. (Soydan and Oner, 2004)

Developing products faster, better and cheaper than competitors had become critical to success in many markets. (Ford and Sterman, 1998) Both managers of technology suppliers and scholars realize that R&D provides science and technology, which serves tomorrow's industry profitably, whereas marketing paves the way for sales of existing technologies to current market. Figure 77 alone indicates that cyclical causal relationships require deep understanding. The budgets to be shared by R&D and marketing vary every period. Technology suppliers undergo excess resource allocation such as over investment in marketing, though companies in that particular industry may not have enough funds for investment due to circumstances in their external environment such as economy in recession. They can over invest in R&D, though industry is not particularly seeking new technologies during that time period. (Soydan and Oner, 2004) It is a dynamic problem, since the trade-off between marketing and R&D changes every time. The extent that technology suppliers achieve synchronization between marketing and R&D resources will increase number of companies in that particular industry they are selling to, and therefore their revenues.

The aim is to provide and explain policies for a technology supplier such that it achieves long term success in having more companies in that particular industry as customer and in increasing revenues. As Sterman (2000) argued, the real value of a system dynamics model is the elimination of problems by changing the underlying structure of the system rather than anticipating and reacting to the environment.

### 4.3.5 Social Networks Causal Loop Module

Innovation diffusion occurs in complex systems where networks connecting system members are overlapping, multiple, and complex. Diffusion occurs most often in heterogeneous zones, i.e., transitional spaces where sufficient differentiation among network members comes to obtain. Such heterogeneous network connections, which comprise the innovation-diffusion system as shown in Figure 81, occur among innovators and other engaged members of target populations (Rogers et.al, 2005).

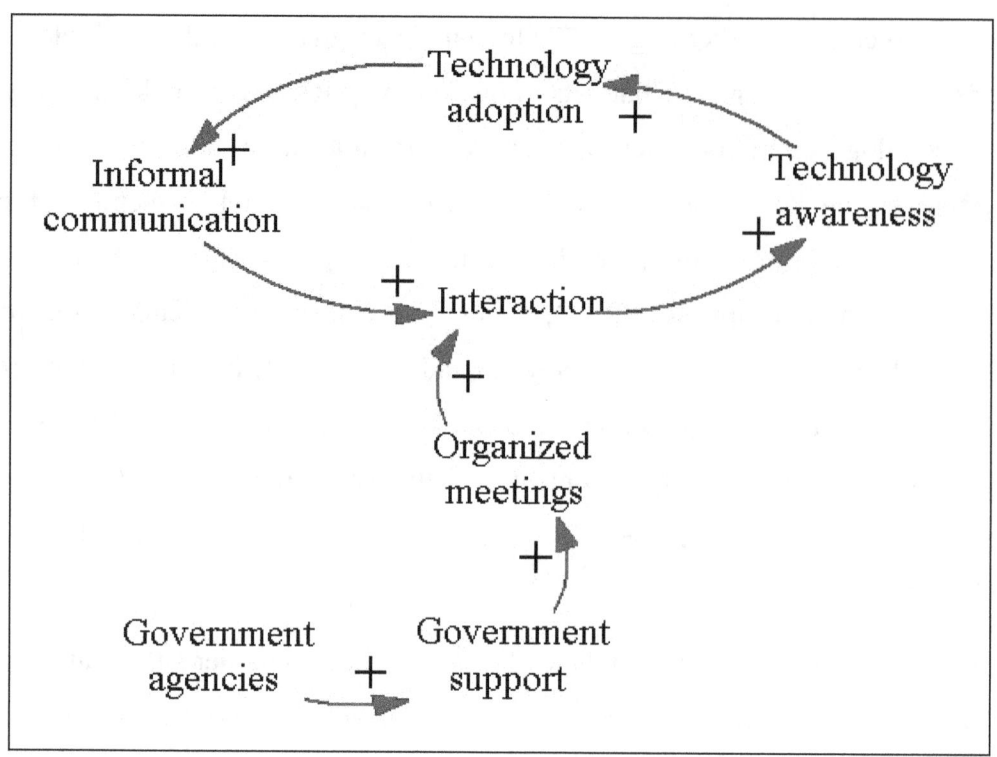

**Figure 81** Social networks

### 4.3.6 Public Policies Loop Module

Public policy is defined as the "The basic policy or set of policies forming the foundation of public laws, especially such policy not yet formally enunciated" (Webster Dictionary, 2008). With a broader perspective public policy may also be defined as efforts designed to influence the content, quality or extent of governmental, private sector activities, profit or nonprofit activities of significant public interest.

By using their back- grounds, experiences, and activities that occupy their attention people develop, carry, react to, and modify ideas. People become attached to those ideas over time through a social-political process of converting their ideas into good currency (Van de Ven, 1986). This process is introduced as a trigger for the emergence of public policies (Schon, 1971) as illustrated in Figure 82.

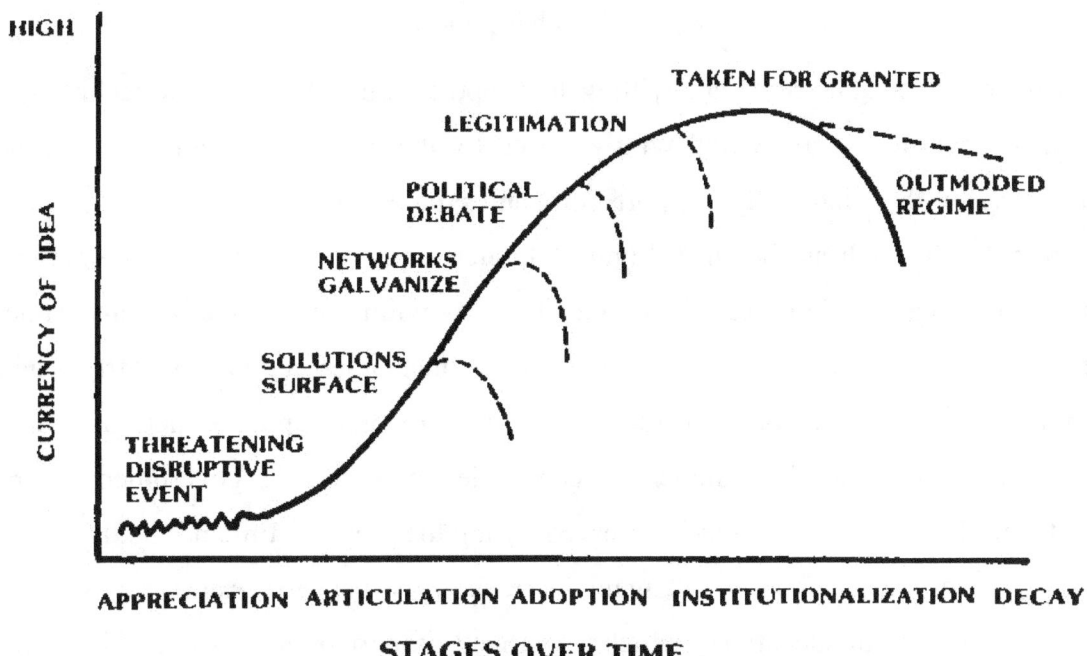

**Figure 82** Lifecycle of ideas in good currency
(Adapted from Schon, 1971)

As elaborated more in technology and market areas of innovation diffusion, the role of expectations influence diffusion of technology. For a given price and new technology, companies in the market will delay adoption of new technology, if the expected future price is lower and more improvement is anticipated. (Rosenberg, 1976) Complementing Rosenberg's arguments, causal loops of technology diffusion show dynamic changes in expectations during technology lifecycle.

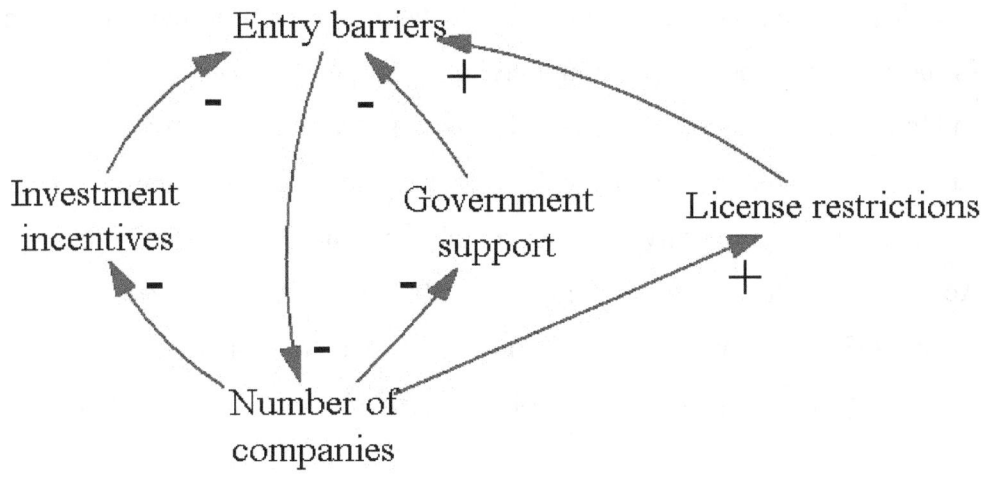

**Figure 83** Public policies

When government authorities are willing to support companies for new technologies, they usually provide tax credit with respect to the investment amounts for new technology, or they indirectly support companies investing in technology via public procurements. Though as shown in Figure 83, such support initiatives reduce the entry barriers for companies in order to deploy technology within their organizations. Though as entry barriers investing in new technology decline, other companies start to adopt technology as well. Since one considers the volume of public procurement as more or less fixed, increase in the number of companies may reduce government support allocated to those companies, which deserved during the previous time period. Hence less available government support will again increase entry barriers. Another government method is investment incentives, which is utilized as part of macroeconomic policies such as unemployment, trade policy. When government provides too many investment incentives towards a particular industry, then new companies will be established as a result of lower entry barriers of that industry. When number of companies increases excessively due to several reasons, government can place license requirements in order to regulate the industry. Hence the barriers to enter the particular industry become higher and have a negative effect on the total number of companies.

Since innovation means sustainable development, increased welfare and employment for national economies, not only governments put emphasis on factor conditions that foster innovation but also European Commission, as supra-national institution, states that both research & development and innovation should take in each European Union member country's political, financial and commercial agendas. As part of Lisbon strategy, European Union aims to develop new policies for R&D and information society, to speed up structural reforms for innovation and competitiveness, to create common European market to be the most competitive, most dynamic and knowledge-based economy in the world. According to OECD studies, more than 50% of growth in developed economies during 1970-1995 corresponds to innovation and innovativeness. Hence public policies, as outlined in Figure 84, enable various tools that influence firms' innovation activities.

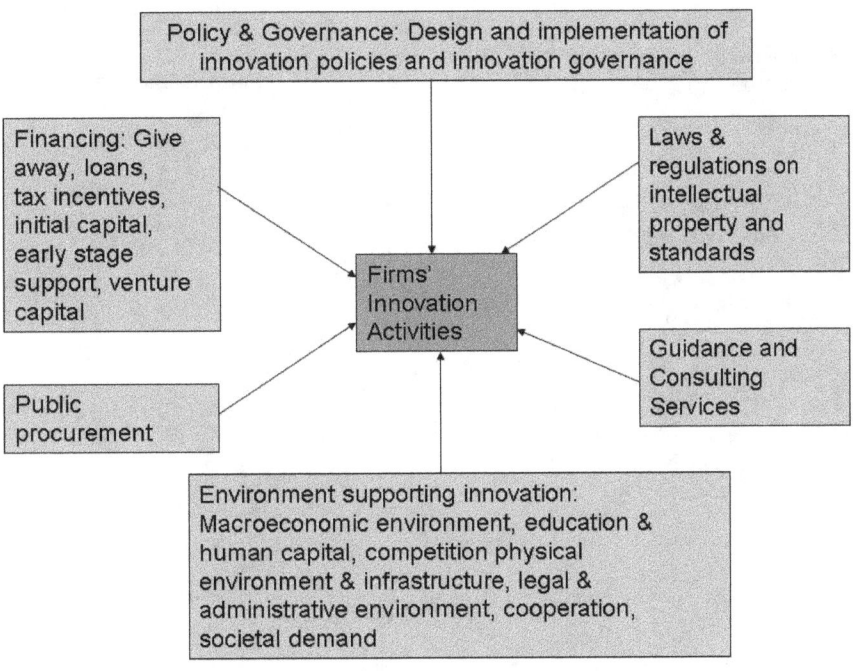

**Figure 84** Public policies Affecting Firms' Innovation Activities
(Adapted from: Şirin Elçi, 2006)

Lisbon strategy, being a major example by European Union, government authorities place higher priority on innovation policies and governance. National innovation systems are networks of public authorities, universities and non-governmental organizations that develop policies for innovation management and also measure the performance of innovation policies. Further, governments establish laws and regulations that help companies in their innovation activities and that protect R&D efforts such as intellectual property. As discussed in previous paragraphs, governments design public policies that support innovation by companies. A main tool of these strategies, as displayed in Figure 85, is financial support that governments make available to companies.

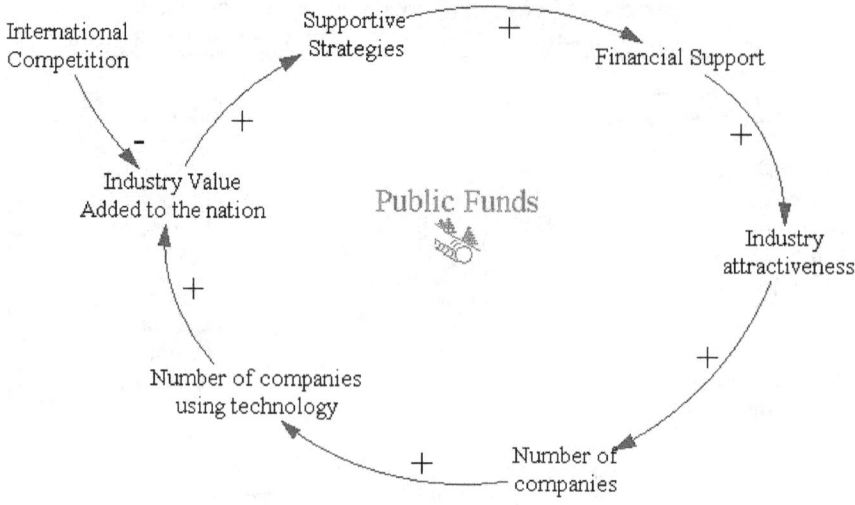

**Figure 85** Public funds

Financial support can provide companies cash and/or benefits in various ways such as tax incentives or cash for investment in technology, which increases industry attractiveness. Hence both number of companies increases in general, and companies willing to use new technology spread either such that economic value added by the particular industry increases. Another way of financial support is that government authorities carry out public procurement as shown in Figure 86.

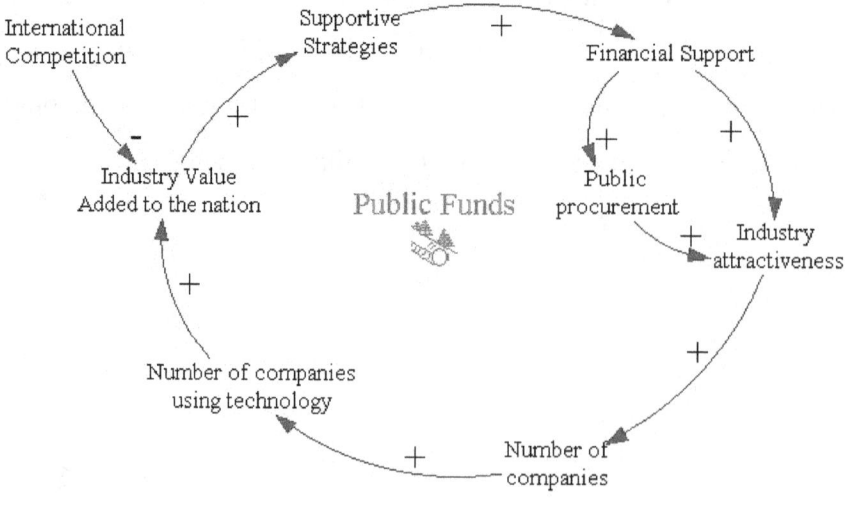

**Figure 86** Public funds and procurement

Further, governments have legislative and law enforcement capabilities such that they facilitate firms' innovative activities via regulatory framework. Government agencies also provide consulting services to companies such that they provide feedback to legislative authorities either. This second loop named law enforcement is displayed in Figure 87.

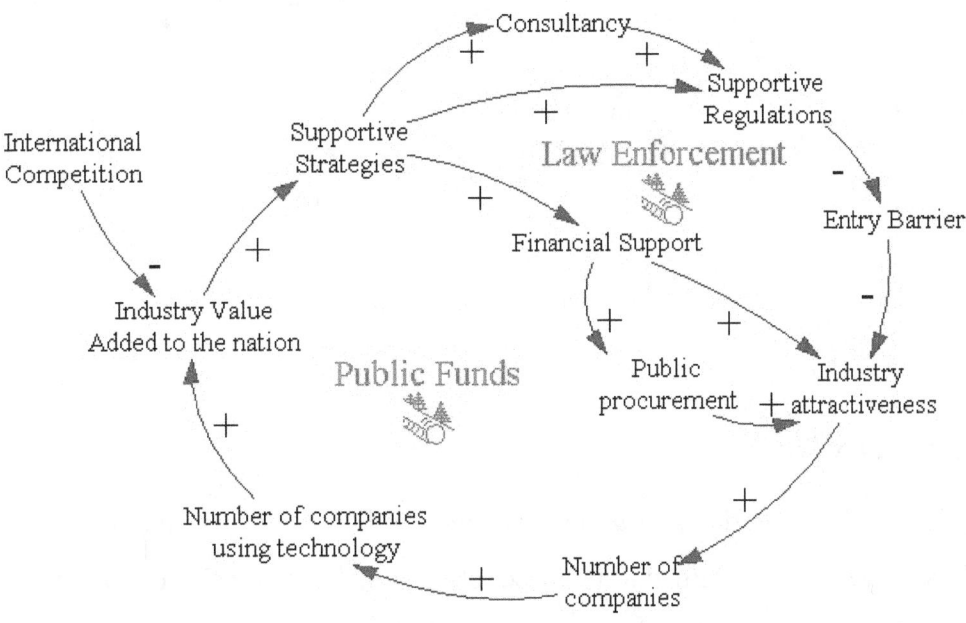

**Figure 87** Law enforcement

An extension the law enforcement loop is the regulation for intellectual property such that patents and other intangible assets provide benefits to innovative firms. Consequently, they get protected from a competition for a while by the means of regulations. Due to higher entry barriers innovative firms will receive additional benefits. This outlines tools and methods, how public policies can stimulate or slow down technology diffusion as summarized in Figure 88.

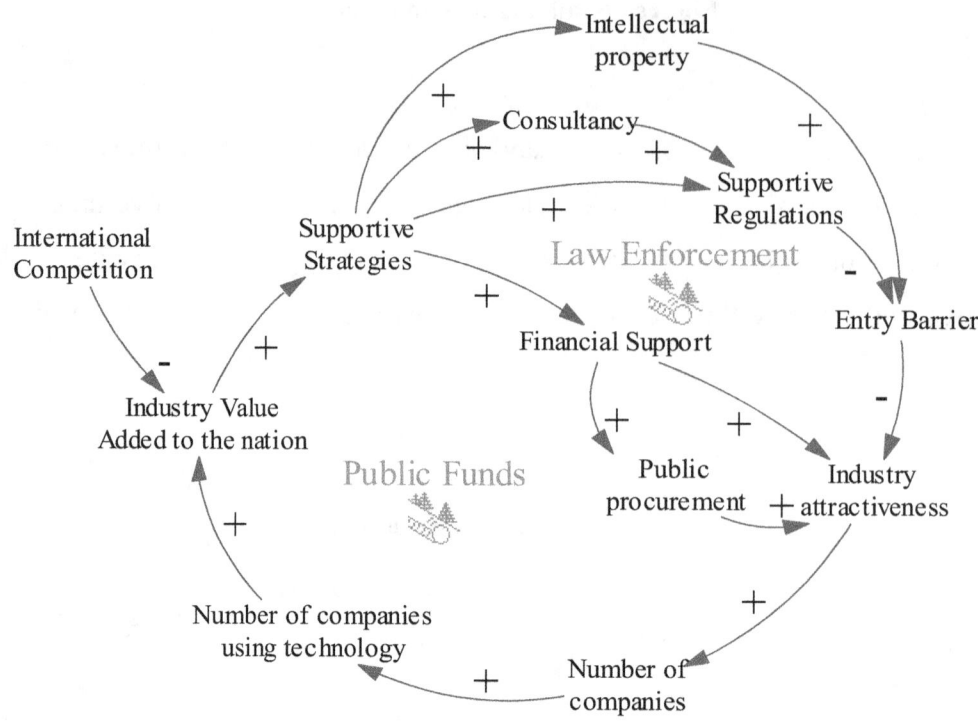

**Figure 88** Public Policies

## 4.4 Technology Suppliers

When a firm sells its products, it generates **revenue** by charging **price per unit** for **unit sales**, since buyers are presumed to be price takers and there is lack of competition during the initial lifecycle stages for those products. Based on firm's income resulting from **profit margin**, the firm will establish a **total expenditure budget** for company activities. A firm will decide upon various budget items and allocate a **production budget** by a certain **production budget fraction**. **Production cost factor** is an exogenous variable that may take various factors affecting production cost into account. After fixing on production budget, the firm will make number of units produced, such that production cost of unit new technology becomes available. These causal relationships are displayed in Figure 89.

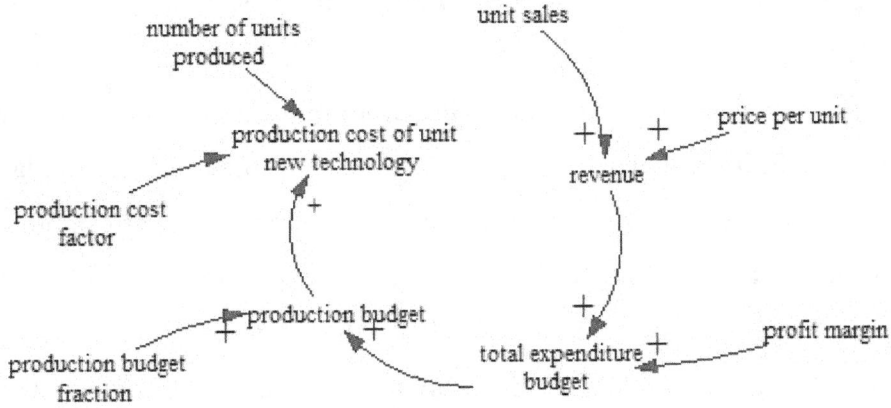

**Figure 89** Cause-Effect Relations in Production

In order to close the loop, a link has to be added. Before carrying on, the stock-and-flow diagram of the relations that are mentioned in the previous paragraph are displayed in Figure 90. **Price per unit** has been set as 20 Euro, whereas **unit sales** is 100 units per month. Profit margin is assumed 10% such that total expenditure budget is 90% of revenue. Production budget is assumed 20% of total expenditure budget and production cost factor is taken as 1 EUR/unit such that cost of production occurs as units are produced.

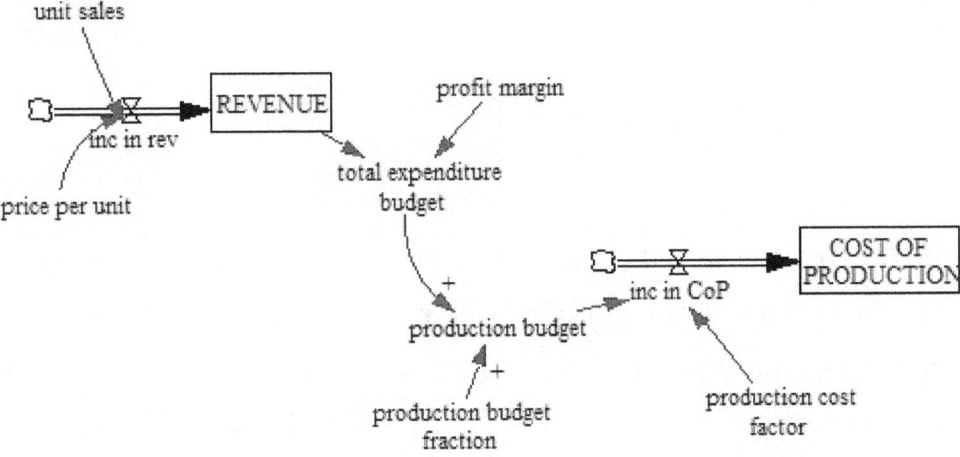

**Figure 90** Stock-and-flow Relations in Production

Since there are no opposite relationships among variables, both revenue and cost of production increase indefinitely. However, since there is no causal loop, revenue does not relate to time, which accumulates steadily, therefore expenditure and cost of production appear to rise indefinitely, which is unrealistic and can be observed as simulation output in Figure 91 the above stock-flow diagram. It becomes obvious that establishing stock-flow relationships out of causal loop diagram requires more rigorous thinking about cause and effect relationships among variables and whether particular variables are missing. Otherwise, simulating interactions among variables lack meaningful outcomes.

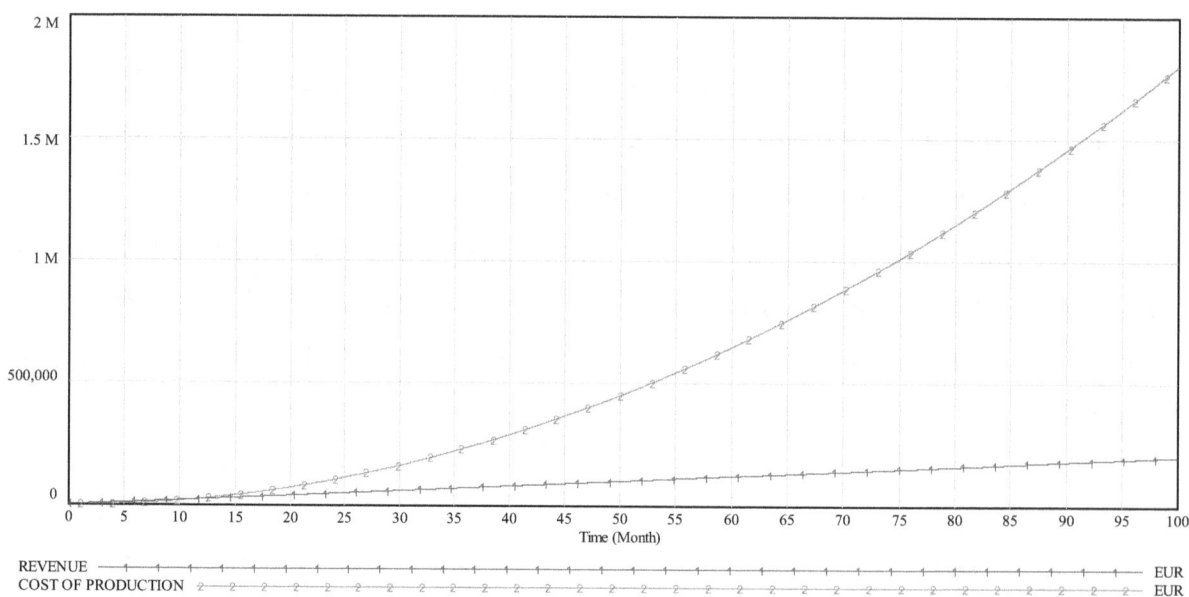

**Figure 91** Revenue and Cost of Production

A firm's production loop should consider that firms have to make profit, such that **price per unit** should be above **production cost of unit new technology**. When talking about new technology, that process innovation is a product from the firm's perspective selling that technology. Although **unit sales** also depend on technology lifecycle, number of units produced determines the limit of sales. However, pricing is major problem for high technology products and there are four major pricing policies (Maier, 2002):

- Penetration pricing: $p^{pen}(t) = c^s(t).\Pi.(1 + a.e^{-t/\tau})$;
- Myopic profit maximization: $p^{opt}(t) = c^s(t).\varepsilon_t/(\varepsilon_t-1)$, $\varepsilon_t$ is elasticity of demand;
- Skimming price: $p^{skim}(t) = p^{opt}(t).(1 + a.e^{-t/\tau})$;
- Full cost coverage: $p^{fcc}(t) = c^s(t).\Pi$

For simplicity, price is considered as a single variable, since a firm has to set **price per unit** for profit. A firm generates revenue each month such that a causal loop arises. Secondly, firms do not decide about their expenditure budget based on their existing profits, however revenue is a major factor that determines total expenditure budget. These relationships are shown in Figure 92.

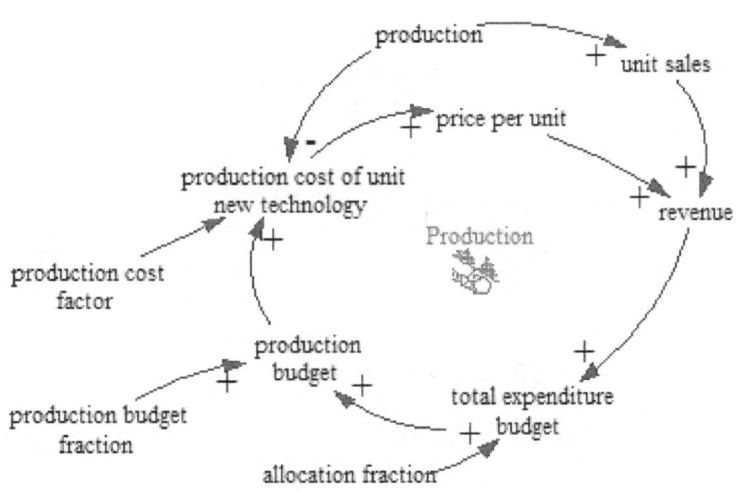

**Figure 92** Production Loop

A firm decides on a certain **total expenditure budget** via **allocation fraction** from **revenue** after retaining some profits. Taking a certain **production budget fraction** into account, **production budget** becomes available. **Budget allocation to production** together with **production cost of unit new technology** determines actual amount of **production** for that particular time period (in this case: month). When firms produce a new product, it is available in stock. Even high technology products can remain as **units in stock** as a delay period until they become **unit sales**. According to the full cost coverage pricing policy (Milling, 2002), a firm sets a **price per unit** for its product by considering a **profit markup** on its unit production cost. When a firm sells its high technology products, it generates cash as **revenue**. The firm settles on **total expenditure budget** for the next time period taking **revenue** belonging to the current period as one factor into account. Figure 93 explains the production loop as a stock-and-flow diagram.

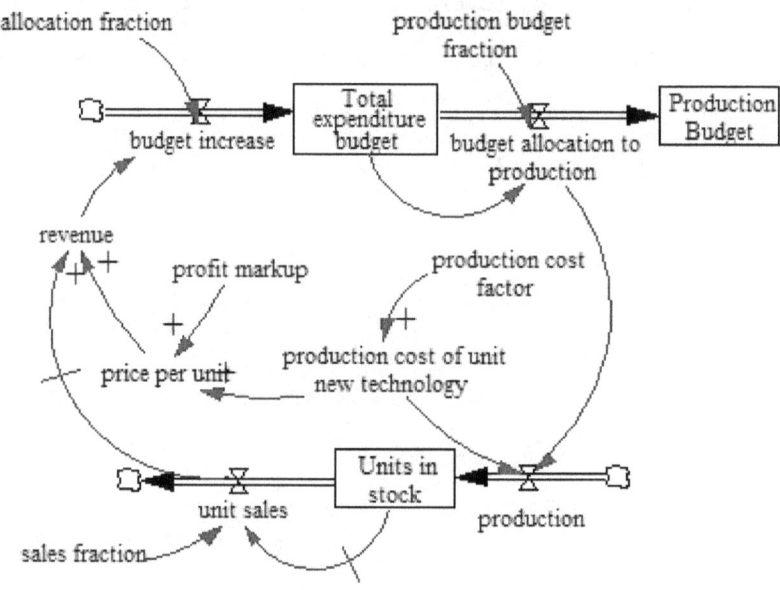

Figure 93 Stock-and-flow production loop

As shown in Figure 93, stock-and-flow diagram of production loop indicates **budget allocation to production** as a flow variable from an initial **total expenditure budget** of 100 EUR. Assuming 50% production budget fraction, budget allocation to production (initially: 100 EUR x 50% = 50 EUR/month) and **production cost of unit new technology** of 1 EUR/unit determines monthly **production** volume. Production lead time is assumed twelve months, which is typical for capital equipment. Since a sale of new technology does not take place instantly, **unit sales** are carried out by assuming a **sales fraction** of 90% from **units in stock** (initially 10 unit) waiting in warehouse around three months. The full cost coverage pricing policy is applied on **price per unit** (1.2 EUR/unit), such that **profit markup** of 20% is added on **production cost of unit new technology**, whereas price per unit and unit sales make up **revenue**. **Revenue** is assumed to be available to the firm four months after **unit sales**. **Allocation fraction** from **revenue** to **total expenditure budget** is set as 50%. The simulation results for a period of two years, i.e. 24 months are displayed in Figure 94.

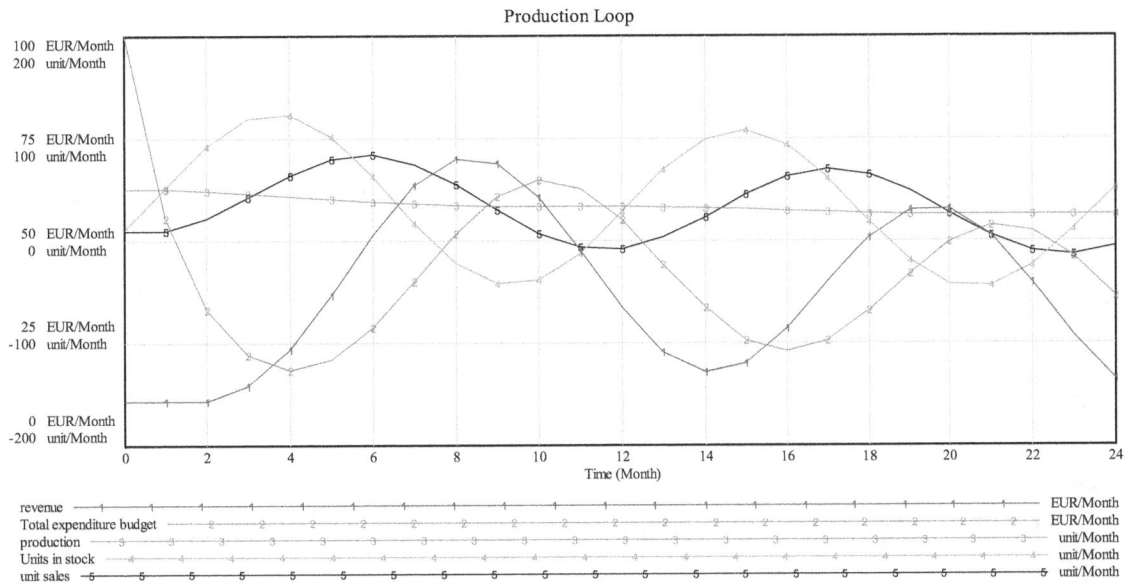

**Figure 94** Production Loop

**Revenue, total expenditure budget** and **units in stock** show oscillatory behavior. However, these material delays bring out a weakness of the model such that **units in stock** and **unit sales** become negative during these delays. This inconsistency is overcome by inserting check that unit sales happen upon available units in stock. Incorporating this assumption, the outputs for **revenue** and **total expenditure budget**, as shown in Figure 95, are in declining trend as previously. Since production loop is reinforcing, the decline in revenues can only be attributed to less production and therefore less budget allocation for production. **Allocation fraction** of 50% practically indicates that a firm allocates remaining 50% as net profit. Therefore budget allocation to production remains small and each month budget becomes less since production and revenue become lower. Companies who sell high technology products have at least around 30% operating profit according to TAYSAD. Since what remains from budget allocation for expenditure can be regarded as net profit, allocation fraction as a parameter must have a higher value. If **allocation fraction** is set as 80%, **unit sales** decline slightly. But when **profit markup** is made as 30% instead of 20% in addition to **allocation fraction**, production loop becomes reinforcing towards growth in line with the conventional numbers given by automotive parts manufacturers' executives. The effects of these two parameters on unit sales are clearly visible in Figure 96.

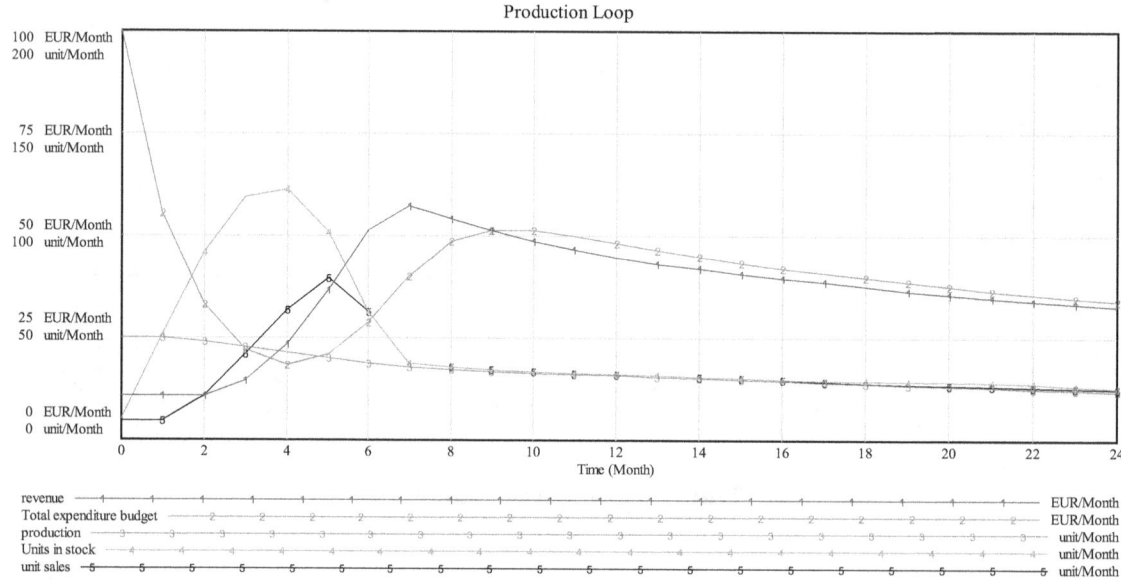

**Figure 95** Production Loop with non-negative stock

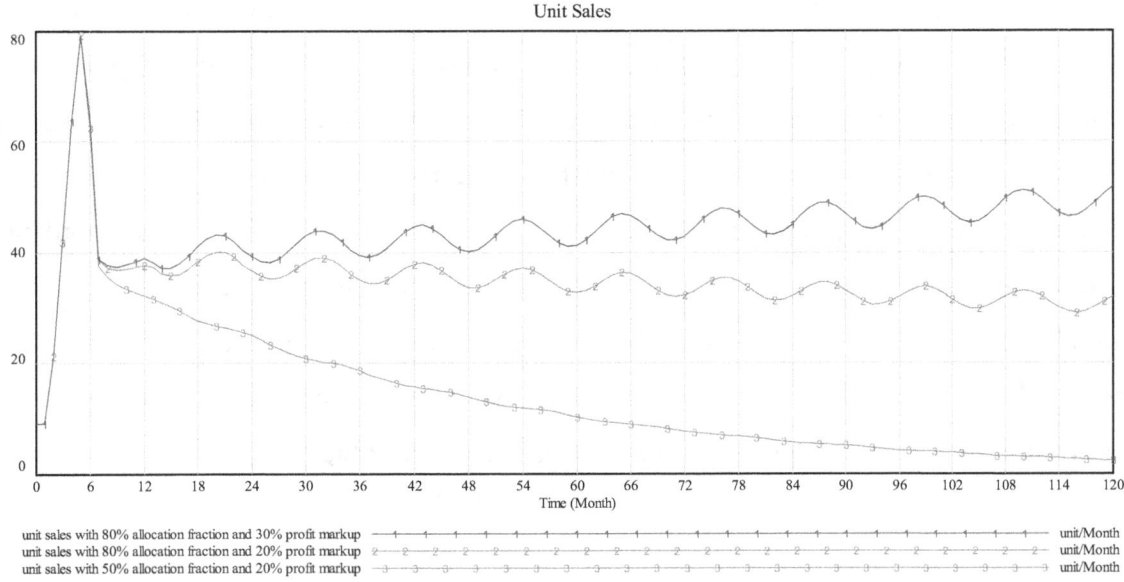

**Figure 96** Effect of production budget allocation and profit on sales

### 4.4.1 System Dynamics Model of Technology Diffusion

At the end of the model development efforts and comprehensive literature and executive reviews, the final model is illustrated in Figure 97. Technology supplier who sells capital equipment as new technology to firms in an industry, e.g. automotive parts manufacturers, establishes an expenditure budget and allocates its resources among the three major functions: production, R&D and marketing. Since the focus is on a single main product of technology supplier, research and development is about improving processes to produce that particular technology. Therefore **use of R&D process budget** is the allocation of R&D budget, such that use of R&D product budget is not considered in this model, since new product/technology development is a completely different area of study. The originating problem which resulted in this system dynamics model is whether a technology supplier can produce new technology and foster diffusion of that particular technology by analyzing effects of its decisions about budget allocation, price and capacity such that technology supplier can carry out new decisions with respect to adoption decisions by firms in the Turkish automotive parts manufacturer industry. If **orders received** exceed **capacity**, **production** continues though backlog accumulates. If **backlog** exceeds current **capacity**, **capacity adjustment** results in investment for capacity. Since capacity investment is a quite broad subject in production management, the financial resources are assumed to be exogenously included in **total expenditure budget**, since budget allocations to production, research & development and marketing make up a maximum of 85% of the budget. **Capacity step** simply indicates the time period until a technology supplier decides to increase its capacity, whereas **time to adjust capacity** indicates the necessary period that additional capacity becomes available. **Capacity** determines the maximum level of production, i.e. **potential production**, whereas **desired production** points out planned amount of production based on **use of production budget** and **production cost of unit new technology**.

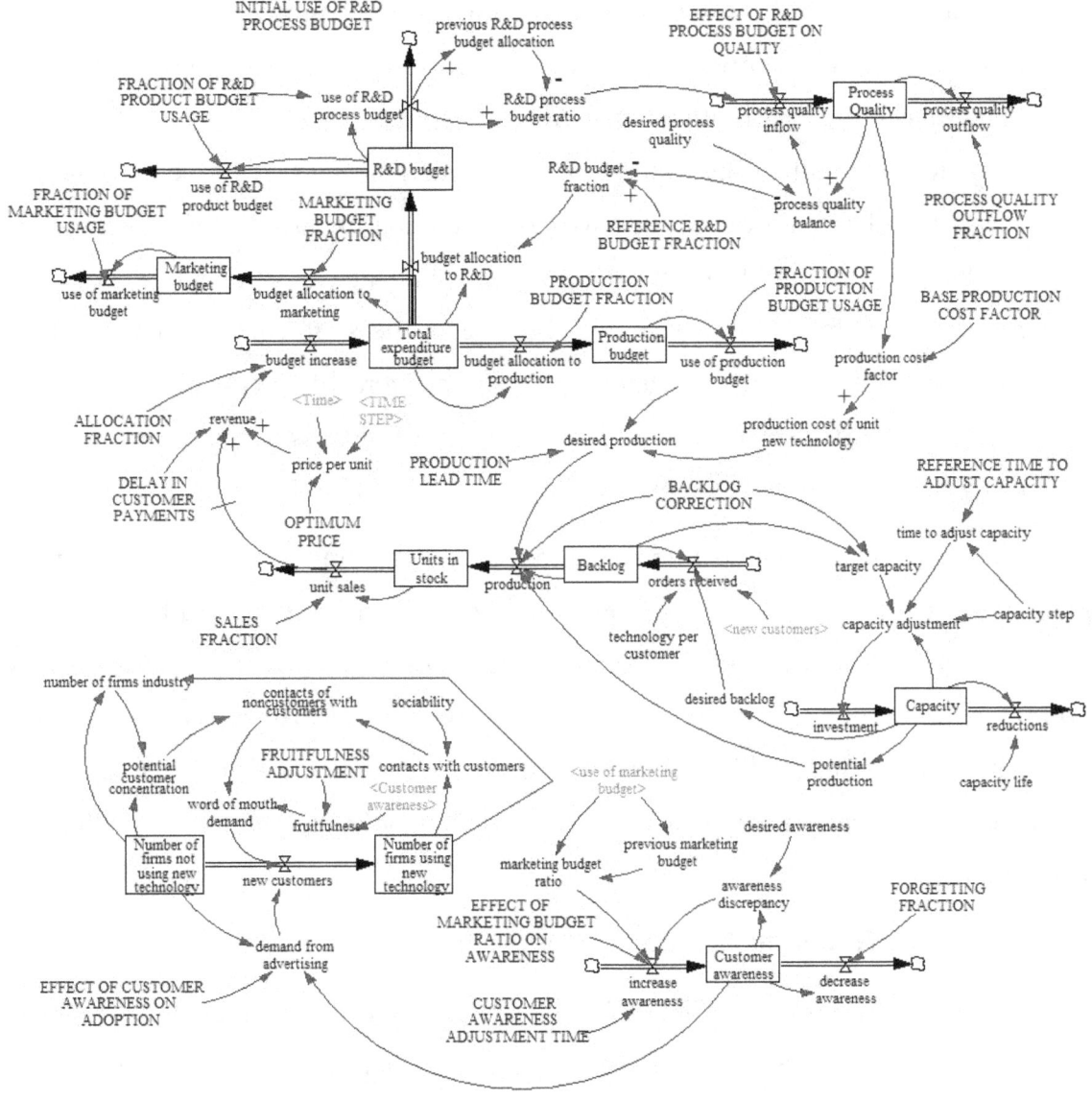

**Figure 97** Supplier's System Dynamic View on Innovation Diffusion

Technology supplier's marketing activities interact with firms in a particular industry such that each firm becomes **new customers** of that new technology. **Budget allocation to marketing** ensures that **use of marketing budget** contributes to firms' **customer awareness** about new technology. Once customer awareness is at a sufficient level, **demand from advertising** leads to new customers. As **number of firms using new technology** increases, **word of mouth demand** increases, because:

1. Absolute **number of contacts of noncustomers with customers** increases among automotive parts manufacturers, since **sociability** of firms using new technology initiates **contacts with customers**. When there are less **number of firms not using new technology**, contacts among user and non-user firms have to decline.
2. That particular contact between a user firm and non-user firm of new technology results in adoption decision by that particular non-user firm is named as **fruitfulness**. Fruitfulness indicates the effectiveness of contacts among firms using and not using new technology such that word of mouth demand occurs. Increase in **customer awareness** leads to more fruitfulness, since it enables faster progress across stages of innovation decision according to Rogers (2003).

Firms' demand for new technology is quantified as **new customers** during each month as time step, which is the total effect of demand from advertising and demand from word of mouth. Assuming that each firm buys new technology only once, **technology per customer** is set as one. Therefore **new customers** determine **orders received** by that technology supplier in a particular month, if backlog is not greater than capacity. Otherwise, orders received are 10% less than total demand in that particular month, i.e. new customers.

### 4.4.2 Simulation Results of Technology Diffusion

The parameters used during the simulation of technology diffusion model are given in Table 12. The simulation period is 10 years or 120 months. Since new technology means process innovations for firms in automotive parts manufacturing industry, its diffusion takes at least several years. Each firm needs to make an investment when a technology supplier carries out marketing activities.

**Table 12** Parameters used during the simulations

| Variable Name | Initial Value |
|---|---|
| Simulation Period | 120 month |
| Allocation Fraction | 80% |
| Total Expenditure Budget | 1,000,000 EUR |
| Production Budget | 500,000 EUR |
| R&D Budget | 100,000 EUR |
| Initial Use of R&D Process Budget | 100,000 EUR |
| Production Budget Fraction | 50% / month |
| Reference R&D Budget Fraction | 10% /month |
| Marketing Budget Fraction | 10% /month |
| Fraction of Production Budget Usage | 1 |
| Fraction of R&D Product Budget Usage | 0 |
| Fraction of Marketing Budget Usage | 1 |
| Effect of R&D Process Budget on Quality | Table lookup with [(0,0)-(2,1)],(0.3,0),(0.4,0.05),(0.5,0.1), (0.6,0.15),(0.7,0.2), (0.8,0.25),(0.9,0.3), (1,0.35),(1.1,0.45),(1.2,0.5),(1.3,0.55), (1.4,0.6),(1.5,0.65),(1.5,0.65),(1.6,0.7), (1.7,0.8),(1.8,0.85),(1.9,0.9),(1.95,0.95), (2,1) |
| Process Quality Outflow Fraction | 1% / Month |
| Desired Process Quality | 0.99 |
| Base Production Cost Factor | 30,000 EUR/unit |
| Production Lead Time | 12 Month |
| Optimum Price | 100,000 EUR/unit |
| Delay in Customer Payments | 4 Month |
| Sales Fraction | 1 / Month |
| Units in Stock | 10 unit |
| Backlog | 0 unit |
| Backlog Correction | 1 / Month |
| Reference Time to Adjust Capacity | 0.4 Month*Month / unit |
| Capacity Step | 40 unit / Month |
| Capacity | 2 unit / Month |
| Capacity Life | 25 year |
| Number of Firms Not Using New Technology | 1000 company |
| Number of Firms Using New Technology | 10 company |
| Sociability | 3 |
| Fruitfulness Adjustment | 0.1 company / Month |
| Effect of Customer Awareness on Adoption | Table lookup with [(0,0)-(1,0.02)],(0,0),(0.1,0.0012), (0.2,0.0032),(0.3,0.0056),(0.4,0.0084), (0.5,0.0113),(0.6,0.0142), (0.7,0.0164), (0.8,0.0181),(0.9,0.0195),(1,0.0197) |
| Effect of Marketing Budget Ratio on Awareness | Table lookup with [(0,0)-(1.5,1.2)],(0,0.2),(0.15,0.23), (0.3,0.31),(0.45,0.39),(0.6,0.52), (0.75,0.67),(0.9,0.84),(1.05,1), (1.2,1.11),(1.35,1.17),(1.5,1.19) |
| Customer Awareness Adjustment Time | 6 Month |
| Desired Awareness | 1 |
| Forgetting Fraction | 1% / Month |

When the model is simulated, there is demand for new technology by 14 companies during the first month such that **new customers** reach its peak of 60 companies during the fourteenth and fifteenth months as can be seen in line '1' of Figure 98. Since **number of firms using new technology** becomes 100 from initially 10 within six months only, diffusion of new technology is quite fast. Since **production** remains far behind **orders received**, the exponential increase of **backlog** on line '3' results in steady **capacity adjustment**. Therefore **capacity** continues to increase to 86 unit/Month, until **backlog** becomes less than **capacity** during $46^{th}$ month. Therefore, although there are no **new customers** after $36^{th}$ month, production continues until $49^{th}$ month in order to close **backlog**.

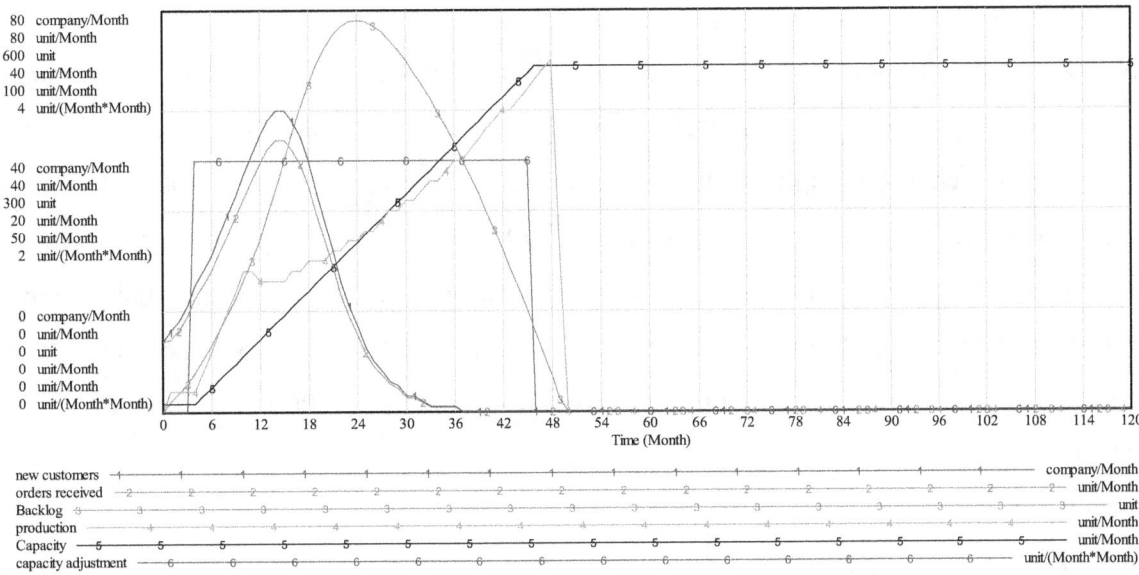

**Figure 98** Simulation Results for Demand, Backlog, Production and Capacity

As discussed in section 4.4, skimming price strategy has been considered in the model from technology supplier's perspective by putting an exponential function setting the price of new technology high and then reducing it as time passes (Maier, 2002). However when price declines too sharply as in Figure 99, a technology supplier cannot benefit lower cost of production as the consequence of improvement in process quality, since price reduction from 200,000 EUR/unit to 100,000 EUR/unit is beyond the rate of decrease in **production cost of unit new technology** from 50,000 EUR/unit to 31,636 EUR/unit.

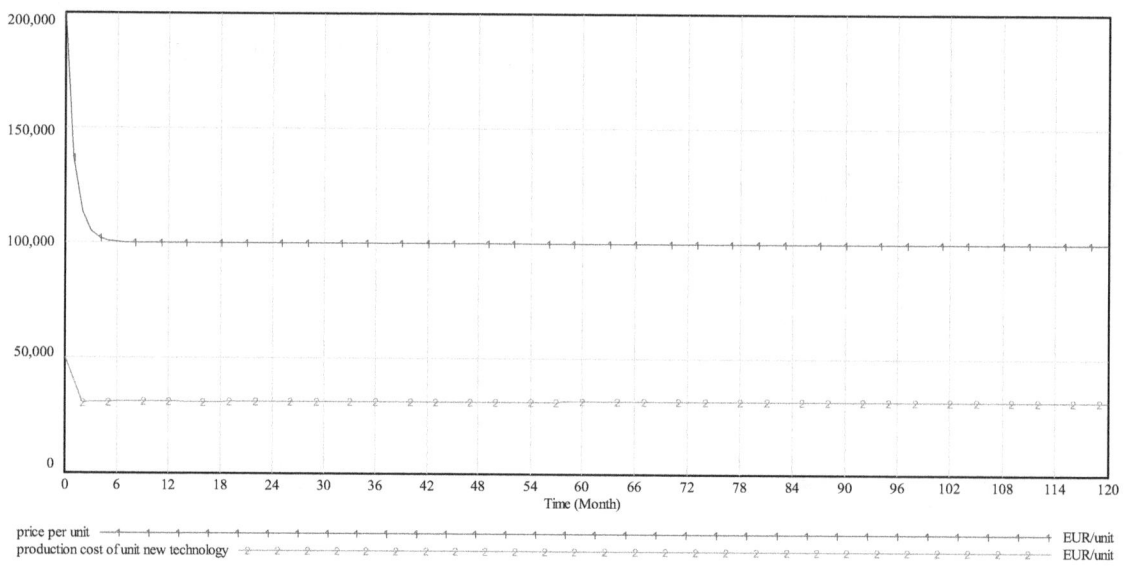

**Figure 99** Price and Cost of New Technology

Since production cannot meet demand due to capacity, lack of increase **unit sales** together with declining price per unit decreases revenue. Accordingly, budgets for production, R&D and marketing become less either during the first year as depicted in Figure 100. As **price per unit** becomes stable within seven months and production therefore **unit sales** start to increase, each month's **revenue** continues to increase as long as **backlog** is beyond **capacity**. Since **production** declines rapidly, **revenue** decreases sharply either with a four months **delay in customer payments** after **unit sales**. Although there is no new sales after 50$^{th}$ month, marketing and R&D budgets are available and used. Similarly there is **use of production budget**, though **production** does not occur, since there is no **orders received**.

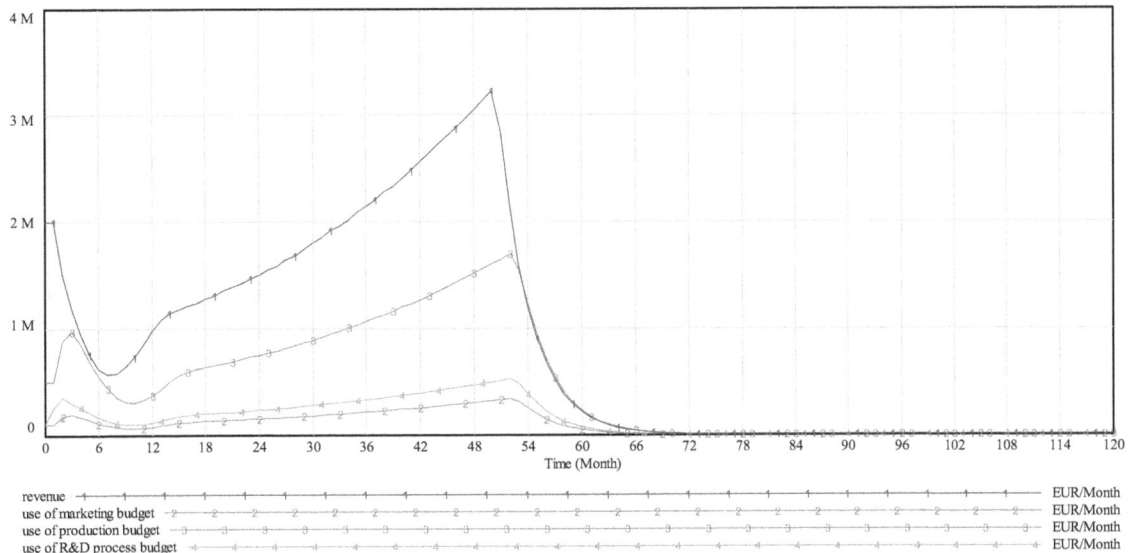

**Figure 100** Simulation Results for Revenue and Budget Allocations

That a technology supplier invests in research and development of its processes results in improvement of **process quality**, which provides a cost advantage when selling new technology. However, corresponding to the S-curve for a particular technology, it cannot be improved forever as shown in Figure 101. Therefore significant increase in **use of R&D process budget** results in initial growth of **R&D budget fraction** and stabilizes after eighteen months have passed. Therefore process quality remains around 95% during the later months of the simulation period. Similarly, **use of marketing budget** indirectly determines customer awareness with an initial value of 0.6. Due to decline in **revenue** during the first year, there is an oscillation of **marketing budget ratio** during the first year, though **customer awareness** continued to increase with a slower speed. When the ratio becomes fixed, **customer awareness** remained stable around 94% until around 50$^{th}$

month, when revenue started to decline. Even though **unit sales** was complete at that time, **customer awareness** continued to **remain around 92%**, since **use of marketing budget** still contributed to the inflow **towards customer awareness** mitigating the effect of **forgetting fraction** as outflow from **customer awareness**.

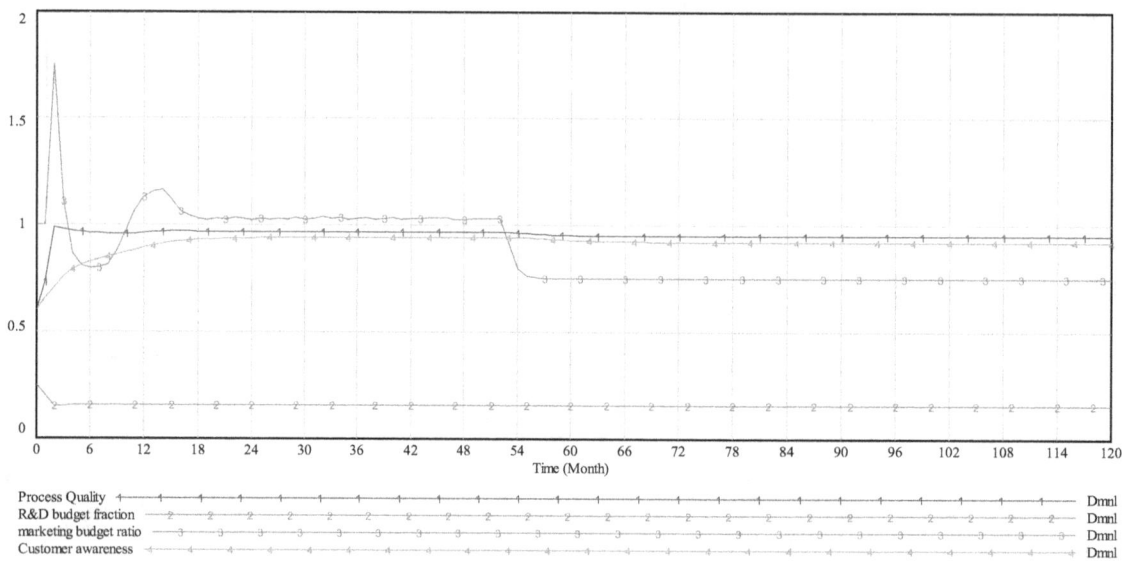

**Figure 101** R&D – Process Quality and Marketing – Customer Awareness

Since new technology is process innovation from the aspect of buyer industry, i.e. automotive parts manufacturer, the technology supplier produces and sells its product as new technology on make-to-order policy. Therefore, **units in stock** have been equivalent to **unit sales** due to **sales fraction** with a value of one. Although high technology products such as CNC machine tools have quite long supply lead times such that production starts upon ordering and buyer firms wait for delivery from six to twelve months, technology supplier can employ other production and pricing policies depending on circumstances. For example, if there is an economic downturn, demand and hence sales may collapse. What is produced can remain in stock instead. Therefore, *policy design and formulation* as the fifth step of modeling process enables new strategies, structures and decision rules for managers selling new technology (Sterman, 2000:104).

Sensitivity analysis in section 4.6 will elaborate policies under different scenarios and given uncertainties after completing *testing* as the fourth step in model validity by discussing about validity and validation tests of this system dynamics model in the next section.

## 4.5 Model Validity

Model validity constitutes an important step in system dynamics methodology. In Merriam-Webster dictionary "valid" is defined as *"well-grounded or justifiable: being at once relevant and meaningful, logically correct"*. In other words, validity implies support by objective truth. Since models are limited, simplified representations of real world, no model can be verified or validated with respect to dictionary definition of validity (Sterman, 2000:846).

The validity of a model can be assessed according to its suitability for a purpose (Forrester, 1961). Thus model validity and validation cannot entirely be based on formal/objective constructs and procedures (Barlas, 1996). That system dynamics has a different approach to model validity, can be attributed to major philosophies of science. The traditional reductionist/logical positivist school considers a valid model as an objective representation of the real system. The model can either be true or false. This school regards validity as a measure of accuracy. Whereas, the relativistic/holistic philosophy of science, which system dynamics belongs to, accepts that validation must have some semi-formal and subjective components (Barlas and Carpenter, 1990).

System dynamics paradigm assumes causality and is holistic and interdisciplinary in nature; models are not true or false but lie on a range of usefulness. Model validation is an ongoing process of building confidence about the usefulness of a model (Barlas and Carpenter, 1990). When validity is related to usefulness with respect to some purpose, validity of model purpose is also assessed (Forrester, 1961:115). Therefore although model validation has been defined as the fourth step in system dynamics modeling, it is dispersed throughout system dynamics methodology from problem identification till implementation of policy recommendations. The validity of the internal structure of the model is crucial. Behavioral validation of a model as reproduction of real system behavior is also important but only after there has been sufficient confidence in the structure of the model. (Barlas, 1996)

With respect to validity, models can be categorized as "causal-descriptive" or "correlational". In correlational models causality in structure is not in the foreground. Validity is assessed whether model output matches the actual output within some range of accuracy. Though causal-descriptive models do not only predict behavior, but also describe how that behavior generated such that ways of changing existing behavior are elaborated (Barlas, 1996). System dynamics models fall in causal-descriptive category. Hence model validity is a relative concept (Forrester, 1961). System dynamics view about validity is in parallel with the relativist philosophy of science. Since validity means sufficiency with respect to a purpose, model validation has informal and subjective aspects (Barlas and Carpenter, 1990). For this study's model validity discussions, Barlas' framework for tests of formal validation will be utilized as shown in Figure 102.

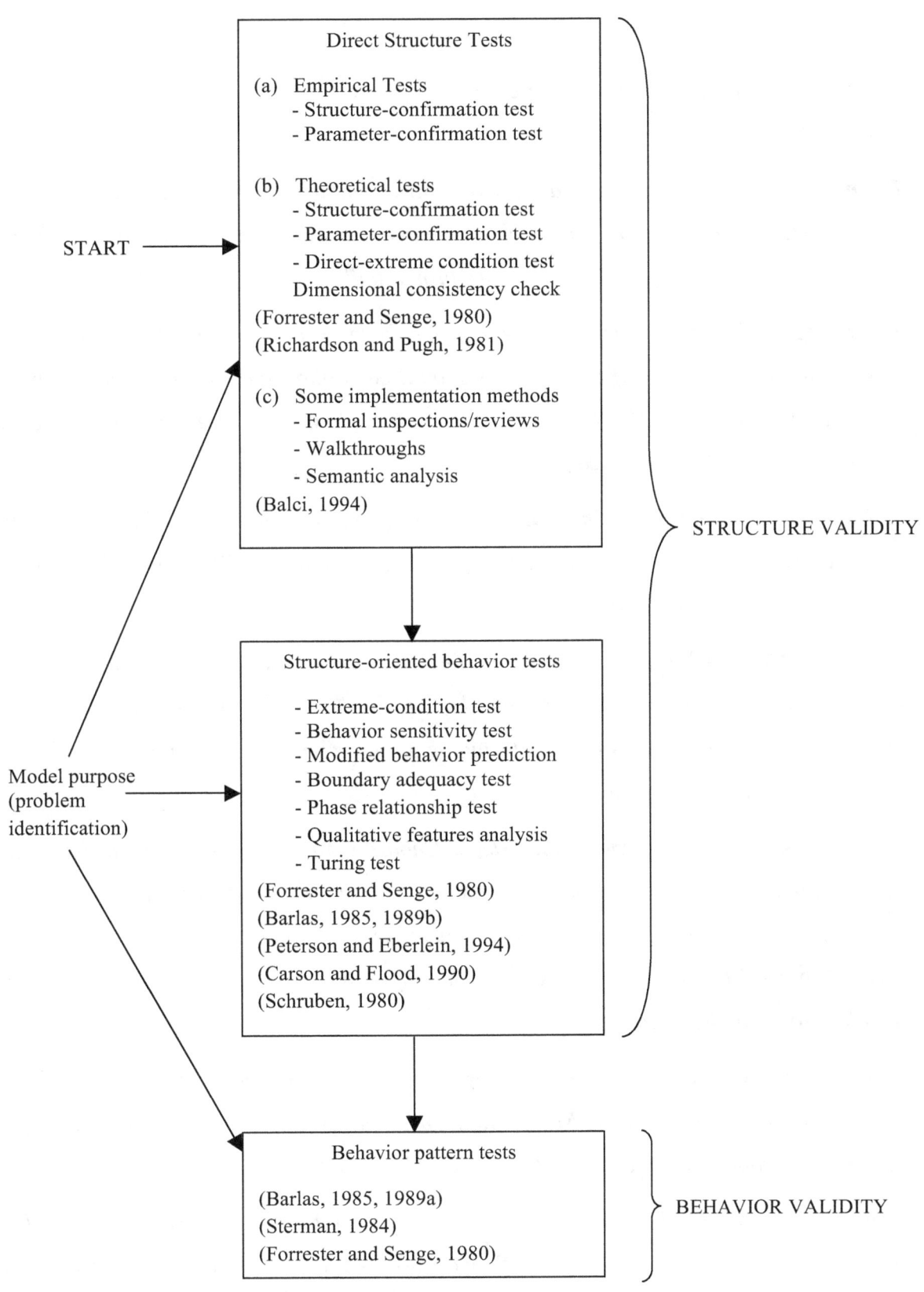

**Figure 102** Overall nature and selected tests of formal model validation (Barlas, 1996)

Lai and Wahbar (2001) provide the following checklist to use when building and simulating models:

*1. Units Check:* Computer programs have built-in feature that will check all equations for consistency in units. One must check models for dimensional consistency before simulating either using the software feature or manually.

*2. Naming Variables:* A naming convention has been proposed by Ventana, the makers of Vensim. The first letter of Stock names should be capitalized; Constants should be in all capitals and names of all other variables, including flows are all lower case. In general, the word "rate" is used for flows.

*3. No Constants embedded in equations:* One must not simplify equations by using numeric constants embedded in equations. A good model will show all constants explicitly as individual elements.

*4. Do Not Mention Parameter Values in The Documentation:* If parameter values are mentioned in the documentation, they will have to be changed every time the equation is changed. This can be tedious and confusing as a reader will see two different numbers if the documentation is not updated.

*5. Choose Appropriately Small Time Steps:* Choose the time step to be about one-eight the value of the smallest time constant in the model (the time constant is the reciprocal of a growth or decay fraction). Doing so will increase the frequency at which the software solves the model equations, improving the approximations of continuous time and avoiding some mathematical errors.

*6. Stock Values Can be Changed Only by Flows:* The only model elements with direct connections to stocks are flows. No constants or auxiliary variables should directly enter the stock equation, except for the initial values of the stock.

*7. Every Flow Should be Connected to Auxiliary Variables or to Other Flows:* A flow only increases or decreases a stock. A flow cannot be used as a source of information in a model as it cannot be measured.

***8. Flows Should not be Linked to Auxiliary Variables or to Other Flows:*** *One must not use a flow to provide information to an auxiliary variable.*

***9. Stocks Should Not be Linked to Stocks:*** *A stock is the integral of a flow, to show information transfer between two stocks, connect the first stock to the flow of the second stock.*

***10. Using IF THEN ELSE, MIN/MAX and Other Logic Statements:*** *One must use table functions to avoid discontinuities introduced by such statements.*

***11. Use of Initial Values:*** *When initial values are used in a model, they should be clearly specified and connected to the model.*

***12. Curving Connectors:*** *The connectors that link one variable to another should be curved as a model with curved connectors looks nicer, and the feedback loops are easier to trace.*

Based on the preceding validity discussions in system dynamics literature, the following list is used to analyze the validity of the model:

1. Discussion of the purpose and usefulness of the model (section 4.1);
2. Boundary selection (section 4.4);
3. Dimensional Consistency Check (section 4.5.1);
4. Extreme Condition Test (section 4.5.2);
5. Applying Lai and Wahbar (2001)'s checklist (section 4.5.3).

### 4.5.1 Dimensional Consistency Check

Dimensional consistency of the model is tested using Vensim software. Vensim offers "model check" and "unit check" utilities to check the model and whether the units used in the model are consistent, i.e. left hand side of the equations are same with the right hand side of the equations. These tests are applied and Vensim verified that the model is dimensionally consistent. Model equations and units are given in Appendix I.

### 4.5.2 Extreme Condition Test

The model should be robust in the case of extreme variations. For example, if use of R&D process budget is zero, process quality declines. Vensim offers "Reality Check" function which is an extreme condition testing environment. Reality Check equations are statements such as: "If this happens, then that must happen". The following test conditions are defined and tested using Reality Check function of Vensim:

- When *use of production budget* is zero, production budget should be zero.
- When *capacity* is zero, *reductions* should be zero.
- If *number of firms not using new technology* is zero, *orders received* should be zero.

Reality check is run and no failures are observed. Thus the model passed the reality check. The results displayed by Vensim is as follows:

- 3 successes and 0 failures testing 3 Reality Check equations,
- The Reality Check Index as run is 0.000619195,
- Closeness score is 100.0% on 2 measurements.

### 4.5.3 Applying Lai and Wahbar's Checklist

Table 13 displays the results after Lai and Wahbar's checklist had been applied.

Table 13 Lai and Wahbar's checklist applied to the model

| Item | Comment |
| --- | --- |
| Units Check | Vensim unit check applied. Passed the test |
| Naming Variables | Naming conventions are applied. |
| No Constants embedded in equations | All constants are outside the equations. There is only one exception |
| Do Not Mention Parameter Values in The Documentation | Only the source of parameter values is mentioned. |
| Choose Appropriately Small Time Steps | Smallest time constant is one month. DT used in the model is 0.125 month which is less than one eight of smallest time constant. We run the model with smaller DT's. Although simulation results are slightly different, there is same pattern. Passed the test. |
| Stock Values Can be Changed Only by Flows | No constants or auxiliary variables did enter the stock equation |
| Every Flow Should be Connected to Auxiliary Variables or to Other Flows | Flows are connected to auxiliary variables or other flows. |
| Flows Should not be Linked to Auxiliary Variables or to Other Flows | Flows are not linked to auxiliary variables or other flows. |
| Stocks Should Not be Linked to Stocks | Stocks are not linked to other stocks |

| Using IF THEN ELSE, MIN/MAX and Other Logic Statements | Min function is used in order to ensure production and backlog. |
|---|---|
| Use of Initial Values | Initial values are shown explicitly in the model |
| Curving Connectors | Curves are used so connectors look nicer |

### 4.5.4 Formal Inspections / Reviews

The model was first reviewed in the 12th workshop held on Dec 2008 in Yeditepe University under the supervision of the thesis advisor Assist. Prof. M. Atilla Öner and with the participation of recent Ph.D. fellows working on system dynamics. Following the first review, the model is constantly updated and reviewed during the system dynamics workshops held by Yeditepe University Management Application and Research Center (MARC).

The model was also reviewed by the general manager of DMG Gildemeister Turkey as a follow up session after the expert executive interview.

### 4.5.5 Replicability

Documentation is one of the most important pragmatic issues for modelers such that results can be understood and then replicated by others. It allows critique and extension of models (Sterman, 2002). Replication is rarely done in social and management sciences. Therefore the documentation for the model in section 4.4 is available in appendices according to model documentation guidelines by Sterman (2000:856).

### 4.5.6 Behavioral Tests

The logical sequence of behavior pattern validation is followed (Barlas, 1996). The budget allocation among R&D, marketing and production is adapted from Soydan and Oner (2004)'s study on resource allocation between R&D and marketing. Although the model differs from Soydan and Oner's model, the behavioral patterns that firms become users of new technology and effect of marketing on customer awareness and adoption are equivalent.

## 4.6 Sensitivity Analysis

Results of sensitivity analysis are presented. They are simulation runs which enable managers and public policy-makers to assess how much the behavior (or problem) changes as a result of changes in selected parameters, inputs, and initial stock values.

There are three types of sensitivity (Sterman, 2000):

1. **Numerical sensitivity** exists when a change in assumptions changes the numerical values of the results
2. **Behavior mode sensitivity** exists when a change in assumptions changes the patterns of behavior generated by the model
3. **Policy sensitivity** exists when a change in assumptions reverses the impacts or desirability of a proposed policy

Morecroft and Sterman (1994) suggest that "simulations provide consistent stories about the future, but not predictions". In this section we are going to analyze these consistent scenarios.

### 4.6.1 Expenditure Budgets

In order to analyze the effect of budget allocation on production, R&D and marketing, we let allocation fraction parameter to change between 0.65 and 0.95 where its normal value is 0.80. Figure 103 illustrates that production has initially been immune to budget allocation, since capacity has initially been behind desired production. What remains from allocation fraction can be considered as net profit of a firm. Therefore allocation fraction provides the funds for a firm's activities in three corporate functions: *production*, *research & development* and *marketing*. The effect of downsizing budgets for higher profits may have various implications in the future. Reducing allocation fraction disproportionally extends backlog as shown in Figure 104 and causes more increase in capacity, which is displayed in Figure 105. In short, increasing allocation fraction has diminishing returns.

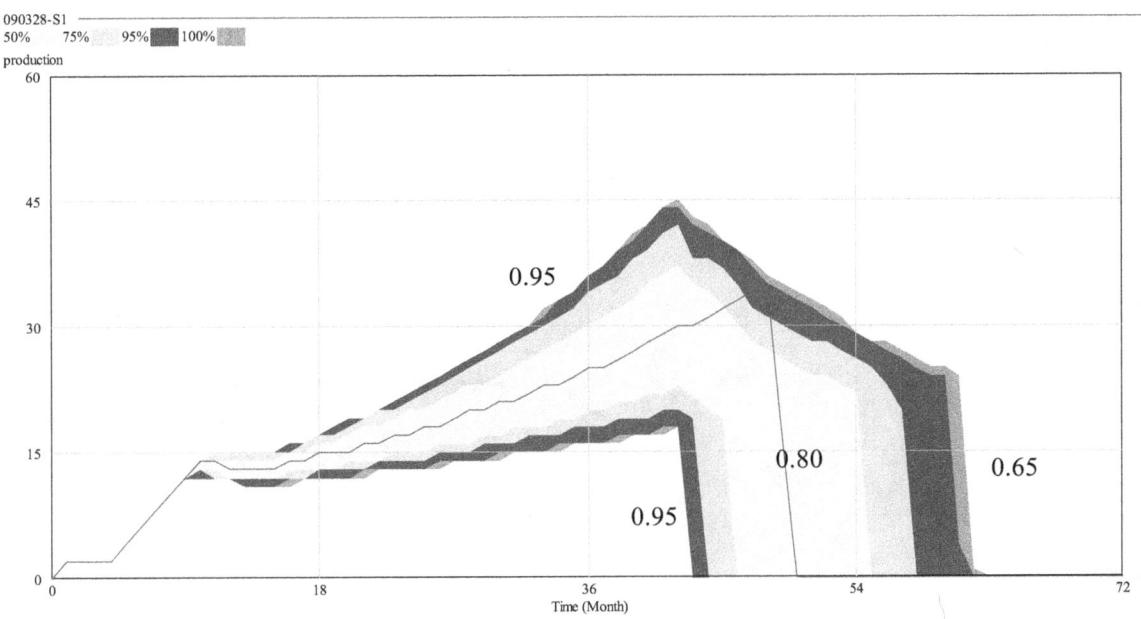

**Figure 103** Sensitivity Analysis: Effect of Allocation Fraction on Production

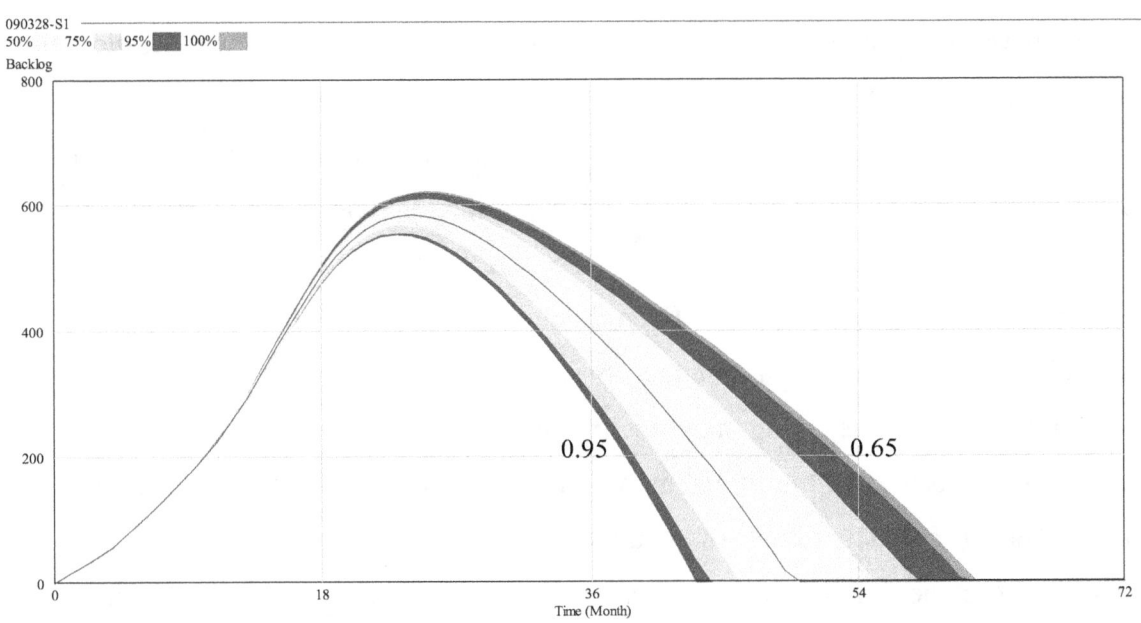

**Figure 104** Sensitivity Analysis: Effect of Allocation Fraction on Backlog

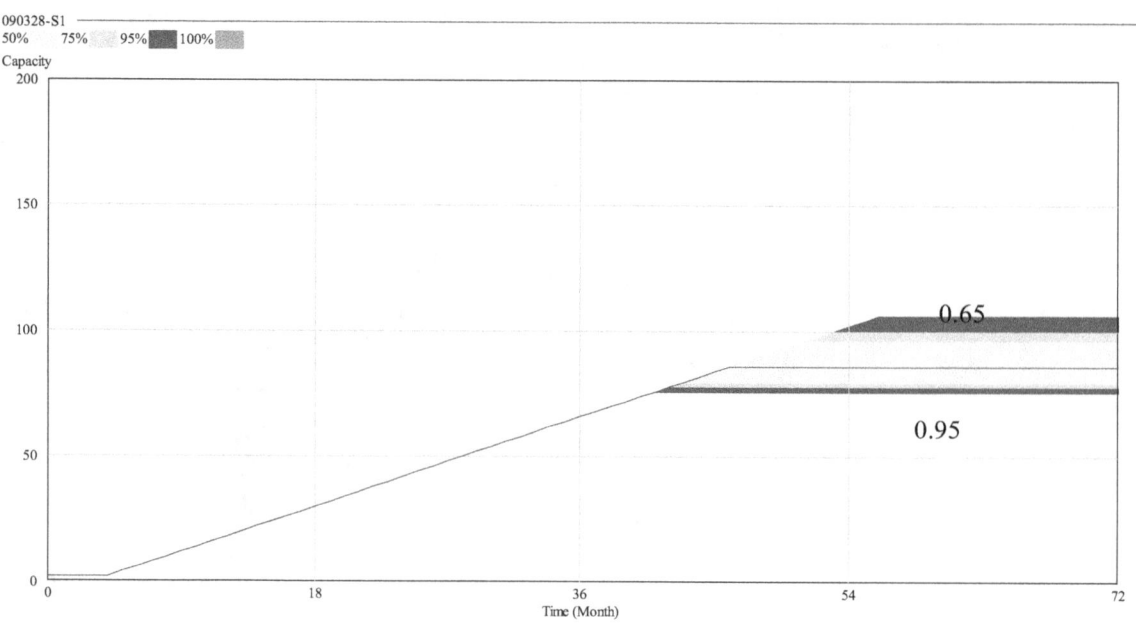

**Figure 105** Sensitivity Analysis: Effect of Allocation Fraction on Capacity

Since increase in **process quality** depends on **R&D process budget ratio**, **allocation fraction** indirectly affects it. However, process quality that can be viewed in Figure 106 has overall not been influenced. There have been only minor changes in process quality, while revenue has been growing fast. After production has ended, process quality declines later, when allocation fraction has become higher. **Total expenditure budget** incorporates company equity, either. Even though there is no revenue, financial reserves (accumulated in total expenditure budget) make **use of R&D budget** available for some time. **Number of firms using new technology** reaches 100 companies within five months, 500 companies within fifteen months and 900 companies in twenty three months. Hence diffusion speed is about 18 months until 90% of firms become users of new technology from the time when 10% of firms in an industry are users of new technology. Sensitivity analysis does not affect diffusion speed.

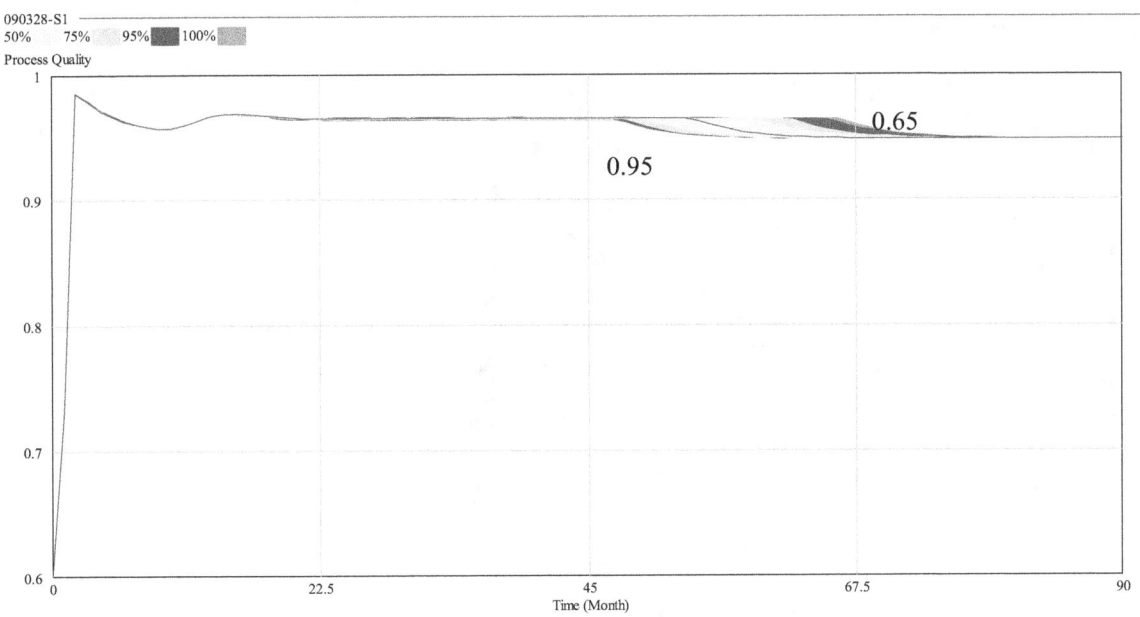

**Figure 106** Sensitivity Analysis: Effect of Allocation Fraction on Process Quality

**Production budget fraction** fluctuates between 40% and 60%, while its usual value is 50%. Peak production levels are before 48$^{th}$ month, if **budget allocation to production** increases or decreases as shown in Figure 107. Since production is apparently determined by desired production, increase or decrease in production has a proportional effect on backlog according to Figure 108. Increasing/decreasing **production** reduces/boosts **backlog** and therefore cause less/more **investment** in capacity. Nonetheless, increase in **capacity** becomes useless in either way, since use of production budget conduced desired production only less than capacity, i.e. potential production. In Figure 109, peak capacity becomes less due to fewer backlogs as the consequence of more production. The opposite case should occur usually. Therefore manufacturing of capital equipment as new technology requires steady policy formulation and implementation by technology suppliers with respect to demand.

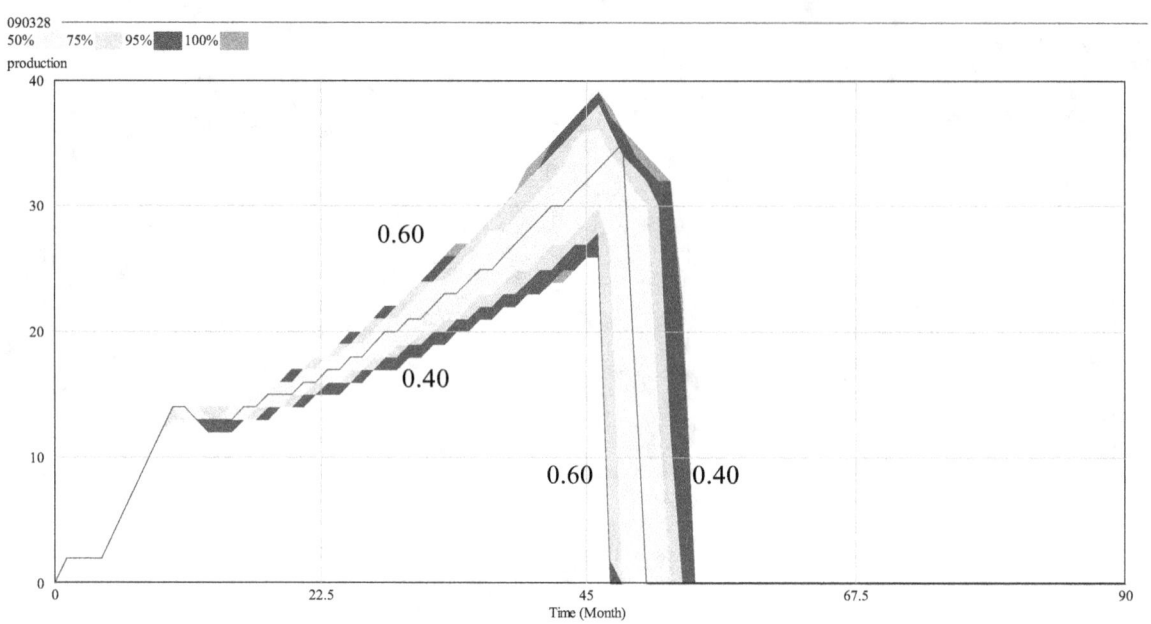

**Figure 107** Sensitivity Analysis: Effect of Production Budget Fraction on Production

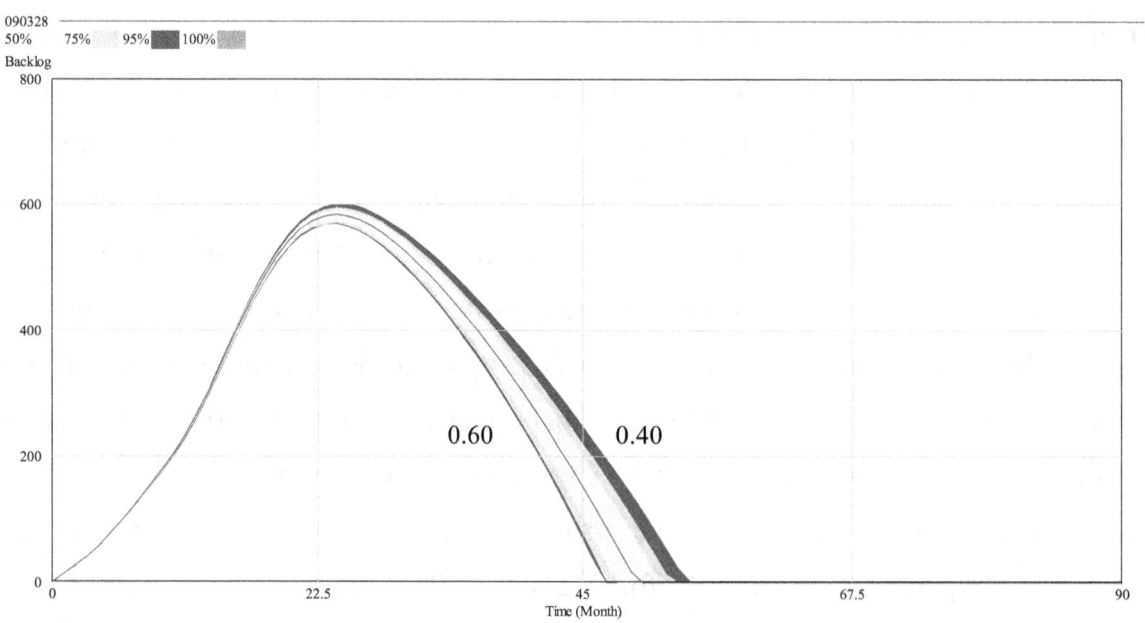

**Figure 108** Sensitivity Analysis: Effect of Production Budget Fraction on Backlog

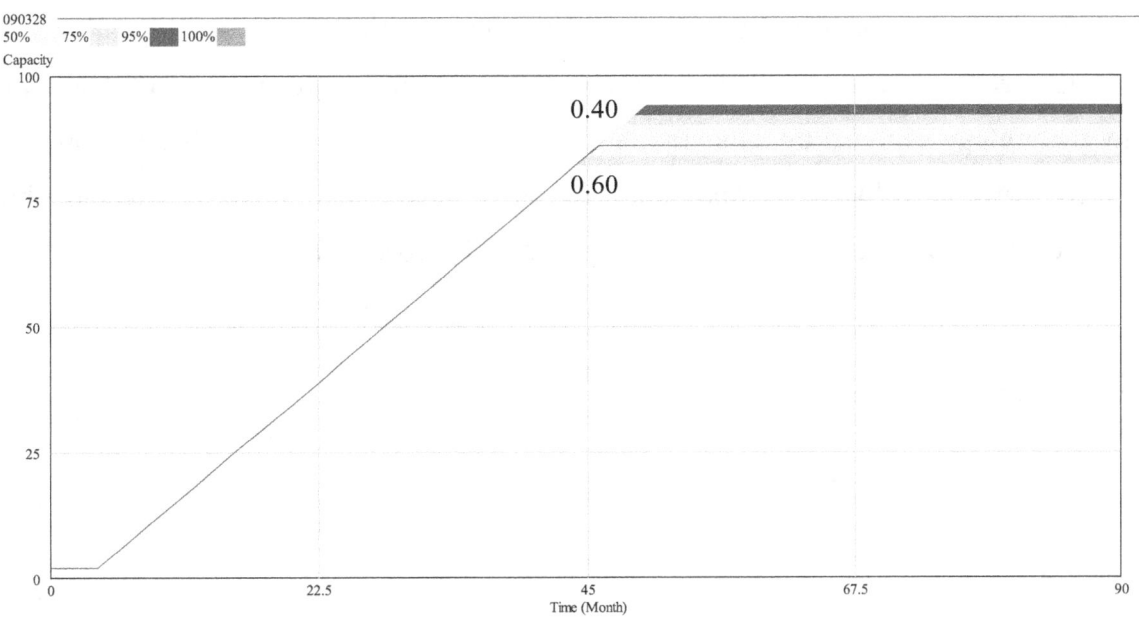

**Figure 109** Sensitivity Analysis: Effect of Production Budget Fraction on Capacity

Usually high technology firms allocate around 10% and even more of their turnover to research and development. As discussed in executive interviews and simulated in the system dynamics model, technology suppliers selling new technology capital equipment have at least 30% gross profit. Hence 10% allocation to R&D with respect to turnover can almost be regarded equivalent to **reference R&D budget fraction** of 15% with respect to **total expenditure budget**. When **reference R&D budget fraction** changes between 5% and 25%, it effects on **process quality** and **production cost of unit new technology** are illustrated in Figure 110, Figure 111 and Figure 112. When reference R&D budget fraction becomes less than 15%, there is less sudden increase in **use of R&D process budget** during the initial months, because **R&D process budget ratio** is slightly above or below one. There is only negligible fluctuation in process quality, after R&D budget ratio has become stable. After all **production** has been converted to **unit sales**, lower **reference R&D budget fraction** has the consequence that **R&D process budget ratio** reaches its equilibrium level 75% in later periods.

Having **reference R&D budget fraction** more than 15%, boosts R&D process budget ratio. Since investment in processes has diminishing returns, **process quality** is not sensitive to changes in **R&D process budget ratio**. Therefore there is a limit in reducing cost of production for a technology supplier which is clearly in the simulation run demonstrated in Figure 112. In this system dynamics model, **production cost of unit new technology** declined by a maximum of 40%. Since increasing use of R&D process budget may not always be possible, executives' convention is applicable that improvement in production processes may lead 20-30% cost advantage.

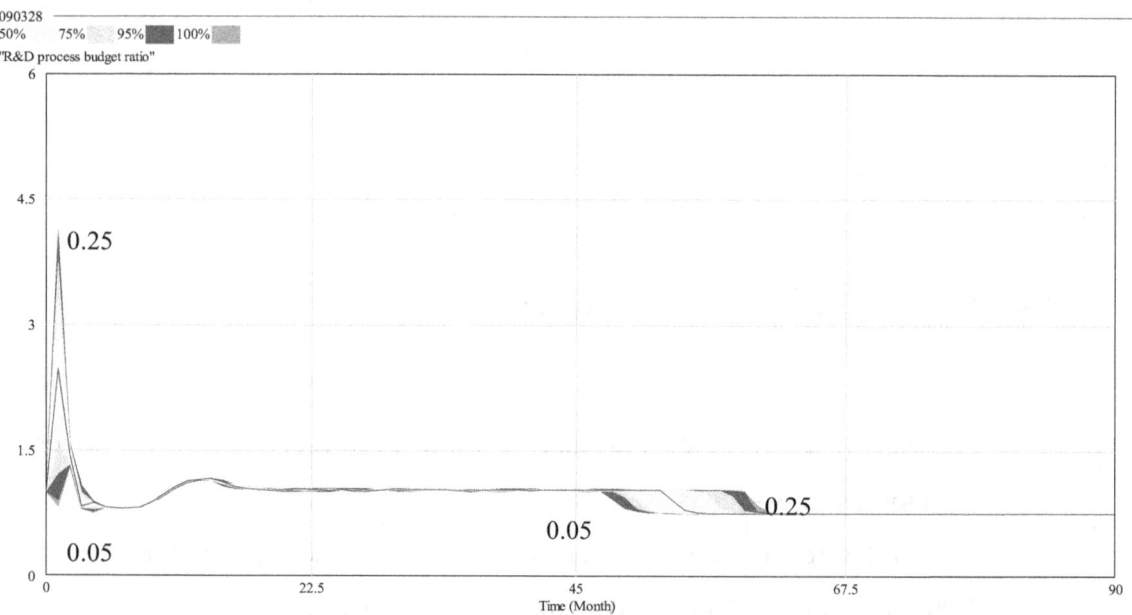

**Figure 110** Sensitivity Analysis: Effect of Reference R&D Budget Fraction on R&D Process Budget Ratio

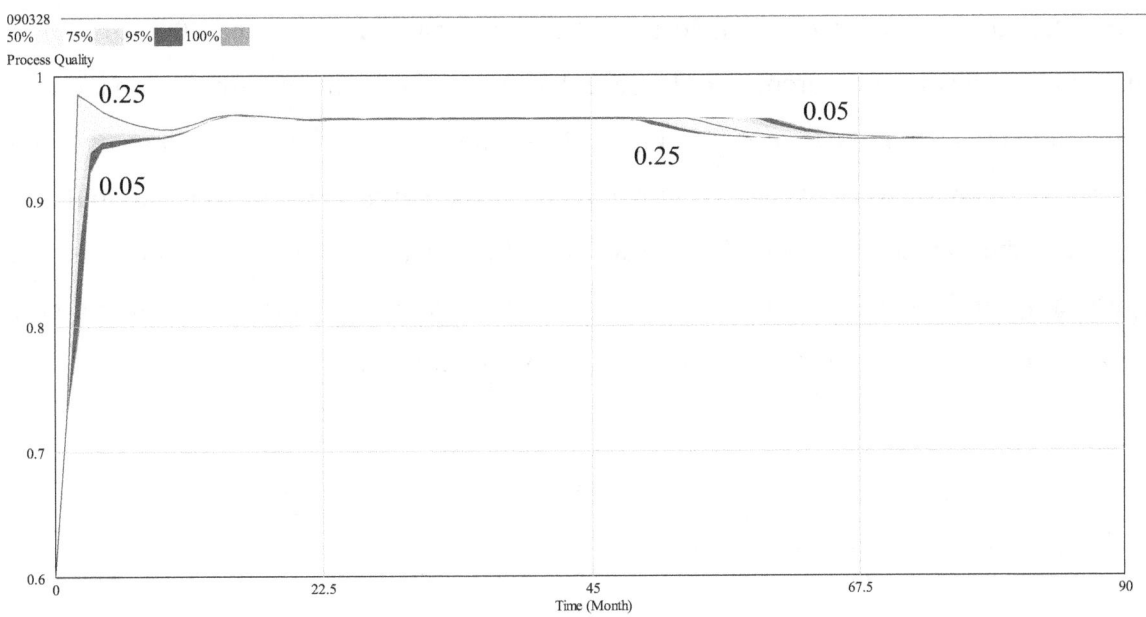

**Figure 111** Sensitivity Analysis: Effect of Reference R&D Budget Fraction on Process Quality

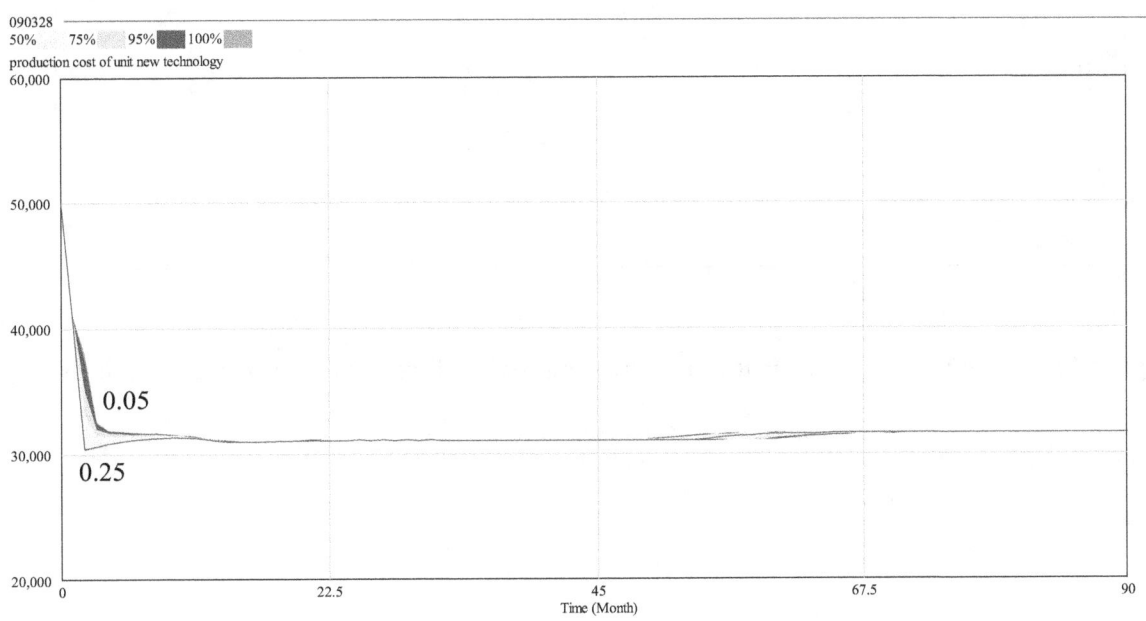

**Figure 112** Sensitivity Analysis: Effect of Reference R&D Budget Fraction on Production Cost

Marketing is needed such that buyer firms get aware about new technology. There is a considerable amount of literature about R&D and marketing regarding their joint effectiveness (Souder and Chakrabarti, 1978). In the system dynamics model, **marketing**

**budget fraction** has been determined as 10%. If it is simulated between 0% and 20%, sensitivity of customer awareness is limited due to the formula for effect of marketing budget ratio on awareness as shown in Figure 113. The reason is that even if a technology supplier would not carry out marketing activity, i.e. marketing budget fraction would be zero, customer awareness would increase as 0.2. Since customer awareness is not significantly influenced, Figure 114 reveals that there is negligible change in new customers during each month, i.e. demand for new technology.

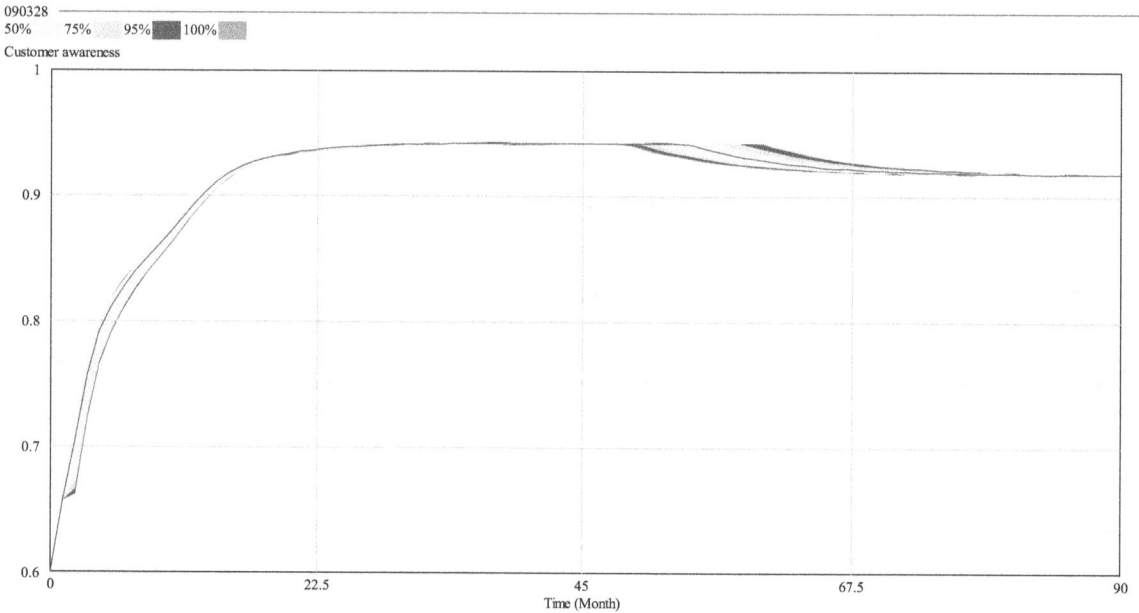

**Figure 113** Sensitivity Analysis: Effect of Marketing Budget Fraction on Customer Awareness

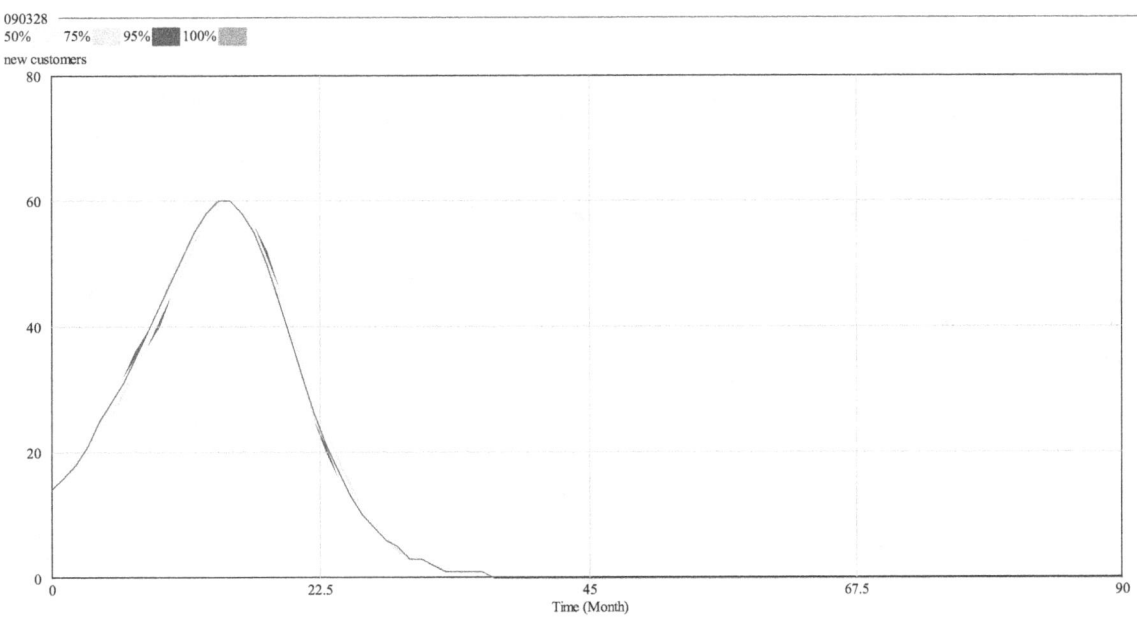

**Figure 114** Effect of Marketing Budget Fraction on New Customers

### 4.6.2 Process Quality and Production

When a technology supplier does not invest in its production and/or business processes, process quality gets worse, since tools and equipment for manufacturing get older. Therefore improvement in process quality requires ongoing research and development, either. When simulating the model, **process quality outflow fraction** has been a constant of 1% per month. When the parameter is let to take variable values to take between zero and 5% per month, **process quality** would remain stable close to **desired process quality** of 99% as shown in Figure 115. However, increasing outflow fraction results in greater fluctuations in process quality, and process quality declines considerably when production ends. When **process quality outflow fraction** increases, it brings about increase in R&D budget allocation as goal seeking behavior of process quality towards desired process quality. However, with less outflow fraction, use of R&D budget declines much faster since process quality becomes higher. These non-symmetric effects on **use of R&D process budget** can be viewed in Figure 116.

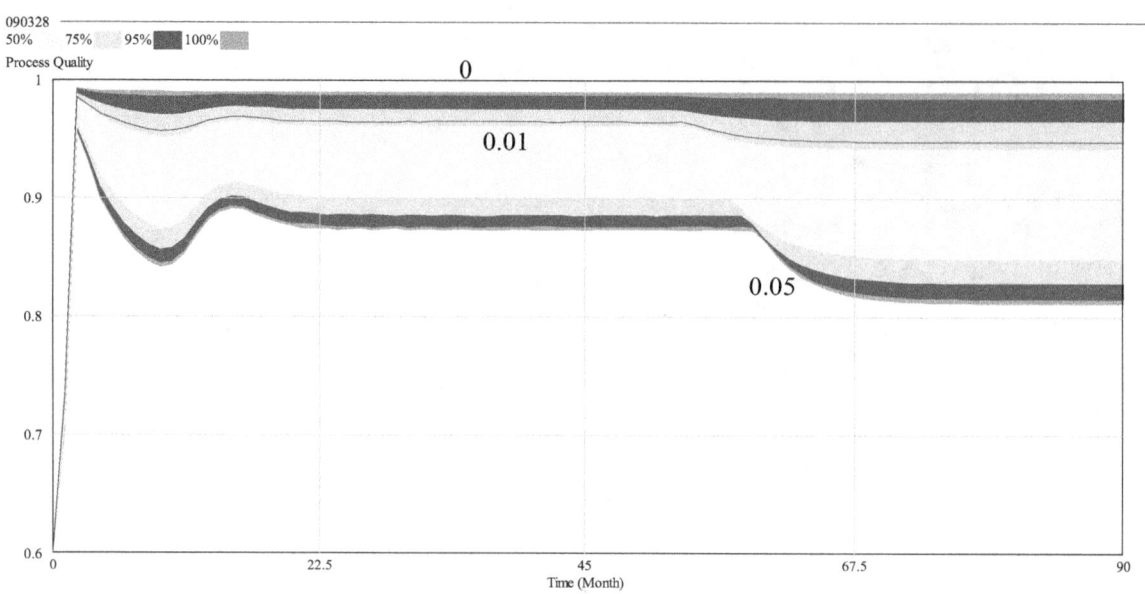

**Figure 115** Sensitivity Analysis: Effect of Process Quality Outflow Fraction on Process Quality

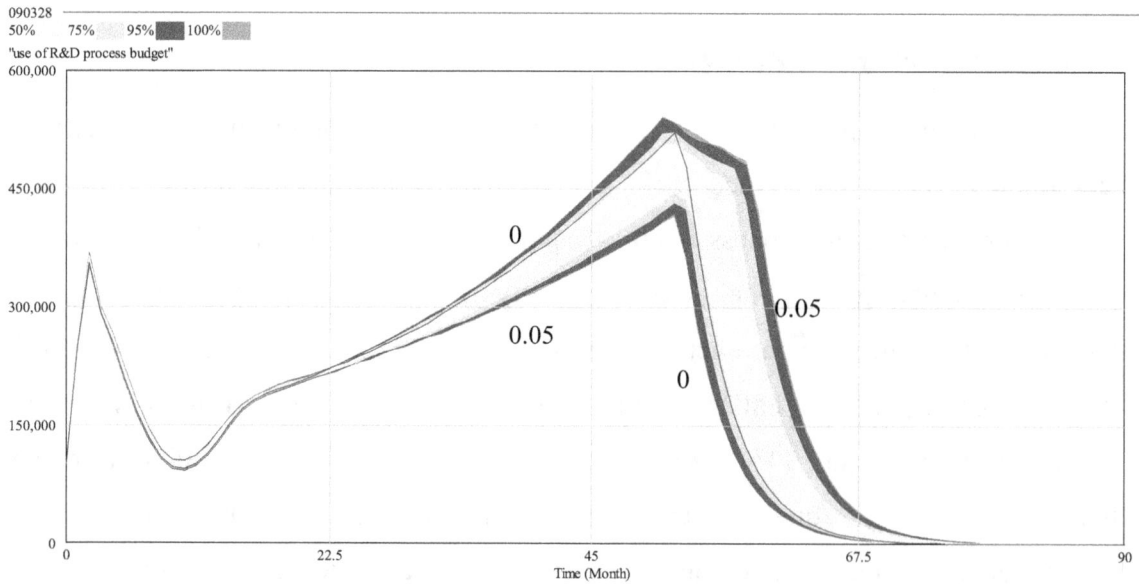

**Figure 116** Sensitivity Analysis: Effect of Process Quality Outflow Fraction on R&D Process Budget

### 4.6.3 Capacity and Backlog

The value of **capacity step** has been forty during the simulation of the system dynamics model. However, as displayed in Figure 117 and discussed in section 4.6.1, since **desired**

**production** determines **production** and is less than capacity, capacity cannot provide its purpose to close backlog, simulating capacity step between the values of 10 and 70 does not change the pattern for capacity, as shown in Figure 118. Therefore inreasing capacity step has only a marginal impact on extending capacity, whereas Figure 119 gives an idea that decreasing capacity step makes production higher during the initial months such that **backlog** becomes less.

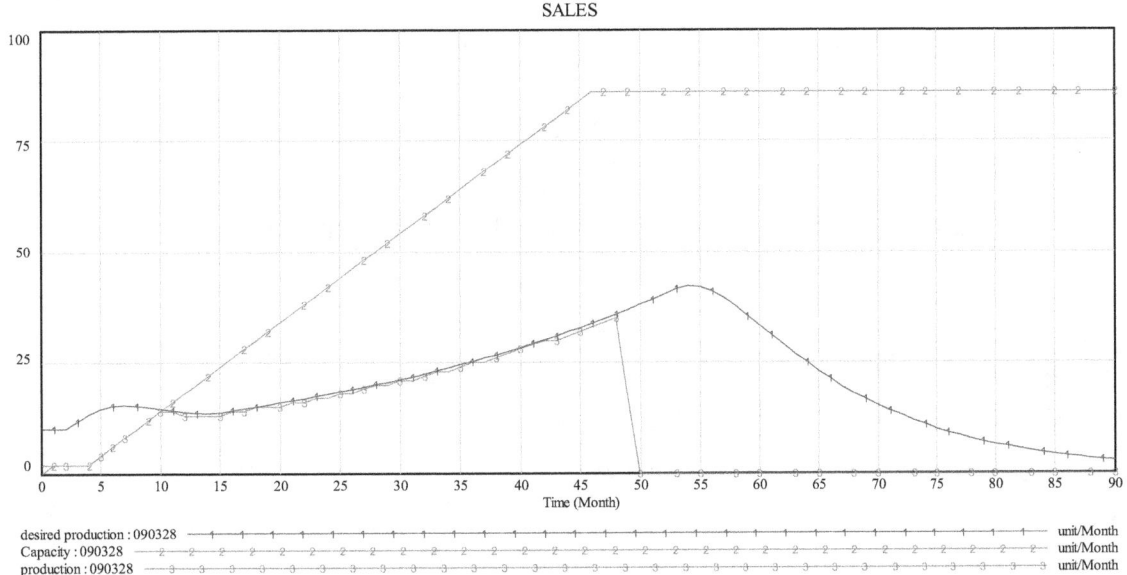

**Figure 117** Desired Production and Potential Production

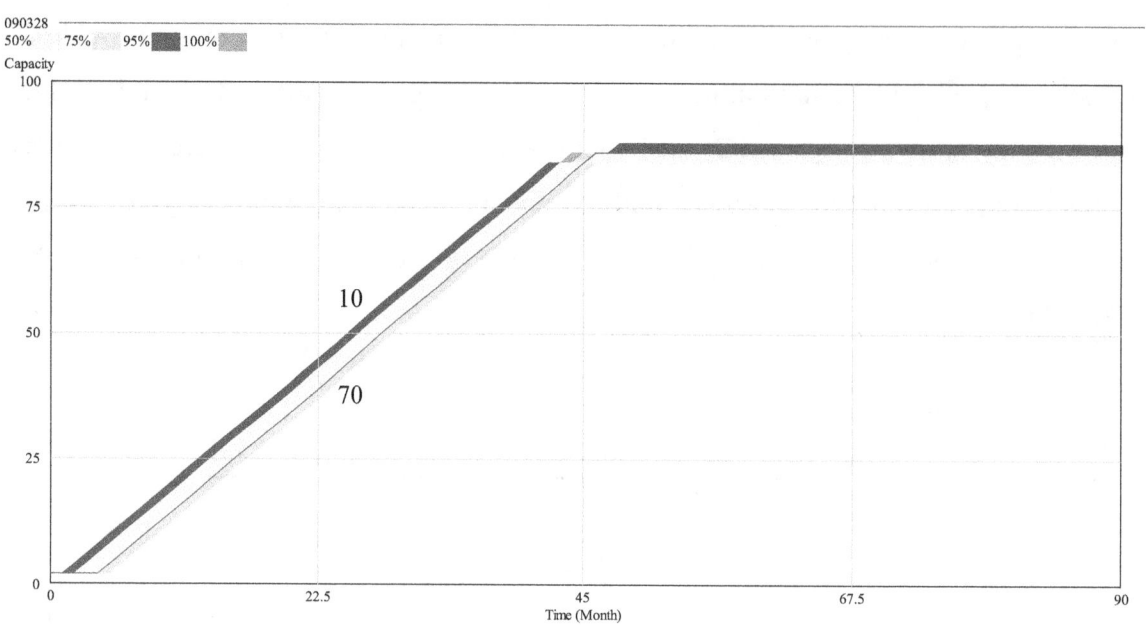

**Figure 118** Sensitivity Analysis: Effect of Capacity Step on Capacity

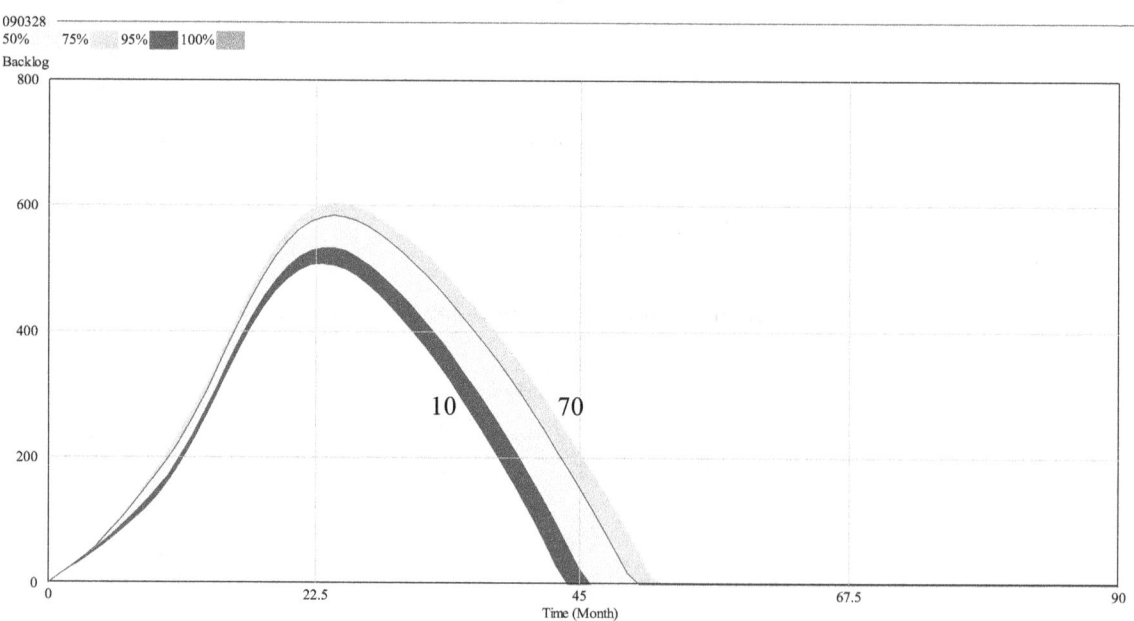

**Figure 119** Sensitivity Analysis: Effect of Capacity Step on Backlog

According to the relationship between capacity and production, although the structure is correct, there appears to be a decision problem. According to executive interviews, time period for capacity step is presumed to be sixteen months. Hence having **reference time**

**to adjust capacity** is 0.4 unit/month resulted in defining **capacity step** as 40 unit/Month (i.e. 40 x 0.4 = 16 months). There is backlog due to demand for new technology by firms in an industry. Due to relatively large amount of backlog with respect to initial capacity of 2 units per month, capacity adjustment starts only after when target capacity equivalent to backlog exceeds capacity step of 40 units per month, as shown in Table 14. Further Figure 117 shows that investment in capacity becomes useless, since production is available only according to production budget. Therefore **time to adjust capacity** may differ depending on circumstances regarding technology, industry characteristics. In summary, related parameters can be adjusted and updated when analyzing diffusion of innovations in different industries.

**Table 14** Simulation Results for Demand, Backlog and Capacity

| Time (Month) | 0 | 1 | 2 | 3 | 4 | 5 | 6 | 7 |
|---|---|---|---|---|---|---|---|---|
| capacity adjustment | 0 | 0 | 0 | 0 | 5 | 5 | 5 | 5 |
| new customers | 14 | 16 | 18 | 21 | 25 | 28 | 31 | 35 |
| Backlog | 0 | 14 | 26.4 | 40.6 | 57.5 | 78 | 99.2 | 121.1 |

Accordingly, capacity decision has to be considered. Another important factor that the system dynamics model took demand as an independent phenomenon such that number of firms using new technology occurs even though part of orders received is lost by the technology supplier due to large amount of backlog. Therefore, the model equations are changed slightly. First, **orders received** is made equivalent to **new customers**. If backlog exceeds capacity, demand in that period becomes only 70% of the integer sum of **word of mouth demand** and **demand from advertising**. Secondly, **target capacity** is not any more equivalent to backlog amount by changing the value of **backlog correction** to 1% instead of one. Accordingly, the value of **capacity step** is changed to four (4) instead of forty (40), since decision about increasing capacity The slightly modified model is presented in Figure 120. The table lookup function for effect of marketing budget ratio on awareness is updated such that increase in **customer awareness** is not possible when **budget allocation to marketing** becomes zero. For ease of reference, this updated model's parameters and initial values are presented in Table 15 showing changes in grey background.

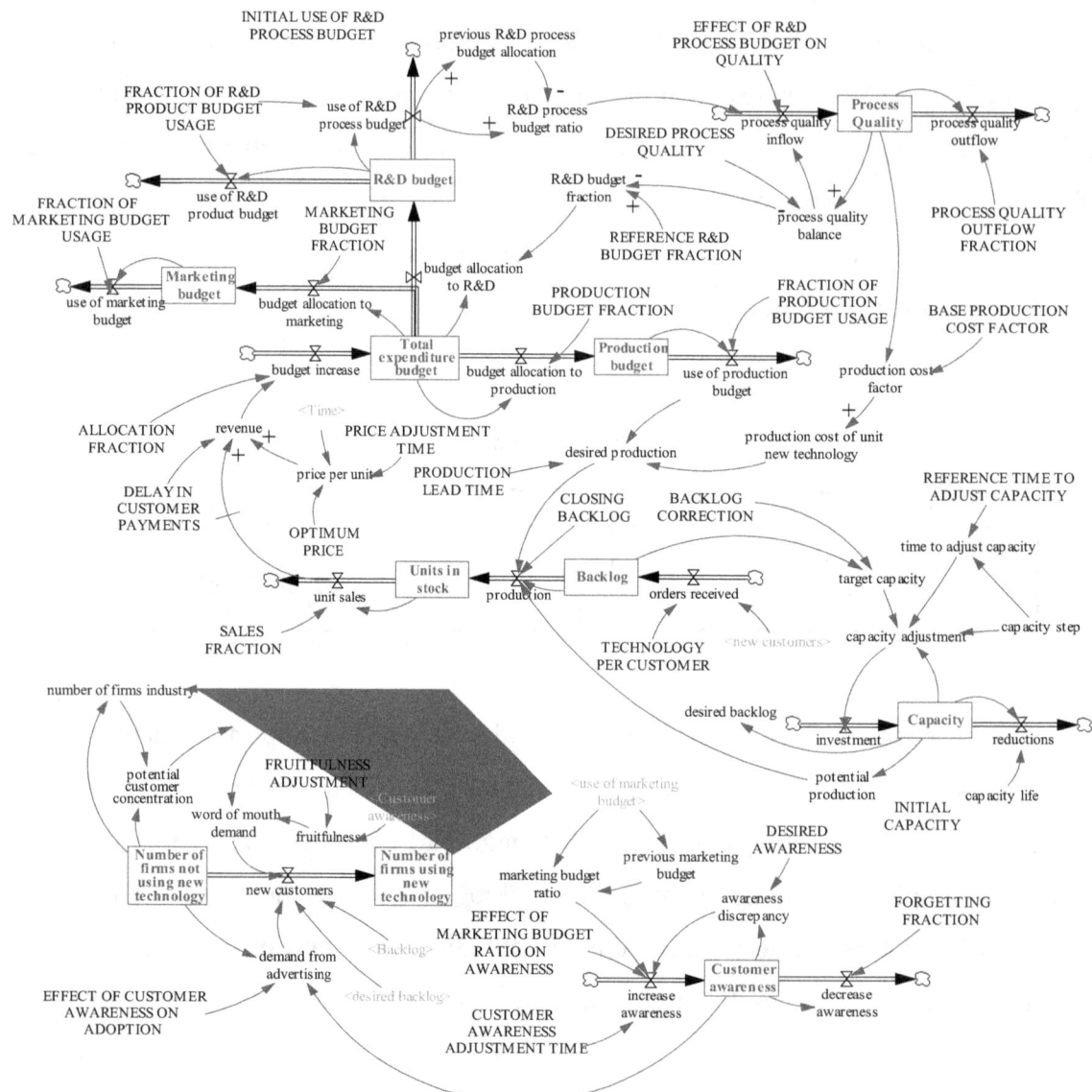

**Figure 120** Updated System Dynamics Model

**Table 15** Parameters and Values in the Updated Model

| Variable Name | Initial Value |
|---|---|
| *Simulation Period* | *90 month* |
| Allocation Fraction | 80% |
| Total Expenditure Budget | 1,000,000 EUR |
| Production Budget | 500,000 EUR |
| R&D Budget | 100,000 EUR |
| Initial Use of R&D Process Budget | 100,000 EUR |
| Production Budget Fraction | 50% / month |
| Reference R&D Budget Fraction | 10% /month |
| Marketing Budget Fraction | 10% /month |
| Fraction of Production Budget Usage | 1 |
| Fraction of R&D Product Budget Usage | 0 |
| Fraction of Marketing Budget Usage | 1 |
| Effect of R&D Process Budget on Quality | Table lookup with [(0,0)-(2,1)],(0.3,0),(0.4,0.05),(0.5,0.1), (0.6,0.15), (0.7,0.2), (0.8,0.25),(0.9,0.3), (1,0.35),(1.1,0.45), (1.2,0.5),(1.3,0.55), (1.4,0.6),(1.5,0.65),(1.5,0.65), (1.6,0.7), (1.7,0.8),(1.8,0.85),(1.9,0.9),(1.95,0.95), (2,1) |
| Process Quality Outflow Fraction | 1% / Month |
| Desired Process Quality | 0.99 |
| Base Production Cost Factor | 30,000 EUR/unit |
| Production Lead Time | 12 Month |
| Optimum Price | 100,000 EUR/unit |
| Delay in Customer Payments | 4 Month |
| Sales Fraction | 1 / Month |
| Units in Stock | 10 unit |
| Backlog | 0 unit |
| *Closing Backlog* | *1 / Month* |
| *Backlog Correction* | *0.01 / Month* |
| Reference Time to Adjust Capacity | 0.4 Month*Month / unit |
| *Capacity Step* | *4 unit / Month* |
| *Initial Capacity* | *4 unit / Month* |
| Capacity Life | 25 year |
| Number of Firms Not Using New Technology | 1000 company |
| Number of Firms Using New Technology | 10 company |
| Sociability | 3 |
| Fruitfulness Adjustment | 0.1 company / Month |
| Effect of Customer Awareness on Adoption | Table lookup with [(0,0)-(1,0.02)],(0,0),(0.1,0.0012), (0.2,0.0032), (0.3,0.0056),(0.4,0.0084), (0.5,0.0113), (0.6,0.0142), (0.7,0.0164), (0.8,0.0181),(0.9,0.0195),(1,0.0197) |
| *Effect of Marketing Budget Ratio on Awareness* | *Table lookup with [(0,0)-(1.5,1.2)], (0,0),(0.211009,0.0842105), (0.344037,0.157895),(0.472477,0.289474), (0.619266,0.468421),(0.75,0.67),(0.889908,0.847368), (1.05,1),(1.2,1.11),(1.35,1.17),(1.5,1.19)* |
| Customer Awareness Adjustment Time | 6 Month |
| Desired Awareness | 1 |
| Forgetting Fraction | 1% / Month |

The previous model had an initial capacity of 2 unit/Month. Since **capacity adjustment** occurs according to the differentiation among **capacity**, **target capacity** and **capacity step**, initial capacity is an important parameter. When simulations are carried out for different values of **initial capacity** between two and ten, simulation results for capacity adjustment are shown in Figure 121, whereas change in capacity during the simulation runs is put forward in Figure 122. When initial capacity is 2 unit/Month and 4 unit/Month, there are two times or one time capacity adjustment respectively reaching a maximum capacity of 6 unit/Month. If initial capacity is 6 unit/Month or above, **capacity** remains at the same level implying no decision for increasing/adjusting capacity, since **target capacity** is below the threshold determined via **capacity step**. Therefore, **initial capacity** will remain 4 unit/Month for following sensitivity analyses from here on. A supplier targeting a potential market comprising 1000 companies for selling its product as new technology can initially have a yearly capacity of 48 units which can serve the target buyer industry over a lifecycle of twenty years. The interaction between demand, production and backlog will lead to decision related to capacity.

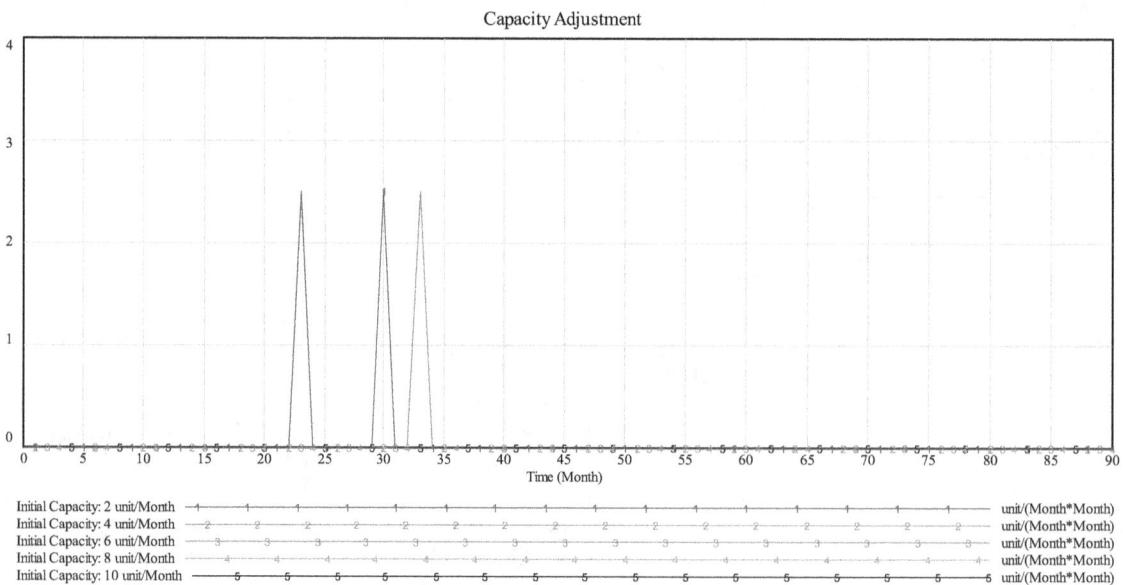

**Figure 121** Effect of Initial Capacity on Capacity Adjustment

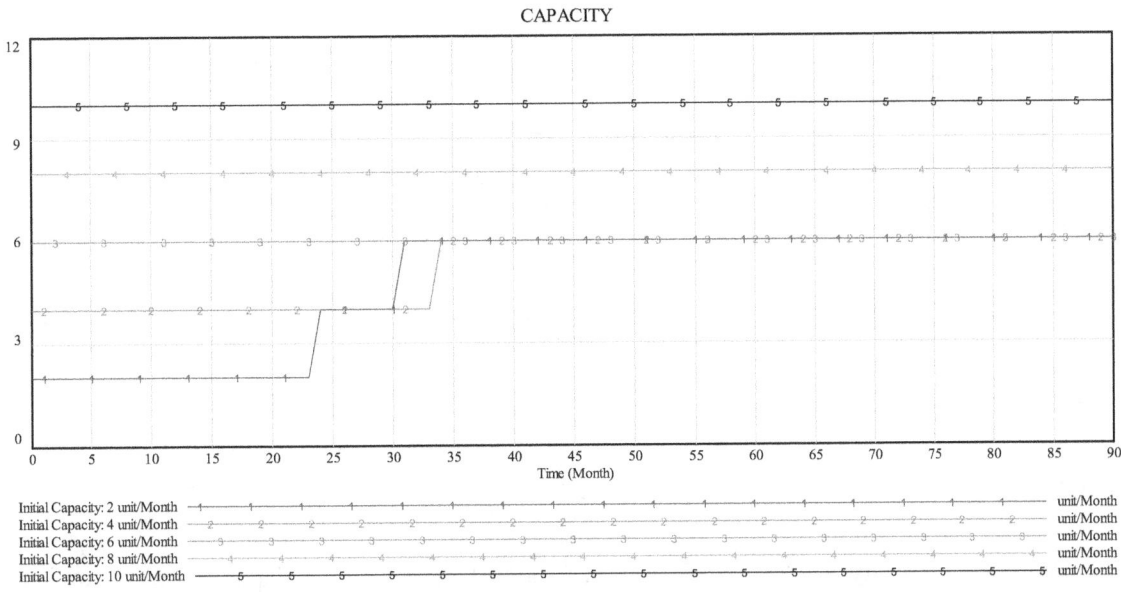

**Figure 122** Effect of Initial Capacity on Capacity

Capacity decision in the system dynamics model is based on **capacity step** and **reference time to adjust capacity**, such that **time to adjust capacity** becomes 1.6 months (instead of 16 months with respect to the previous system dynamics model). Sensitivity analyses on **reference time to adjust capacity** between zero (0) and six (6) leads time to adjust capacity vary from immediate to 24 months. Keeping **capacity step** constant as 4 unit/Month, causes capacity adjustment to occur at the same time interval as displayed in Figure 123, since **backlog** remains same until that time period. Hence longer reference time to adjust capacity leads to greater capacity in Figure 124, since increasing available capacity takes longer. However, greater capacity enables much more **production** as shown in Figure 125. Therefore **revenue** increases much more since backlog is closed earlier, since earlier **unit sales** implies more expensive **price per unit** as viewed in Figure 126. Since demand is much higher than capacity, there is always backlog. Therefore diffusion of new technology is not affected by sensitivity analysis on **reference time to adjust capacity**.

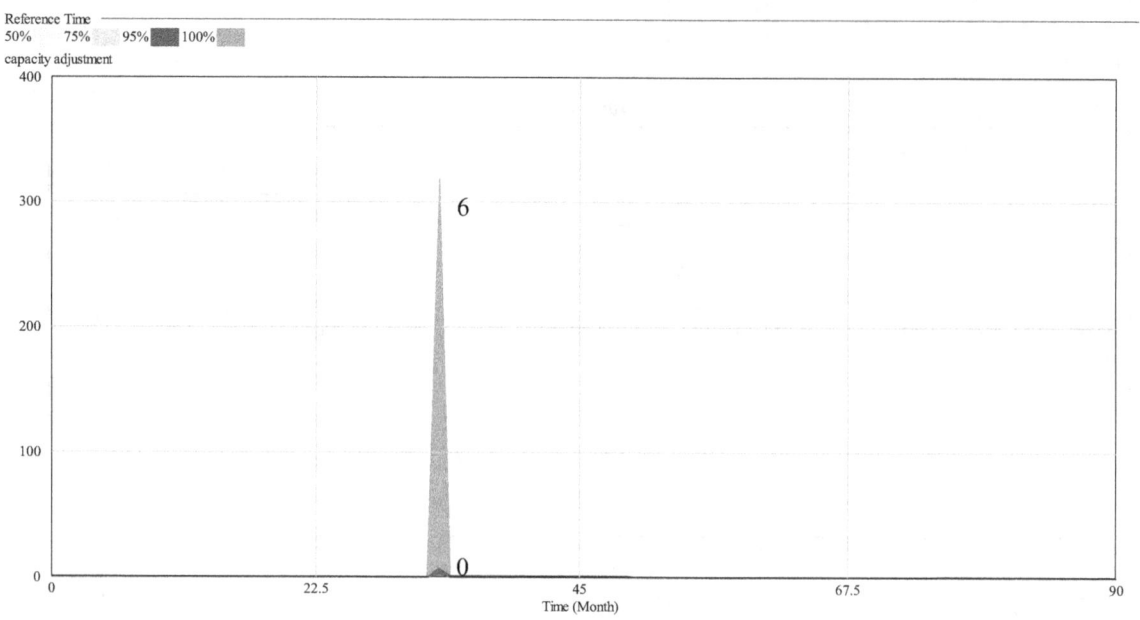

**Figure 123** Sensitivity Analysis: Effect of Reference Time to Adjust Capacity on Capacity Adjustment

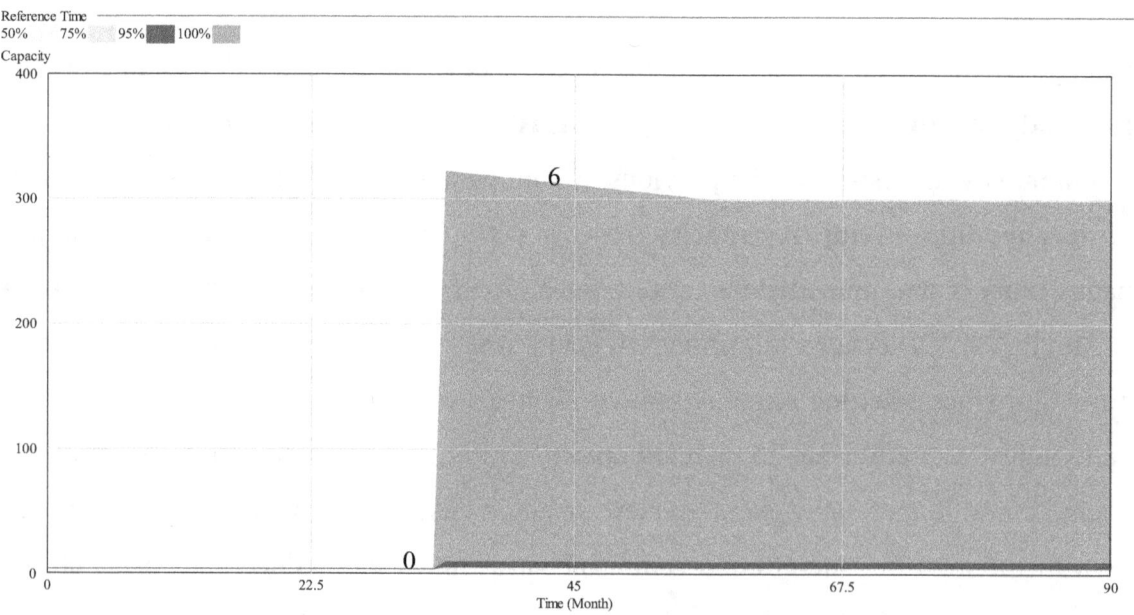

**Figure 124** Sensitivity Analysis: Effect of Reference Time to Adjust Capacity on Capacity

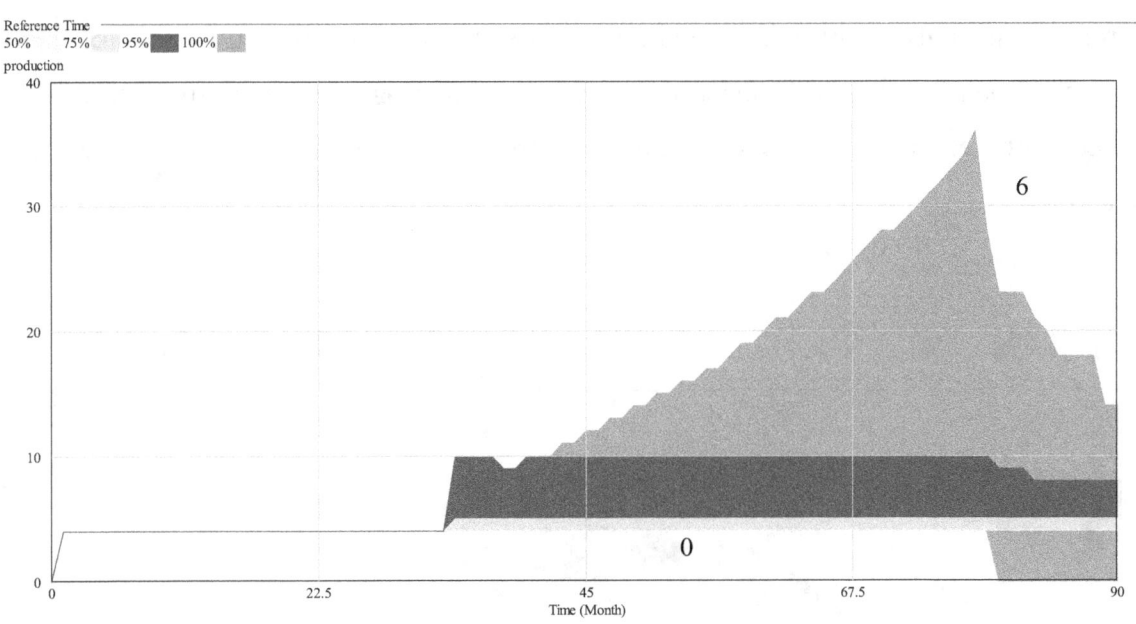

**Figure 125** Sensitivity Analysis: Effect of Reference Time to Adjust Capacity on Production

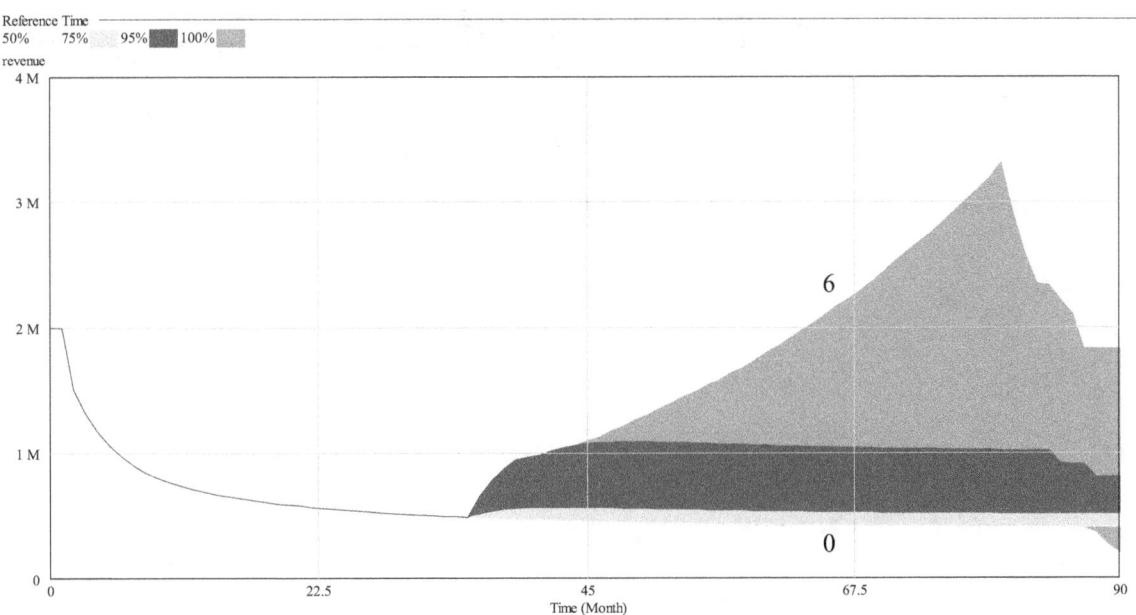

**Figure 126** Sensitivity Analysis: Effect of Reference Time to Adjust Capacity on Revenue

One of the main assumptions in the model is that a firm buys a single technology. Therefore **technology per customer** is set as one. However a firm who is buying new technology as process innovation can have more of the same technology when it grows.

Therefore sensitivity analysis is carried out between the values zero and five. Since there is more demand, there is exponential growth in **backlog** as shown in Figure 127. Consequently **capacity** and **production** increase as in Figure 128 and Figure 129, respectively.

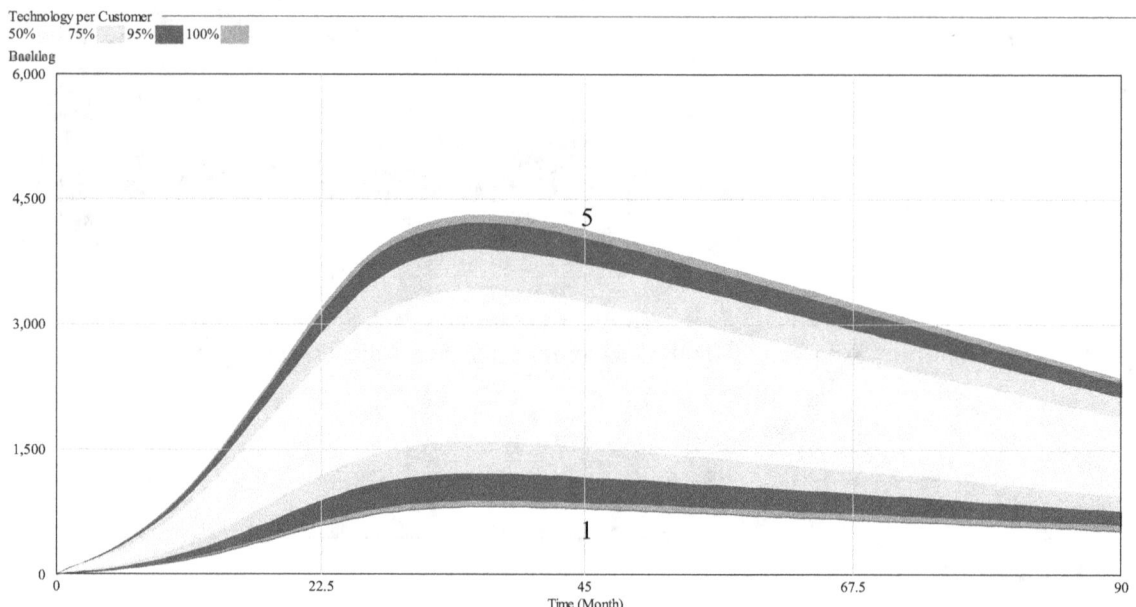

**Figure 127** Sensitivity Analysis: Effect of Technology per Customer on Backlog

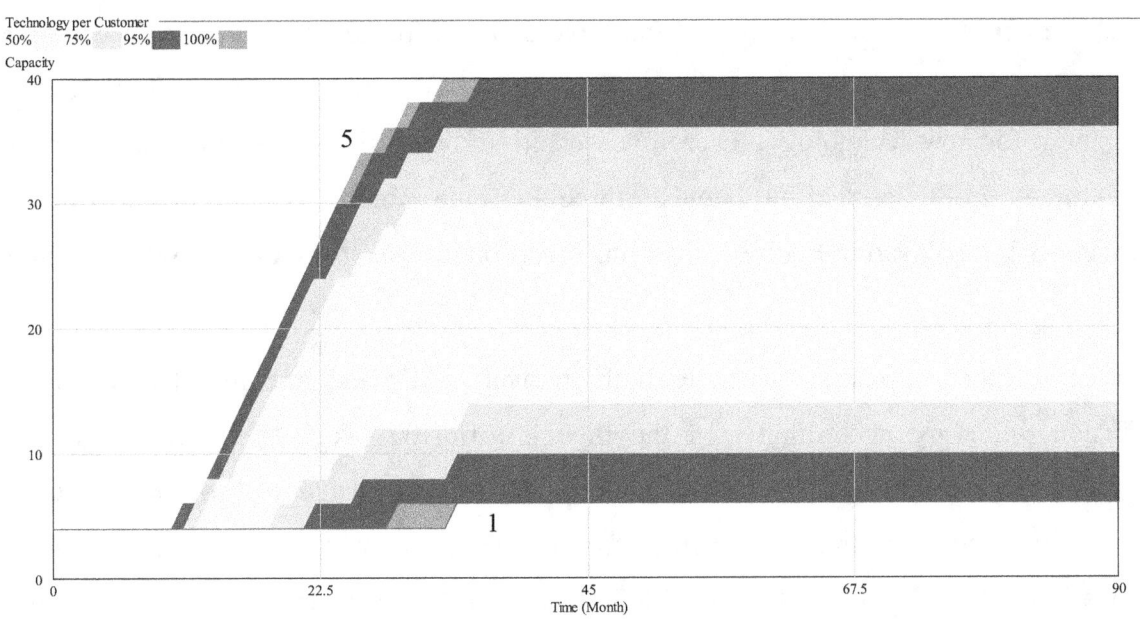

**Figure 128** Sensitivity Analysis: Effect of Technology per Customer on Capacity

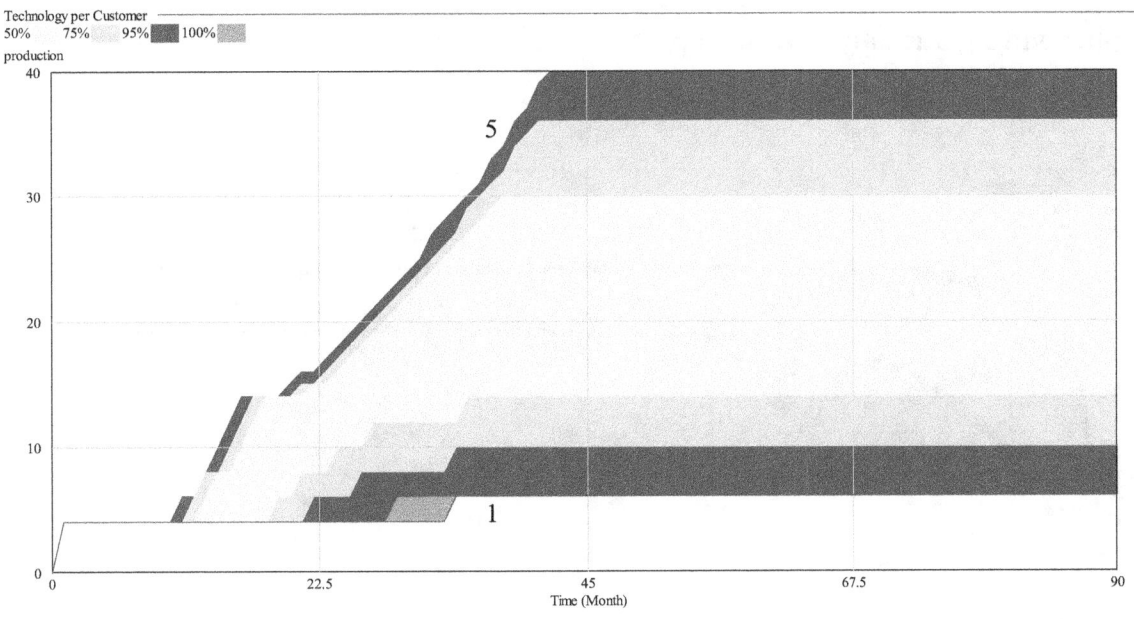

**Figure 129** Sensitivity Analysis: Effect of Technology per Customer on Production

### 4.6.4 Marketing and Demand

Demand for new technology can be influenced via technology supplier's marketing efforts. In the model, there is awareness of new technology before a firm can adopt it which influences both innovative and imitative demand for new technology. Depending on industry characteristics, marketing efforts may have different yields in terms of awareness for new technology. Therefore, sensitivity analysis on **customer awareness adjustment time** is carried out between three and nine months. Its effect on **customer awareness** is displayed in Figure 130 and its effect on **new customers** is shown in Figure 131.

Since customer awareness influences both innovative demand and imitative demand, diffusion will vary accordingly. In the model, diffusion takes 19 months that 500 companies in an industry adopt new technology. **Customer awareness adjustment time** can be attributed to the time period spent for knowledge and persuasion stages during an innovation decision process (Rogers, 2003:169). If customer awareness adjustment time differs at the above extreme values, i.e. 3 months versus 9 months, 90% diffusion takes place varies between 26 and 35 months, as shown in Table 16. Since price has a declining trend due to technology lifecycle, earlier or later sales of new technology by a technology supplier will significantly have an impact on revenue.

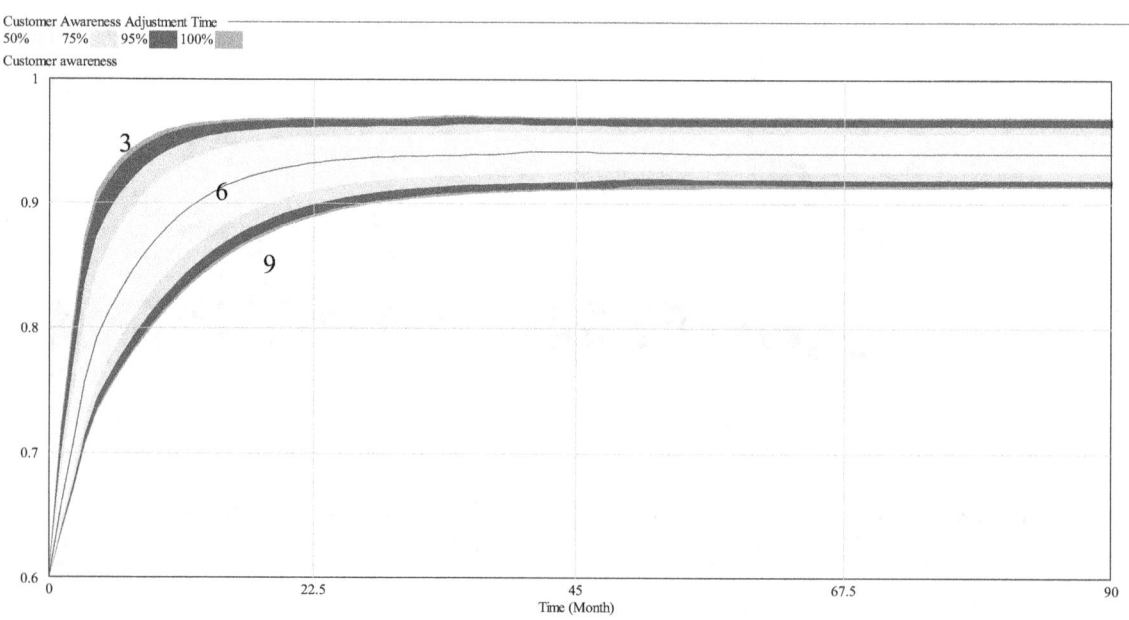

**Figure 130** Effect of Customer Awareness Adjustment Time on Customer Awareness

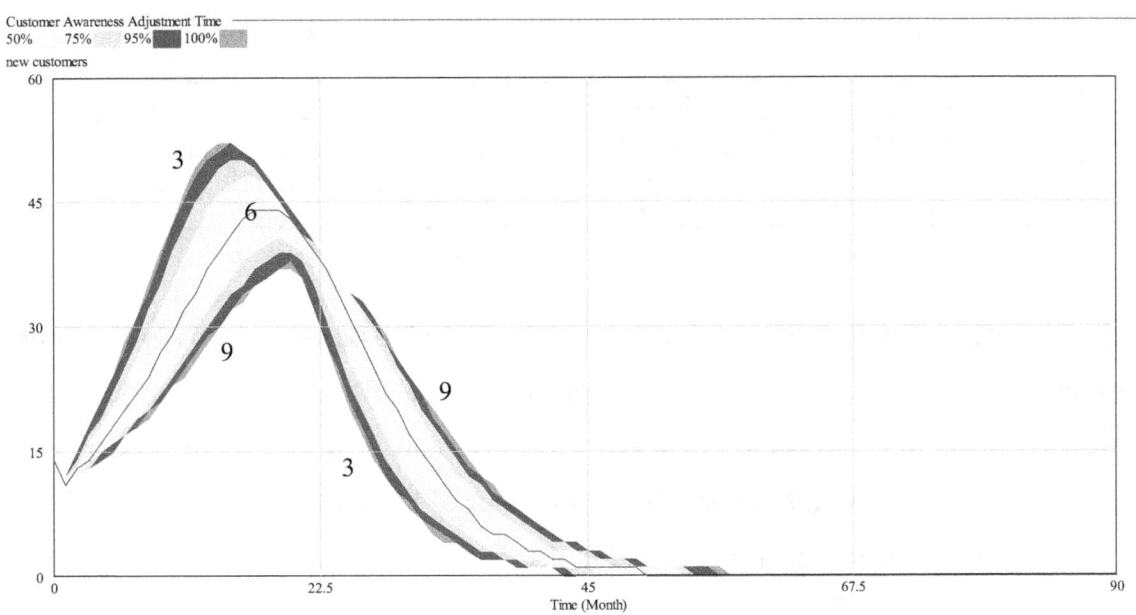

**Figure 131** Effect of Customer Awareness Adjustment Time on Demand (i.e. New Customers)

**Table 16** Effect of Customer Awareness Adjustment Time on Diffusion

| Number of Firms Using New Technology | 10 | 100 | 500 | 900 |
|---|---|---|---|---|
| Month for Customer Awareness Adjustment Time= 6 | 0 | 7 | 19 | 31 |
| Month for Customer Awareness Adjustment Time= 3 | 0 | 6 | 16 | 26 |
| Month for Customer Awareness Adjustment Time= 9 | 0 | 7 | 21 | 35 |

When **forgetting fraction** is simulated between 0 and 0.02 as sensitivity analysis, **customer awareness** reaches maximum or remains below 90% accordingly as shown in Figure 132. Therefore when customer awareness gets away faster, there is less peak demand and diffusion speed becomes slower as depicted Figure 133. In that case, Figure 134 displays that backlog increases slower but decreases slower, either.

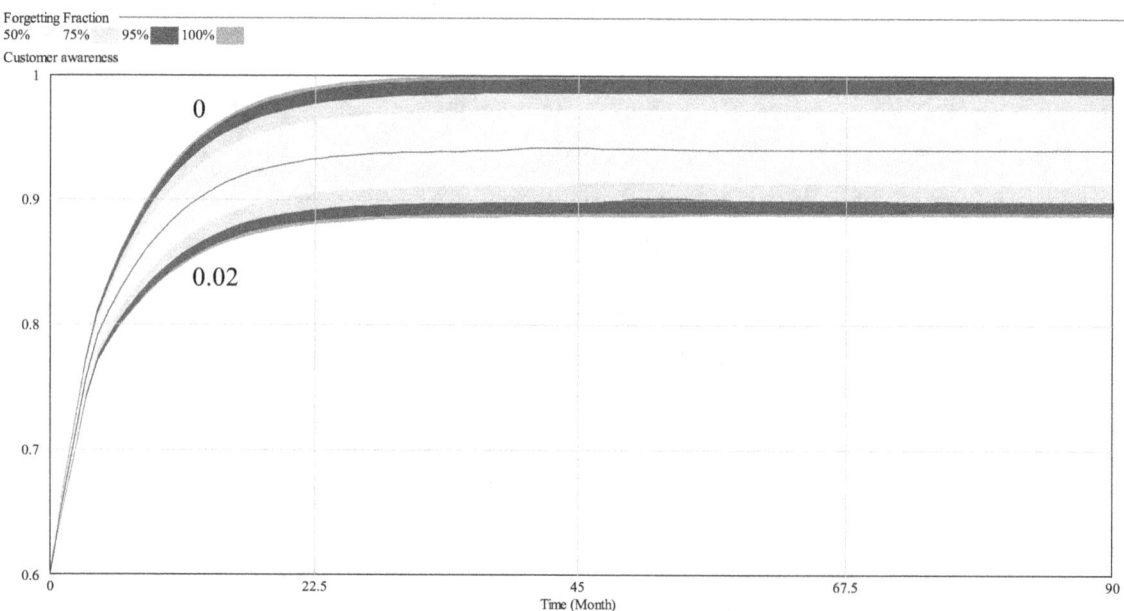

**Figure 132** Effect of Forgetting Fraction on Customer Awareness

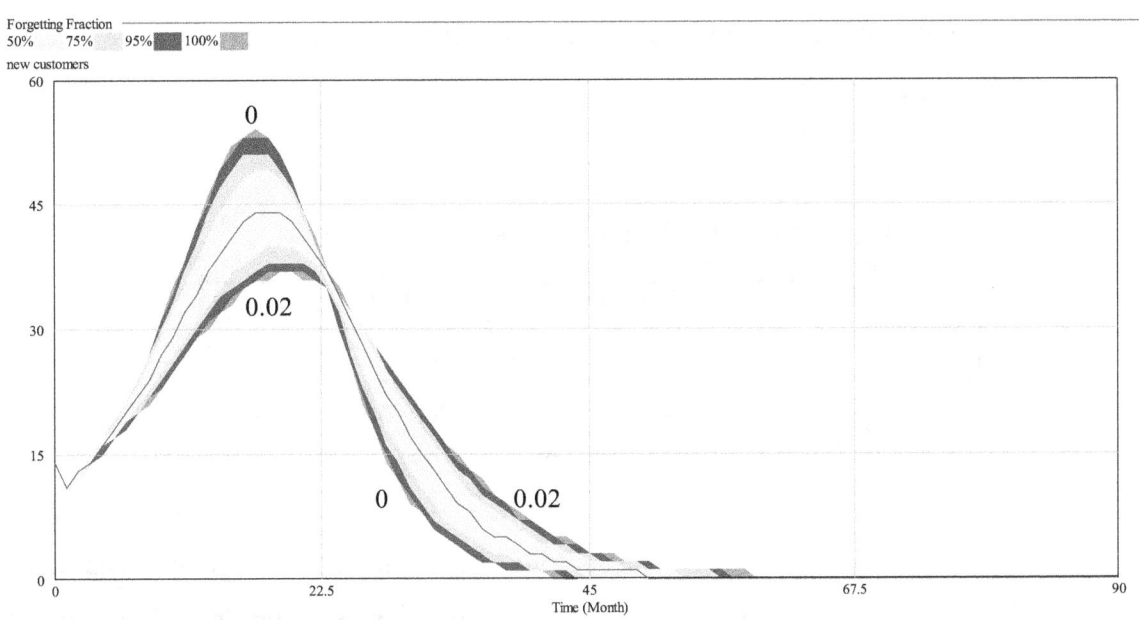

**Figure 133** Effect of Forgetting Fraction on Demand (i.e. New Customers)

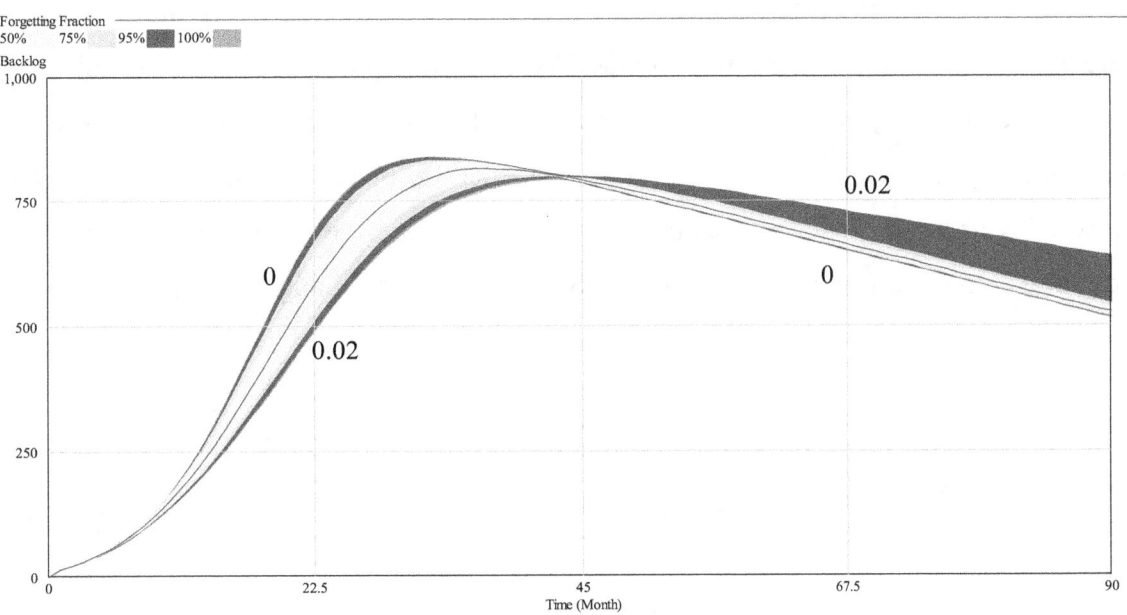

**Figure 134** Effect of Forgetting Fraction on Backlog

Similar to adjustment time for customer awareness, change in **forgetting fraction** leads to differences in **customer awareness**. Therefore diffusion speed is affected as shown in

Table 17. Sensitivity analysis on **forgetting fraction** has more or less symmetric effects on diffusion o new technology.

**Table 17** Effect of Forgetting Fraction on Diffusion

| Forgetting Fraction | Time for adoption from 10% till 90% of firms |
|---|---|
| 0% | 20 months |
| 1% | 24 months |
| 2% | 28 months |

**Sociability** is the average number of contacts by a particular firm using new technology with other firms in that industry such that other firms adopt new technology due to word of mouth. When a firm having adopted new technology has more or less contacts per month, other firms will follow earlier or later according to sensitivity analysis for sociability for the parameter values between 1 and 5 as graphically shown in Figure 135, where the model value has been 3 contacts/company/Month. Figure 136 reveals that **backlog** decreases slowly when there is less inter-firm communication in an industry, though increasing sociability has negligible influence on backlog. It can be interpreted that excessive backlog reduces demand. Since backlog pattern does not change, monthly production amount in Figure 137 changes only with respect to changes in capacity.

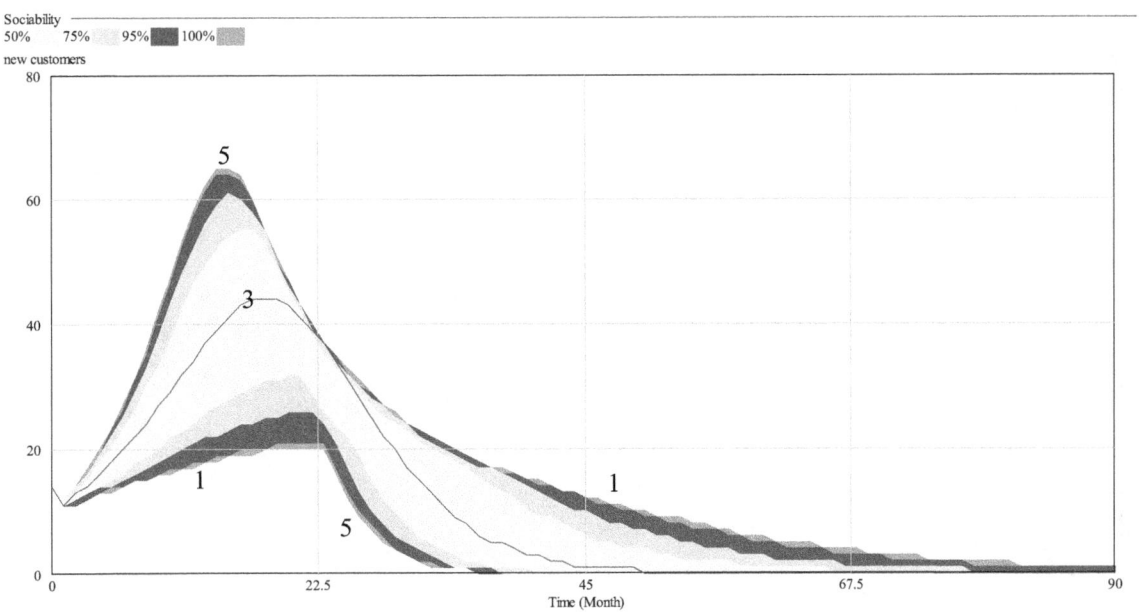

**Figure 135** Effect of Sociability on Demand

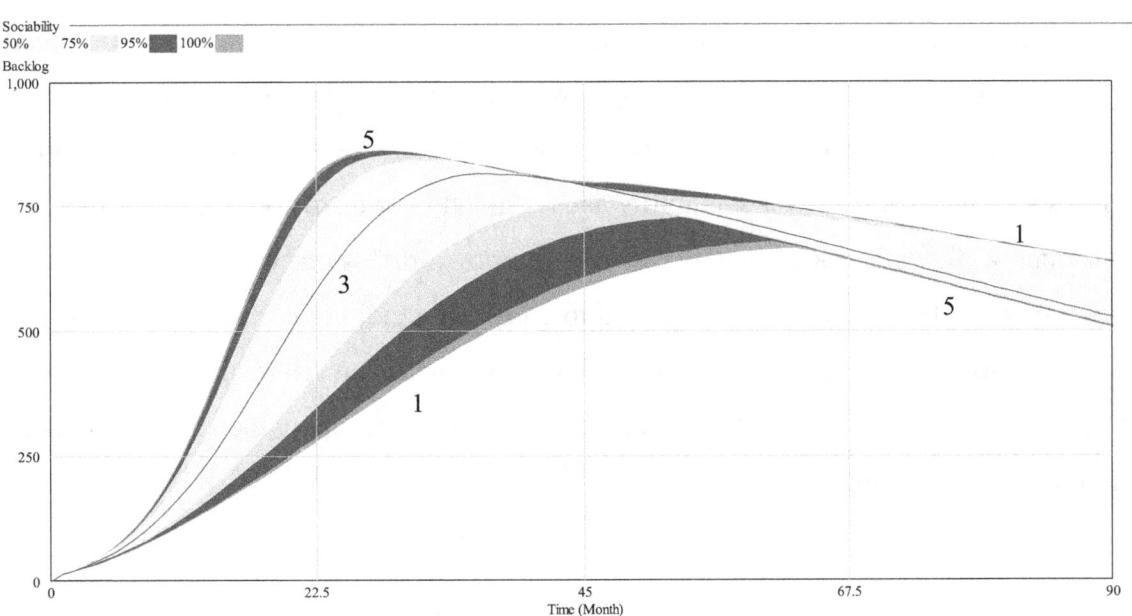

**Figure 136** Effect of Sociability on Backlog

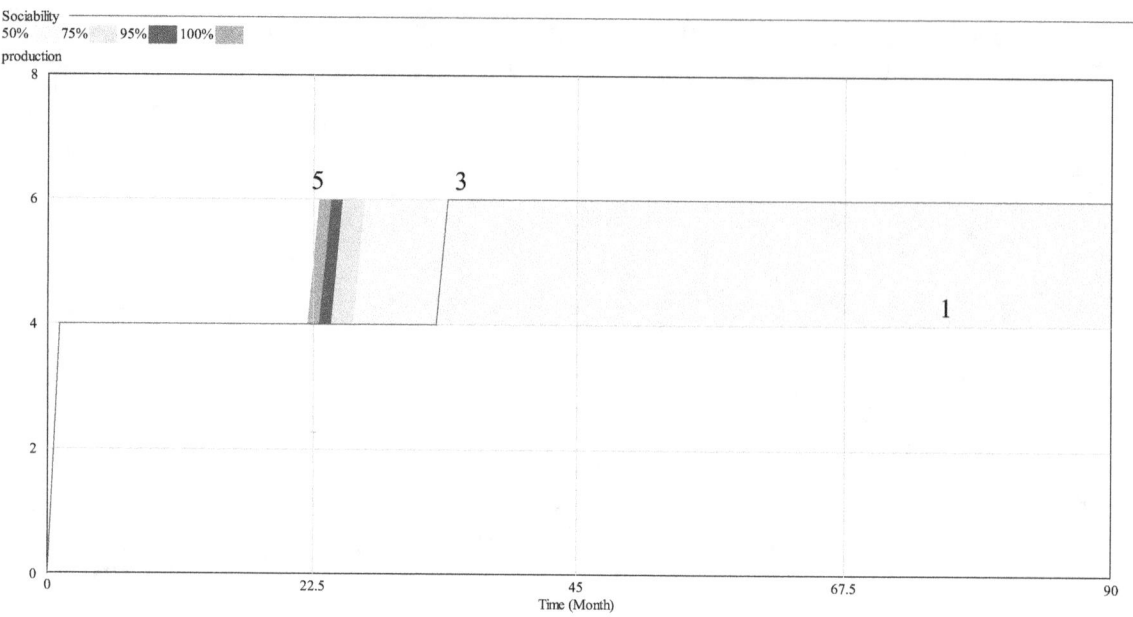

**Figure 137** Effect of Sociability on Production

Table 18 displays effect of sociability on diffusion. Sociability is an indicator of social networks in a particular industry buying new technology. When sociability is lower, diffusion speed is much slower, since word of mouth demand depends on communication links in social networks. Lower sociability causes much later diffusion implying that lack of information flows in social networks will slow down diffusion, whereas the opposite may not be true. Technology suppliers need to consider social networks, whether there is a critical mass for diffusion of new technology based on characteristics of both technology and industry. The model can facilitate deciding upon incentives for early adoption of new technology (Rogers, 2003:361).

**Table 18** Effect of Sociability on Diffusion

| Sociability | Time for adoption from 10% till 90% of firms |
|---|---|
| 1 | 53 months |
| 3 | 24 months |
| 5 | 15 months |

**Fruitfulness** determines the effectiveness of communication among user and non-user firms of new technology such that other firms in an industry adopt new technology due to word of mouth demand. In the model, **fruitfulness adjustment** has the value 0.1 company/contact. If firms in an industry would not possess any awareness about new technology, a firm would imitate new technology after thousand contacts as peer communication within that particular industry. It means that a firm can adopt new technology as the consequence of 10 contacts within that particular industry's peer communication among firms. When sensitivity analysis for **fruitfulness adjustment** is carried out for the values between 0.01 and 0.19, diffusion of new technology varies considerably, as Figure 138 shows change in **new customers** over months. When fruitfulness adjustment is less, **capacity adjustment** may not occur, since there is fewer **backlog**. Sensitivity analysis indicate that price should align demand such that technology supplier makes as much profit as possible. As it can be viewed from Figure 139, revenue decline due to less **price per unit** is reversed earlier, since **word of mouth demand** soars due to higher fruitfulness adjustment. Table 19 shows diffusion of new technology based on sensitivity analysis. When fruitfulness adjustment is 0.01, diffusion speed is 98 months that takes from 100 companies to 900 companies using new technology, whereas it lasts only fourteen months for fruitfulness adjustment of 0.19.

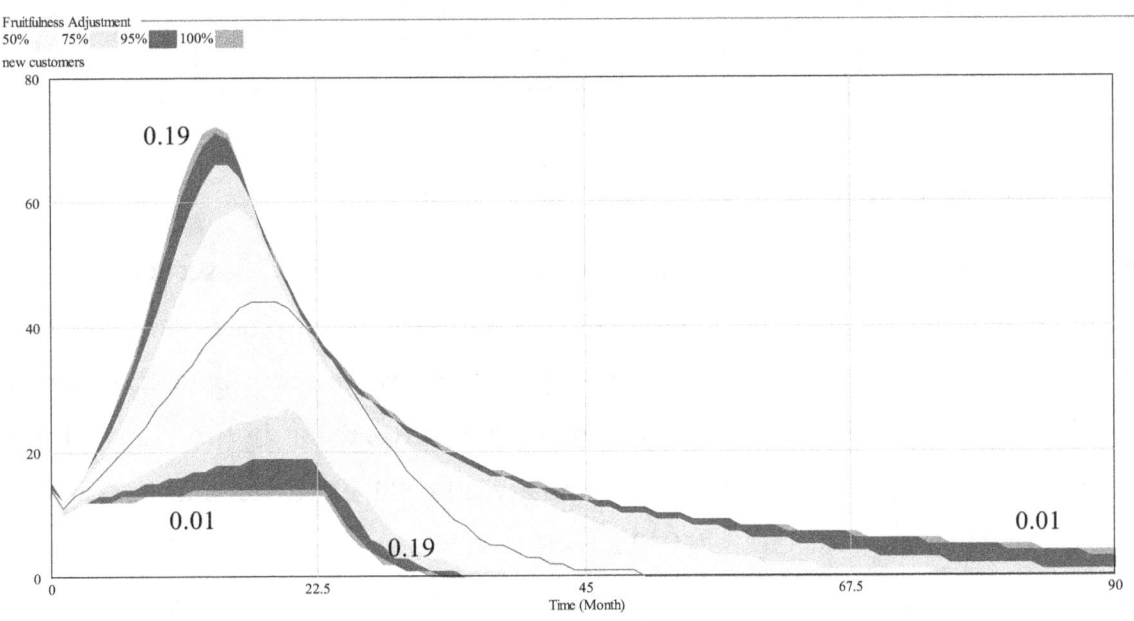

**Figure 138** Effect of Fruitfulness Adjustment on Demand

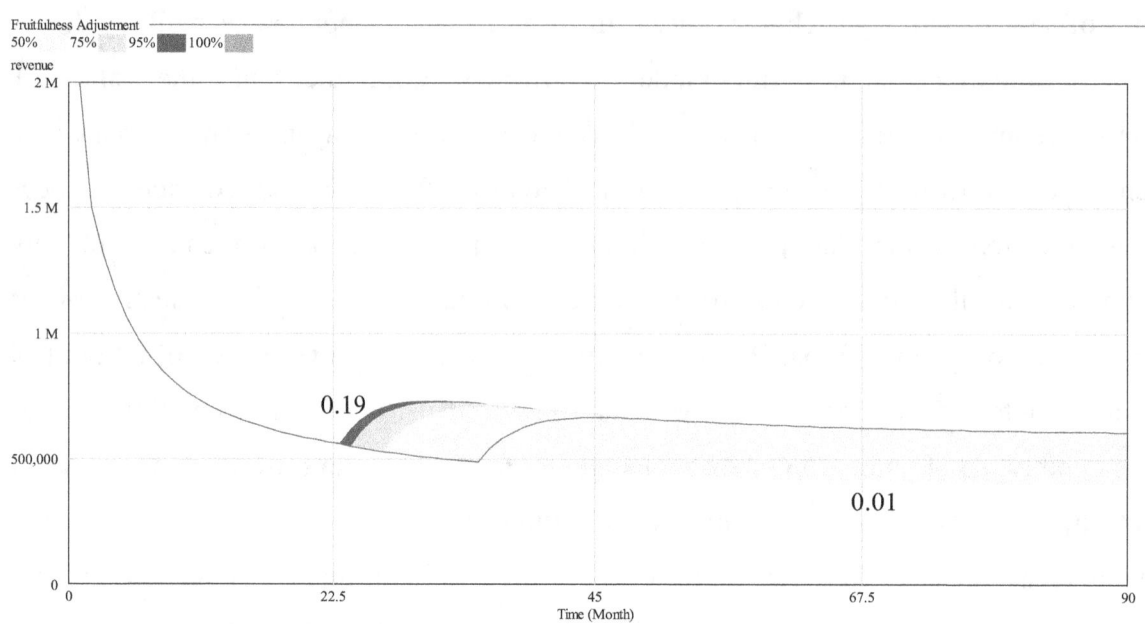

**Figure 139** Effect of Fruitfulness Adjustment on Revenue

**Table 19** Effect of Fruitfulness Adjustment on Diffusion of New Technology

| Fruitfulness Adjustment | Time for adoption from 10% till 90% of firms |
|---|---|
| 0.01 | 98 months |
| 0.1 | 24 months |
| 0.19 | 14 months |

### 4.6.5 Price and Revenue

Since demand for new technology is not price sensitive as discussed in sections 4.2 and 4.4, a technology supplier's pricing policy determines its revenue and therefore profitability over time. In the model, skimming price strategy has been applied, since new technology is initially adopted due to **demand from advertising** by innovative firms (Maier, 2002). In the model, unit price is initially 200,000 EUR declining to 150,000 EUR in 14 months and reaching 120,000 KEUR at 32nd month. Although 40-50% price reductions might be relevant for product innovations towards consumer, technology as process innovation does not become outdated as fast as new consumer products, even though existing technology is substituted by another technology. In this section, sensitivity analyses will be carried out for **delay in customer payments** and **price adjustment time**.

When a technology supplier makes it product sell to a firm, s/he receives payment for those unit sales as **revenue** some time later. In the model this time delay has been considered as four months according to commercial environment in Turkey and expert executive interviews. When **delay in customer payments** is simulated between one and seven months, revenue is more sensitive to later payments as depicted Figure 140. It graphically shows the danger for firms to run out of cash. Therefore time delays in payments cause greater fluctuations in technology suppliers' expenditure budgets as shown in Figure 141.

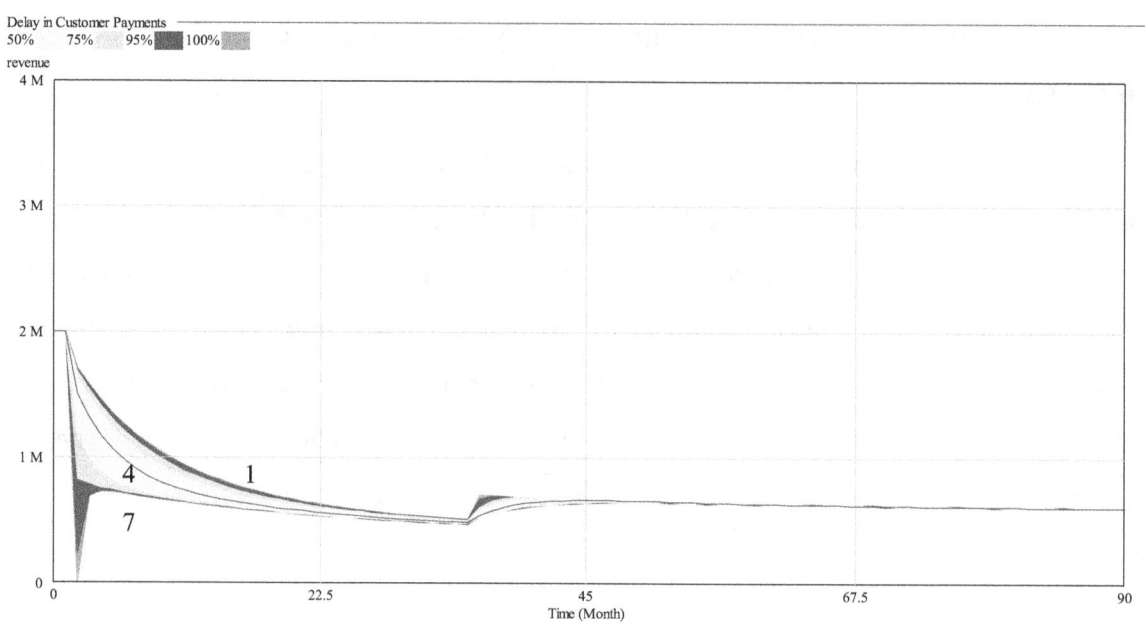

**Figure 140** Effect of Delay in Customer Payments on Revenue

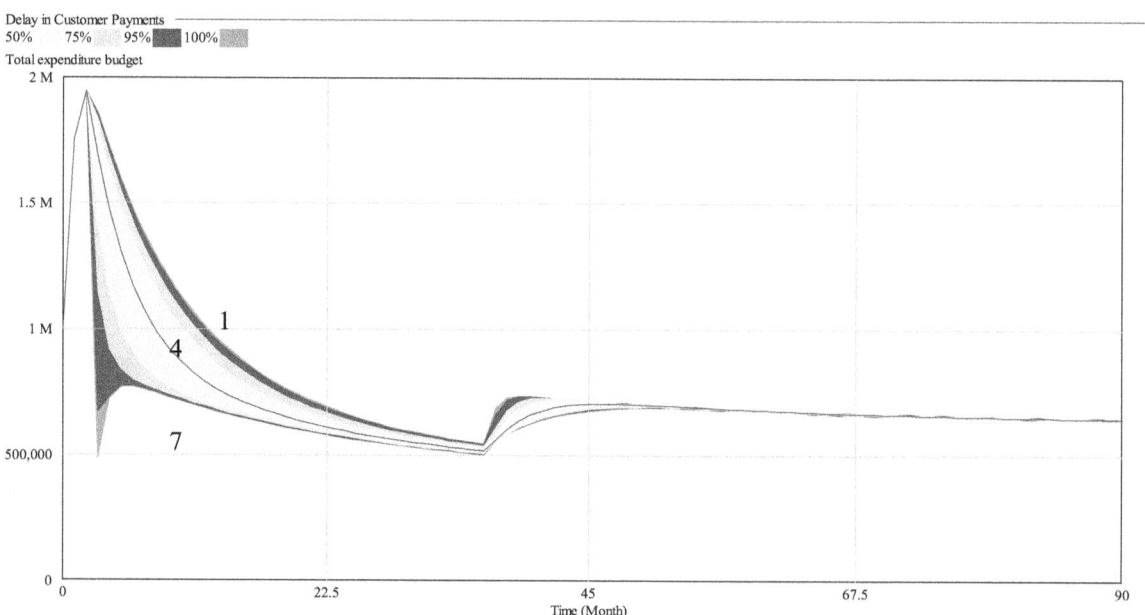

**Figure 141** Effect of Delay in Customer Payments on Total Expenditure Budget

The model enables to evaluate different pricing policies such as constant price, marginal pricing, optimum pricing, since they can be simulated by embedding appropriate price formulas. Hence, the model overcomes the major shortcomings of conventional price theory focusing on the short-term (Robinson and Lakhani, 1975). A manager of technology supplier can make his/her own dynamic price model by taking the evolution of its target market into account and having insights in fixed and variable cost such that the model helps a manager in deciding upon pricing policies.

When **price adjustment time** is simulated between zero and forty months, Figure 142 displays its effect on **revenue**. When **price adjustment time** is longer, **price per unit** decreases slower. Initial decline in **revenue** always occurs, since **unit sales** are initially 10 units, while price is at highest level. Since sales indirectly depend on capacity, a technology supplier's turnover continues to decrease as price for new technology becomes less. When there is **capacity adjustment** during 34$^{th}$ month, **revenue** starts to increase from 36$^{th}$ month on.

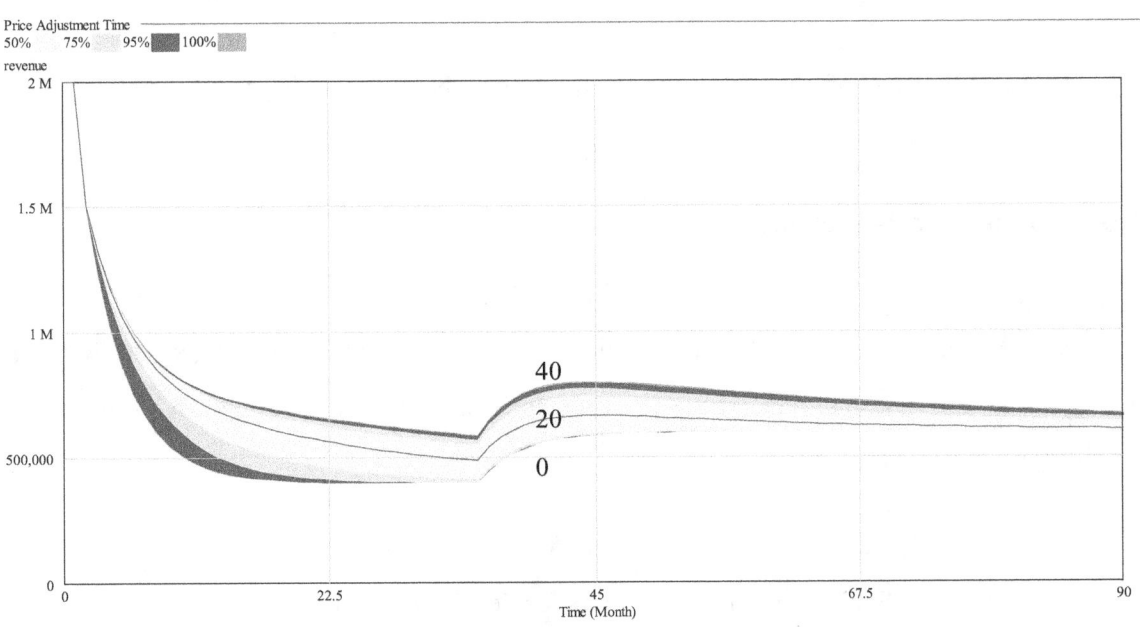

**Figure 142** Effect Price Adjustment Time on Revenue

There is a pattern comprising initial decline and then slight increase of revenue due to more sales. This pattern changes only when initial conditions are changed. In the model there are initially ten companies using new technology. Therefore sales have been 10 unit of new technology at the beginning of simulation. When initial number of firms is simulated between zero and twenty companies as sensitivity analysis, its effect on total revenue along a technology's lifecycle is nonlinear as shown in Figure 143.

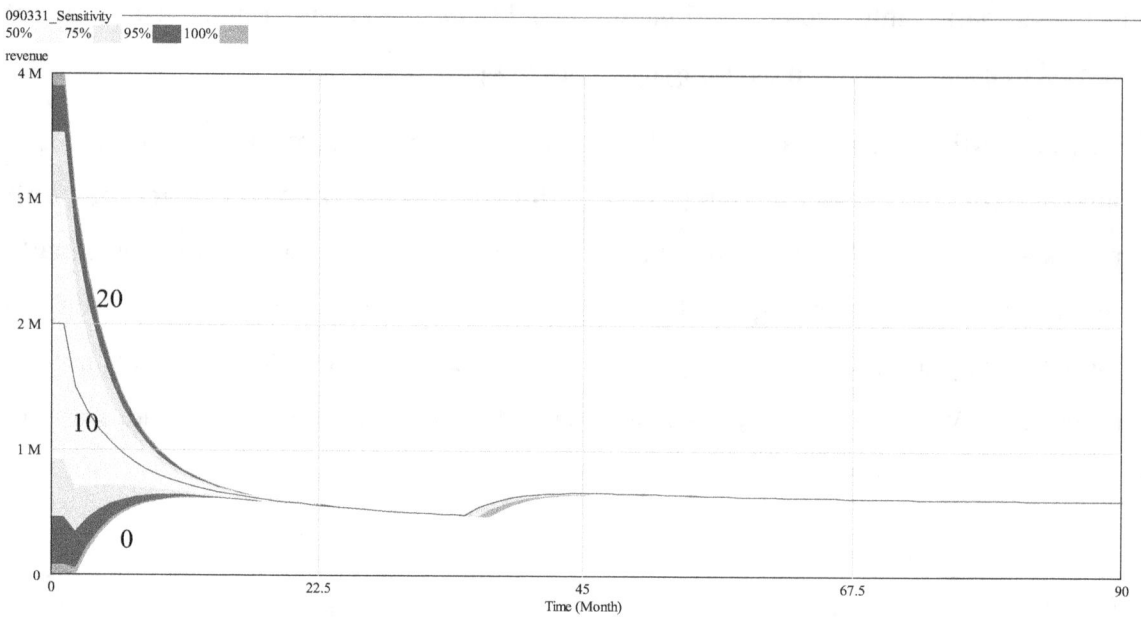

**Figure 143** Effect of Initial Number of Firms Using New Technology on Revenue

### 4.6.6 Comprehensive Results

Previous sensitivity analyses focused on effects in model variables with regard to changes of a single model parameter. In this section, all model parameters discussed will be exposed to sensitivity analysis. Table 20 presents the parameter values and ranges for sensitivity analyses.

**Table 20** Model Parameters for Sensitivity Analysis

| Parameter | Model Value | Range for Sensitivity |
|---|---|---|
| Allocation Fraction | 80% | 65% - 95% |
| Marketing Budget Fraction | 10% /month | 0% - 20% |
| Production Budget Fraction | 50% /month | 40% - 60% |
| Reference R&D Budget Fraction | 15% /month | 10% - 20% |
| Process Quality Outflow Fraction | 1%/month | 1% - 5% |
| Initial Capacity | 4 unit/Month | 2 - 6 |
| Reference Time To Adjust Capacity | 0.4 Month/unit | 0 - 0.8 |
| Capacity Step | 4 unit/Month | 2 - 6 |
| Customer Awareness Adjustment Time | 6 Month | 3 - 9 |

| Forgetting Fraction | 1%/Month | 0 – 0.02 |
| Sociability | 3 | 1 - 5 |
| Fruitfulness Adjustment | 0.1 | 0.01 – 0.19 |
| Delay in Customer Payment | 4 Month | 1 - 7 |
| Price Adjustment Time | 20 Month | 0 – 40 |
| Initial Number of Firms Using New Technology | 10 company | 0 – 20 |

When there are firms using new technology at time zero, **revenue** fluctuates much more than demand as seen in Figure 144, since it occurs some time later after **unit sales**. Sensitivity analysis on new customers in Figure 145 maintains its overall pattern with respect to standalone changes in model parameters regarding contacts among user firms and non-user firms of new technology as discussed in section 4.6.4. Simulation outputs for sensitivity analysis on other stock variables of the model are presented in Appendix II.

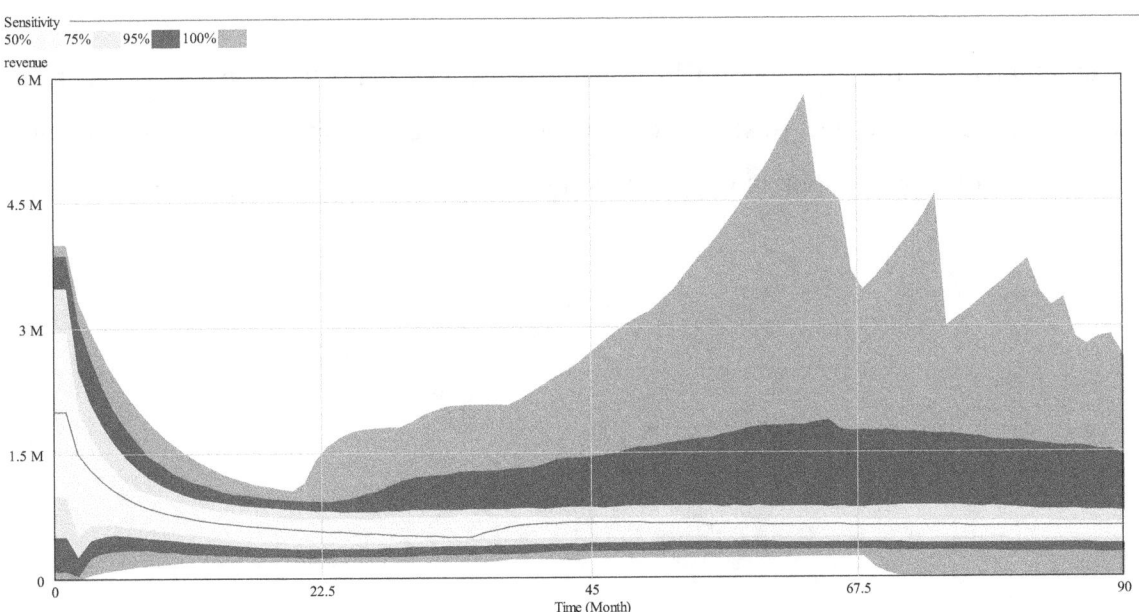

**Figure 144** Sensitivity Analysis: Effect on Revenue

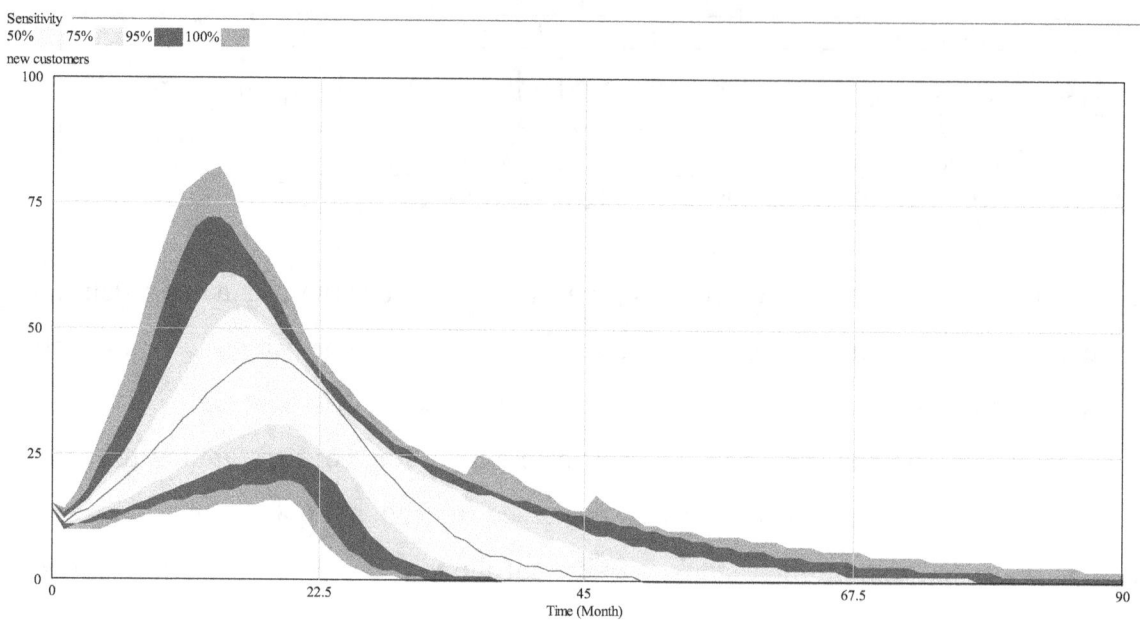

**Figure 145** Sensitivity Analysis on Demand

This cumulative normal distribution in Figure 146 shows that diffusion speed can have greater variance with respect to strategic decisions by a technology supplier such that 900 companies can become adopters of new technology in less than two years or more than eight years.

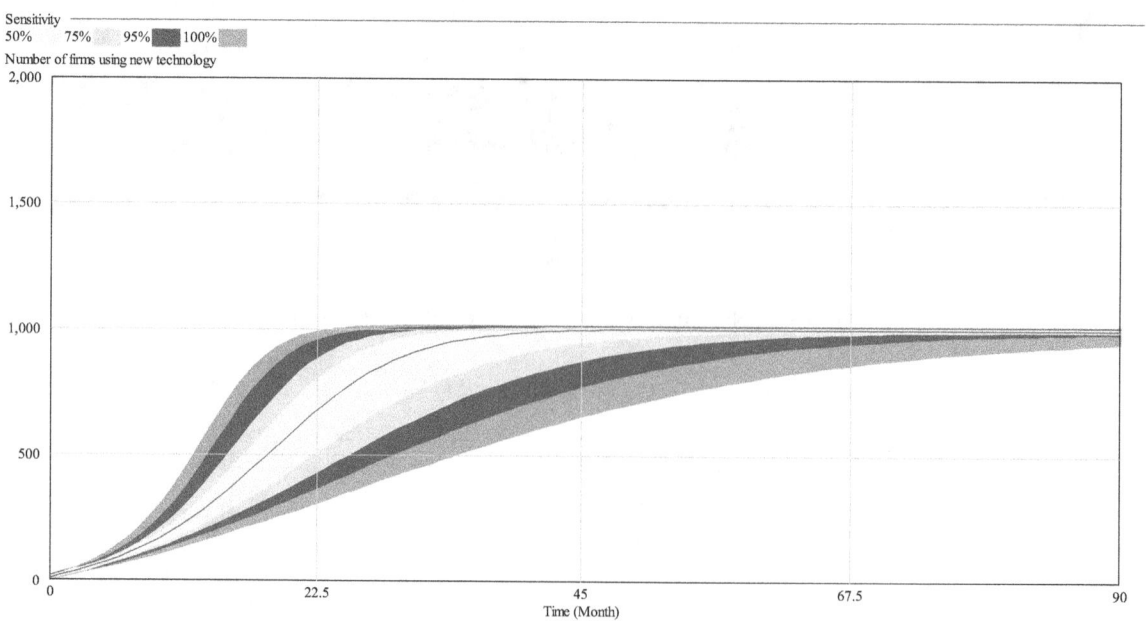

**Figure 146** Sensitivity Analysis on Number of Firms Using New Technology

### 4.6.7 Extended Model

The fluctuation of revenue reminds the researcher about path dependence which states that the end state of any system depends upon initial conditions when it is dominated by positive feedback (Sterman, 2000:351). Therefore prelaunch and postlaunch strategic decisions appear to be much more important. As in this study diffusion of new technology or growth of a new product from supplier perspective can be held back by supply restrictions such as due to limitations in capacity, and capacity decisions can influence the waiting time of potential adopters (Jain, Mahajan and Muller, 1991).

Therefore capacity decision is reconsidered such that capacity adjustment aims to eliminate backlog faster. The updates for the extended model are given in Table 21 referring to Table 15 corresponding to the model in section 4.6.5. Since backlog is reduced with this extended model and investment in capacity stops when market potential becomes less than yearly capacity, technology supplier achieves corporate growth with appropriate pricing policies when comparing Figure 147 with Figure 144 in the previous section. Overall demand increased slightly as shown in Figure 148, since earlier revenue growth leads to increased marketing activities which raise awareness and therefore demand for new technology. Simulation outputs for sensitivity analysis on other stock variables of the model are presented in Appendix III.

**Table 21** Updated Variable & Parameter in the Extended Model

| Updated Variables in Extended Model | 10 |
|---|---|
| Backlog Correction | 0.1 (instead of 0.01) |
| Capacity Adjustment | IF THEN ELSE( target capacity - Capacity - capacity step >0, (IF THEN ELSE( Number of firms not using new technology/12<Capacity , 0 , capacity step)) , 0)/time to adjust capacity |

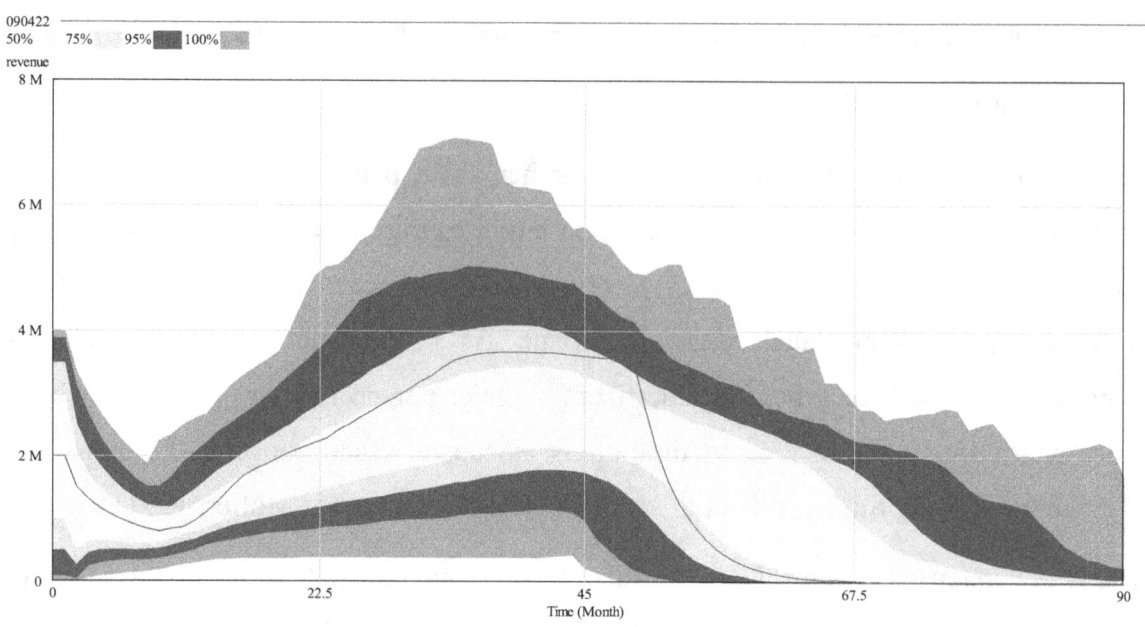

**Figure 147** Sensitivity Analysis of Extended Model on Revenue

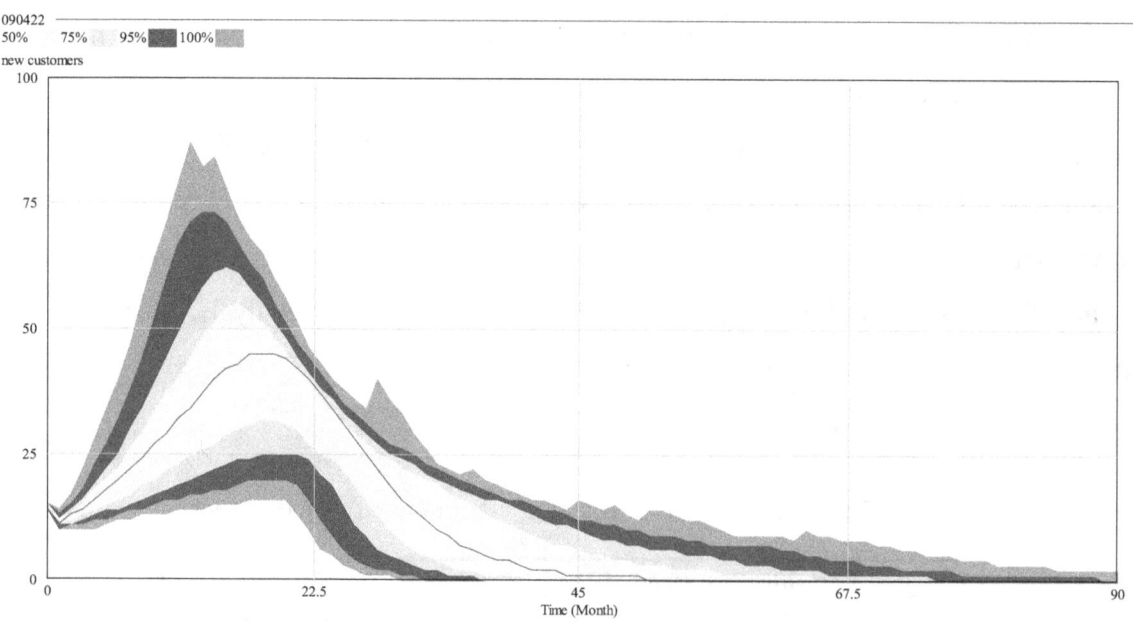

**Figure 148** Sensitivity Analysis of Extended Model on Demand

# 5 CONCLUSION

This final chapter summarizes the entire study by giving a brief overview of the research according to the chapters. It includes the conclusions reached in the context of the conceptual framework, the resulting system dynamics model and the literature of the research study.

Additional key findings of the study are presented according to their methodological, theoretical and practical significance. The strengths and limitations of the study are discussed while possible future research is highlighted. Recommendations will be made and finally some concluding thoughts will be shared in closure of this dissertation.

## 5.1 Brief Overview of Study

This study confirms and improves a relatively new framework on technological innovation diffusion. Originally, the management question focused on how new technology is adopted by firms in a particular industry over time. Therefore automotive supplier industry has been chosen as case study for diffusion of process innovations. However, an industry wide analysis seemed to be complex, since the innovation diffusion framework resulting from literature review categorized five other areas apart from a particular industry as a market for the particular technology itself.

Consequently, the problem has been redefined from the aspect of technology supplier. The management question becomes for technology/innovation supplier about which factors affecting innovation diffusion should be taken into account such that the actions of technology supplier influence diffusion speed. Since this is one of the suggested promising areas of research that understanding of the diffusion of new products will help technology suppliers to develop new product introduction strategies (Mahajan, Muller and Wind, 2000:43), the developed system dynamics model incorporated strategic decisions into extended Bass diffusion model. It opens new perspectives in the diffusion-modeling literature that managers of technology suppliers make their strategic choices when marketing new technology towards firms in a particular industry.

This research integrates demand and supply of new technology that is bought by firms as process innovation. Technology suppliers' decisions on pricing policies significantly influence total lifecycle revenue, when they can change price with respect to demand over time. Similarly, production and capacity decisions may have counterintuitive effects, if company strategies and policies are not formulated rigorously. Initial decisions by a technology supplier may have effects over the whole lifecycle of a technology.

The first chapter is introduction which contextualized this study for the reader, with the research questions (page 3) as the core of the chapter. The researcher puts forward research questions both on practical and theoretical (literature) level.

The second chapter includes a comprehensive literature review that served to inform the reader on technology lifecycles, S-curves and innovation diffusion models from various academic disciplines. The research prioritized diffusion models from marketing and economics. Further, the application of systems thinking started by drawing causal relationships from the literature on innovation diffusion in those disciplines.

The third chapter is about the methodology of the research, which is system dynamics. The researcher aligns system theories in management and organization theory to system thinking and system dynamics as the main set of tools for viewing firms and organization as systems. It briefly explains some tools of system dynamics such as causal loop diagrams and stock flow diagrams and describes the six steps of modeling process whose five steps; namely problem articulation, dynamic hypothesis formulation, simulation model formulation, testing, policy design & evaluation; are followed in the fourth chapter.

The fourth chapter is about the proposed model. It starts by presenting a framework of innovation diffusion first as a general diagram and then shows the relationships among these areas as material and information flows corresponding to system dynamics methodology. For problem articulation, causal loop diagrams are looked upon for each area of innovation diffusion. Formulation of dynamic hypotheses were partly enabled by several interviews with executives from automotive supplier industry as sample user of new technology and machine tools manufacturer as technology supplier. The system dynamics model has been established and simulation results have been interpreted. Some validity tests from system dynamics literature have been applied as model testing.

Sensitivity analyses for various model parameters are run and some arguments are taken for policy formulation and evaluation.

## 5.2 Discussion of Results

The conceptual model of innovation diffusion identified six main areas: technology, industry (adopting and using technology), technology suppliers, end users (as customers of industry), public policies and social network. This study displayed a bird eye view of the complex interrelations among these areas as Figure 60 in section 4.1. Therefore, as briefly mentioned in the previous section, the system dynamics models in sections 4.4 and 4.6 focused on the aspects of technology suppliers, e.g. CNC machine tool manufacturers and the interaction of their decisions with adopter or potential firms in an industry, e.g. automotive parts industry such that variables within and outside control of a technology supplier can be monitored over time. The system dynamics models were built in Vensim software as stock and flow diagrams. Simulation runs and sensitivity analyses enable to monitor changes in all model variables over time.

A firm introduces a new product as innovation in an industrial market as in the example of CNC machine tools in automotive industry. Since the product, i.e. technology is not a consumer good; a firm usually produces it on make-to-order basis. Lead times for producing such industrial goods are relatively long, e.g. twelve months. When demand is more than initially expected, backlog occurs due to relatively lack of competition. Therefore deciding on capacity and the time needed to build capacity become important decision parameters. When operational budget enables production below capacity, there is no use of capacity investment. Different capacity decision may lead to very different outcomes. One of the first results obtained in the study is that demand, which is much above capacity causes excessive backlog. However, capacity adjustment decision determines the level of capacity. When backlog is considered as target capacity, then capacity will reach to unnecessary levels with respect to demand. Therefore policy for capacity investment decision should be based on market potential, cumulative number of adopters and demand at a particular time. Capacity decisions depend on backlog. However, future demand, i.e. potential market should be taken into account. Demand, capacity and backlog phenomena cannot be evaluated simultaneously, since these factors are both inside and outside of a firm producing and selling products as technological innovations. Managers do usually not have the means for rational decision making. For satisficing approach they need rules of thumb. The model gives managers that tool.

Another significant result in this study is the effect of awareness on demand for new technology. Technology suppliers selling innovation need to ensure awareness about their products by potential adopter firms. Since awareness about a technology is relative and has been assigned as a variable of customer awareness with a value range between 0 and 1, marketing budgets may have limited effect. However, marketing efforts can change the effectiveness of awareness towards adoption for new technology. When *customer awareness adjustment time* is reduced from 6 (six) to 3 (three) months, diffusion 10% to 90% takes places within 20 instead of 24 months. Adopter industry characteristics determine the extent of awareness on adoption. When forgetting fraction doubles from 1% to 2%, 50% diffusion of new technology in a particular industry would be delayed by two months: 21 months from the first introduction instead of 19 months. Customer awareness actually represents stages before innovation adoption decision. Since firms in industry are considered in aggregate terms, awareness about new technology has been regarded as depending on industry characteristics. Marketing science focused on stages of innovation decision by consumers. In the model, an S-curve has been utilized as the effect of marketing by technology suppliers on firms' awareness about the new product/technology. Nevertheless, scholars on industrial marketing need to make industry specific analyses to model demand for innovation, i.e. new technology by firms.

Communication within an industry whose firms are going to adopt is expressed as model parameter: *sociability*. When a user firm of new technology establishes contacts with other firms in their industry they create social networks causing word of mouth demand. When an adopter firm has contacts with other firms in that industry, it contributes to word of mouth demand. However when industry characteristics do not favor sociability such that an adopter firm contacts one firm instead of three firms in an industry than 90% diffusion can take place in more than five years instead of tow years. Effectiveness of social networks leading to new adoption is termed as *fruitfulness* of communication. If fruitfulness adjustment increases from 10% to 19%, speed of diffusion increases, since time from 10% to 90% diffusion decreases from 24 months to 14 months. Since these parameters and variables affect word of mouth demand, diffusion speed discussed in the literature changes usually in non-linear way. Because innovation diffusion process is complex, these variables and parameters can be much more in detail.

Demand from advertising and demand from word of mouth are the major driving factors based on extended Bass model. Mathematical models in the literature consider adoption decision as one of the two factors. The system dynamics model considers demand as the combined effect of both factors, which enables demand-supply interaction. Word of mouth demand is also termed as imitative demand that adopters of new technology get in contact with non-adopter firms. The intensity and effectiveness of those social contacts shape diffusion speed of a particular innovation in that industry. Therefore when technology suppliers better understand demand factors of that particular industry, they can test and develop their industry insight by running appropriate model simulations. For different industry characteristics, they can set different model parameters regarding intensity and effectiveness of social contacts betweens user and non-users of a particular innovation, i.e. technology. An initial demand by twenty firms instead of ten firms makes additional revenue of 2 million Euro, which enables management to make other decisions such as allocation of expenditure budgets and investment in capacity. Initial sales with relatively high prices provide economies scale which fosters further corporate growth. Actions in the past always determine the path towards the future.

Selling industrial innovations as new technology is on make-to-order principle. However, business cycles can change such principles, where stocks can pile up when potential adopter firms give up or discontinue using that technology. Declining price implicitly incorporates competition among suppliers of that particular innovation/technology.

In the model, a firm buys a single innovation from a technology supplier. As in the example of CNC machine tools, a firm can buy more than one of the same technology. However, the circumstances of evaluating such additional demand depend on adopter firms' growth and profitability rather than strategic decisions by technology suppliers.

Finally the most important factor is determining appropriate sales price for technology in order to maximize lifecycle profit. The system dynamics model enables managers and policy makers to apply and change various pricing policies over time. If a technology supplier firm reduces its price too early, then its revenues will decline and will never increase, although *unit sales* increase. If firms selling technology find ways to achieve relatively high sales volumes during initial periods with relatively high prices, then those firms possess more funds to allocate more budgets to their operations which further increase sales of that technology. Therefore pricing policies are very important whether a firm marketing innovation/technology grows or not.

Pricing policies determine overall lifecycle profit. The model utilized skimming price strategy reducing *unit price* by 30% during 32 months. Changing price over time with respect to demand requires significant market foresight, which managers need to practice. Delay in customer payments has a non-linear negative effect on revenue, therefore the model displays cases of 'zero revenue' as a combination of other decisions, i.e. bankruptcy. Testing pricing policies such as penetration pricing and myopic profit maximization simultaneously help managers to better understand consequences of their sales strategies. Often managers consider price and cost to be interrelated to each other. Though for an innovation under the circumstances of no competition, price does not need to align to cost of new technology.

## 5.3 Limitations of the Study

In this study, problem formulation took quite long, since synthesizing literature on innovation diffusion going from Table 4 and Table 5 has been almost not possible due to vast amount of literature. The term "diffusion" has not been frequently utilized in some academic disciplines such as economics for the same phenomena. Technological change pointed out the rate of imitation for process innovations, which is now defined as diffusion of an innovation by firms in an industry. Edwin Mansfield's contributions on economics of technical change provide a much better conception of innovation diffusion than Schumpeter's stages of innovation. Therefore, past empirical studies on process innovations by Edwin Mansfield would contribute to building much better models.

Due to time constraints, data collection on diffusion of particular innovations in Turkish automotive parts industry was not possible. Therefore, the researcher had to rely on expert views of executives in related industries. Collecting data about diffusion of process innovations would require an army of researchers probably in the format of a research institute dedicated to studying technical change.

The complexity as of innovation diffusion has been presented in Figure 60 as the framework of the proposed model. Therefore the developed and elaborated system dynamics model could only focus on the area of technology suppliers including partly its interaction with firms in an industry as their market such that managers and policy makers can play a part. Though market dynamics of an industry using technology need to be considered as an exogenous factor, because other areas in the framework such as public policies and social networks require industry-specific research. As explained in methodology a firm, an industry cannot be drawn as system dynamics models on their own. Modeling efforts cannot start without formulation of a problem, which has not been and is definitely not an easy task.

## 5.4 Recommendations for Future Research

Future research will have theoretical, methodological and practical value from an integrated point of view. The researcher certainly believes that Edwin Mansfield's empirical studies should be replicated as longitudinal studies including system dynamics as research method. Success of industrial innovations depends on sales of new products, which is a matter of innovation diffusion and has been the main agenda of this study. There are more industrial innovations based on academic research with respect to the past, and the time period from output of academic research till commercialization of an industrial innovation becomes shorter (Mansfield, 1998). Since Schumpeter's invention-innovation-diffusion trilogy is a non-linear process, systems thinking should be employed about the alignment of academic research to commercial launch of industrial innovations.

Literature on innovation diffusion indicates that higher speeds of diffusion do not necessarily mean socially optimal diffusion rates of innovations. Regarding industrial innovations, firms' investment in new capital equipment may not always be necessary and can hinder an industry's competitiveness in the medium and long term. Therefore public policies are definitely needed to avoid market failures by regulating the speed of diffusion (Stoneman and Diederen, 1994). Government authorities and industry associations should work on policies that aim to maximize social welfare regarding diffusion of process innovations that are adopted by firms in those industries.

Firm selling new technology determined price, since the focus of the system dynamics model has been on suppliers. However, for industrial innovations, where buyer is not price taker, the interaction of supply and demand and its effect on price models can be future research agenda by economics and technology management scholars.

In this research, diffusion of a single innovation/technology has been studied and price has been included for a single technology life cycle. Both price and technological changes shape expectations of both buyers and sellers of innovation which influence diffusion path (Rosenberg, 1976). When a consumer or a firm buys a new product or technology, the benefit of its adoption depends on current price, future movements in prices and the expectations of obsolescence (e.g. launch of next generation or a substitute product/technology). A welfare-optimal diffusion path may be myopic buyer expectations with a monopoly supplier. However such an equilibrium diffusion path is different, if expectations of buyers and sellers are different, and knowing, influencing expectations seems to be crucial in any public policy (Stoneman and Ireland, 1986). Hence modeling efforts need to be carried out about supply and demand interactions during diffusion of an innovation, separately for each industry, since each industry has different problems and issues.

# REFERENCES

1. Abernathy, W.J. and Utterback, J.M. (1978), "Patterns of Industrial Innovation", Technology Review, 80(June-July), 40-47.

2. Abrahamson, E., & Rosenkopf, L. (1993), "Institutional and competitive bandwagons: Using mathematical modeling as a tool to explore innovation diffusion", Academy of Management Review, 18(3), 487–517.

3. Akinola, A. (1986), "An Application of the Bass Model in the Analysis of Diffusion of. Cocoa-Spraying Chemicals among Nigerian Cocoa Farmers", Journal of Agricultural Economics, 37(3), 395-404.

4. Allen, T.J. (1967), "Information Needs and Uses", in Cuadra, C.A. (Ed.), *Annual Review of Information Science and Technology,* Vol. 4, Chicago, IL: Encyclopedia Britannica.

5. Amabile, T., Conti, R. and Coon, H., Lazenby, J. and Heron, M. (1996), "Assessing the work environment for creativity", Academy of Management Review, 39(5), 1154-1184.

6. Arndt, J. (1967), "Role of Product-Related Conversations in the Diffusion of a New Product Journal of Marketing Research", 4(3), 291-295.

7. Arrow, K.J. (1962), "The economic implications of learning by doing", The Review of Economic Studies, 29(3), 155-173.

8. Ayres, R.V. (1989), "The future of technological forecasting", Technological Forecasting and Social Change, 36, 49-60.

9. Bain, A.D. (1963), "The growth of demand for new commodities", Journal of Royal Statistical Society, 126(2), 285-299.

10. Baldridge, J.V. and Burnham, R.A. (1975), "Organizational Innovation: Individual, Organizational and Environmental Impacts", Administrative Science Quarterly, 20(2), 165-176.

11. Baptista, R. (1999), "The Diffusion of Process Innovations: A Selective Review", International Journal of the Economics of Business, 6(1), 107-129.

12. Barabasi, A.L. (2002), *Linked: The New Science of Networks,* Cambridge, MA: Perseus.

13. Barlas, Y. (1996), "Formal aspects of model validity and validation in system dynamics", System Dynamics Review, 12(3), 183-210.

14. Barnard, C. (1938), *The Functions of the Executive,* Cambridge, MA: Harvard University Press.

15. Bass, F. M. (1969), "A new product growth model for consumer durables", Management Science, 15(6), 215-227.

16. Bass, F.M. (1980), "The Relationship Between Diffusion Rates, Experience Curves and Demand Elasticities for Consumer Durables Technical Innovations", Journal of Business, 53(3), 51-67.

17. Beuys, B.L., Kang, W. and Agarwal, R. (1987), "Creating Growth in New Markets: A Simultaneous Model of Firm Entry and Price", Journal of Product Innovation Management, 24, 139–155.

18. Berthon, P., Hulbert, J. M. and Pitt, L. F. (1999), "Brand management prognostications", Sloan Management Review, 40(2), 53-65.

19. Bessant, J. and Rush, H. (1993), "Government Support of Manufacturing Innovations: Two Country-Level Case Studies", IEEE Transactions on Engineering Management, 40(1), 79-91.

20. Betz, F. (1994). *Strategic Technology Management (International ed.)*, Singapore: McGraw-Hill.

21. Bhalla, S.K. (1987), *The Effective Management of Technology*, Reading, MA: Addison-Wesley.

22. Bigoness, W.J. and Perreault, W.D. (1981), "A conceptual paradigm and approach for the study of innovators", Academy of Management Journal, 24(1), 68-82.

23. Boulding, K.E. (1956), "General Systems Theory-The Skeleton of Science", Management Science, 2(3), 197-207.

24. Borgatti, S., & Cross, R. (2003). "A relational view of information seeking and learning in social networks", Management Science, 49, 432-445.

25. Brown, S. and Blackmon, K. (2005), "Aligning Manufacturing Strategy and Business-Level Competitive Strategy in New Competitive Environments: The Case for Strategic Resonance", Journal of Management Studies, 42(4), 793-815.

26. Cagan, T., Oner, M.A. and Basoglu, N. (2003), "Factors Affecting Innovation Diffusion: The Case of Turkish Armed Forces", Proceedings of Portland International Conference on Management of Engineering and Technology, Portland, Oregon, USA.

27. Chang, PL. and Shih, HY. (2005), "Comparing patterns of intersectoral innovation diffusion in Taiwan and China: A Network Analysis", Technovation, 25(2), 155-169.

28. Chai, K.H., Gregory, M.J. and Shi Y. S. (2004), "An Exploratory Study of Intrafirm Process Innovations Transfer in Asia", IEEE Transactions on Engineering Management, 51(3), 364-374.

29. Christensen, C.M. (1997), *The Innovator's Dilemma*, Boston, MA: Harvard Business School Press.

30. Colombo, M.G. and Mosconi, R. (1995), "Complementarity and Cumulative Learning Effects in the Early Diffusion of Multiple Technologies", Journal of Industrial Economics, 43(1), 13-48.

31. Cooper, J.R. (1998), "A multidimensional approach to the adoption of innovation", Management Decision, 36(8), 493-502.

32. Czepiel, J.A. (1974), "Word-of-Mouth Processes in the Diffusion of a Major Technological Innovation", Journal of Marketing Research, 11(2), 172-180.

33. Davies, S. (1979), *The Diffusion of Process Innovations*, Cambridge, UK: Cambridge University Press.

34. Davis, F.D. (1989), "Perceived usefulness, perceived ease of use, and user acceptance of information technologies", MIS Quarterly, 13(3), 319-340.

35. Dawson, R. (2003), *Living Networks: Leading Your Company, Customers and Partners in the Hyper-Connected Economy*, Upper Saddle River, NJ: Prentice Hall.

36. Dodds, W. (1973), "An Application of the Bass Model in Long-Term New Product Forecasting", Journal of Marketing Research, 10(3), 308-311.

37. Drejer, A. (2002), "Towards a model for contingency of Management of Technology", Technovation, 22, 363-370.

38. Duncan, R.B. (1972), "Characteristics of organizational environments and perceived environmental uncertainty", Administrative Science Quarterly, 17, 313-27.

39. Elçi, Ş. (2002), *İnovasyon: Rekabet ve Kalkınmanın Anahtarı*, Istanbul, Turkey: Acar Matbaacılık.

40. Feder, G., O'Mara, G.T. (1982), "On Information and Innovation Diffusion: A Bayesian Approach", American Journal of Agricultural Economics, 64(February), 145-147.

41. Fleisher, C.S. and Bensoussan, B.E. (2003), *Strategic and Competitive Analysis: Methods and Approaches to Analyzing Business Competition*, Upper Saddle River, NJ: Prentice-Hall.

42. Floyd, A. (1968), "A methodology for trend forecasting of figures of merit," in J. Bright (Ed.), *Technological Forecasting for Industry and Government: Methods and Applications*, Englewood Cliffs, NJ: Prentice-Hall. pp. 95-109.

43. Forrester, J.W. (1961), *Industrial Dynamics*, Cambridge, MA: Productivity Press.

44. Forrester, J.W. (1994), "System dynamics, systems thinking, and soft OR, System Dynamics Review", 10(2/3), 245-256.

45. Forrester, J.W., "Counterintuitive behavior of social systems", Technology Review, 73(3), 52-68.

46. Forrester, J.W. (2007), "System dynamics-a personal view of the first fifty years", System Dynamics Review, 23(2/3), 345-358.

47. Freeman, C. (1982), *The Economics of Industrial Innovation*, London: Pinter.

48. Frenzen, J. and Nakamoto, K. (1993), "Structure, cooperation, and the flow of market information", Journal of Consumer Research, 20(3), 360–375.

49. Gable, G. (1994), "Integrating Case Study and Survey Research Methods: An Example in Information Systems", European Journal of Information Systems, 3(2), 112-126.

50. Garcia, R., Calantone, R. and Levine, R. (2003), "The Role of Knowledge in Resource Allocation to Exploration versus Exploitation in Technologically Oriented Firms", Decision Sciences, 34(2), 323-349.

51. Gold, B. (1981), "Technological Diffusion in Industry: Research Needs and Shortcomings", Journal of Industrial Economics, 1, 29(3), 247-269.

52. Gomez, J. and Vargas, P. (2009), "The effect of financial constraints, absorptive capacity and complementarities on the adoption of multiple process technologies", Research Policy, 38(1), 106-119.

53. Goodman, M. (1991), "The Systems Thinking as a Language", The Systems Thinker, 2(3).

54. Goodman, M. (1992), The Do's and Don'ts of Systems Thinking on the Job, The Systems Thinker, 3(6).

55. Goodman, M., Karash, R., Lannon, C., O'Reilly, K.W., Seville, D. (1997), *Designing a Systems Thinking Intervention*, Waltham, MA: Pegasus Communications.

56. Gowrisankaran, G. and Stavins, J. (2004), "Network Externalities and Technology Adoption: Lessons from Electronic Payments", The RAND Journal of Economics, 35(2), 260-276.

57. Götz, G. (1999), "Monopolistic competition and the diffusion of new technology", RAND Journal of Economics, 30(4), 679-693.

58. Green, G.C. and Hevner, A.R. (2000), "The Successful Diffusion of Innovations: Guidance for Software Development Organizations", IEEE Software, 17(6), 96-103.

59. Gregg, J. V., Hassel, C. H. and Richardson, J. T.(1964), *Mathematical trend curves: An aid to forecasting*, Edinburgh: Oliver and Boyd, 1964.

60. Grossman, G.M. and Helpman, E. (1991), "Quality ladders in the theory of growth", Review of Economic Studies, 58, 43–61.

61. Hannan, T.H. and McDowell, J.M. (1984), "The Determinants of Technology Adoption: The Case of the Banking Firm", Rand Journal of Economics, 15, 328-335.

62. Hargadon, A. (1998), "Firms as knowledge brokers Lessons in pursuing continuous innovation", California Management Review, 40(3), 209-227.

63. Hesselbein, F. (2002), *Leader to leader*. San Francisco: Jossey-Bass.

64. Hiebert, L.D. (1974), "Risk, learning, and the adoption of fertilizer responsive seed varieties", American Journal of Agricultural Economics, 56 (4), 764-768.

65. Higa, K., Sheng, O.R.L., Hu, P.J.-H., Au, G. (1997), "Organizational Adoption and Diffusion of Technological Innovation: A Comparative Case Study on Telemedicine in Hong Kong", in *Proceedings of the Thirtieth Hawaii International Conference*, System Sciences, 4, 146-155.

66. Hippel, E. von (2005), "Open source software projects as user innovation networks", In Feller, J., Fitzgerald, B., Hissam, S.A. and Lakhani, K.R. (Eds.), *Perspectives on Free and Open Source Software*, pp. 267-278, Cambridge, MA: MIT Press.

67. Hirooka, M. (2003), "Nonlinear dynamism of innovation and business cycles", Journal of Evolutionary Economics, 13, 549-576.

68. Hobday, M. (1995), "East Asian Latecomer Firms: Learning the Technology of Electronics", World Development, 23(7), 1171-1193.

69. Hobday, M. (1998), "Product complexity, innovation and industrial organisation", Research Policy, 26(6), 689–710.

70. Husserl, G. (1938), "Public Policy and Ordre Public", Virginia Law Review, 25(1), 37-67.

71. Iyigun, M. (2006), "Clusters of invention, lifecycle of technologies and endogenous growth", Journal of Economic Dynamics & Control, 30(4), 687-719.

72. Jain, D.C. and Ram, C.R. (1990), "Effect of Price on the Demand for Durables: Modeling, Estimation, and Findings", Journal of Business and Economic Statistics, 8(2), 163-170.

73. Jaffe, A.B., Newell, R.G. and Stavins, R.N. (2005), "A tale of two market failures: Technology and environmental policy", Ecological Economics, 54, 164–174.

74. Jensen, M. (1988), "Information Cost and Innovation Adoption Policies", Management Science, 34(2), 230-239.

75. Kalafsky, R.V. and MacPherson, A.D. (2006), "The post-1990 rebirth of the US machine tool industry: a temporary recovery?", Technovation, 26(5-6), 665-671.

76. Kalish, S. and Lilien, G.L. (1986), "A Market Entry Timing Model for New Technologies", Management Science, 32(2), 194-205.

77. Kamakura, W. A. and Balasubramanian, S.K. (1988), "Long-term view of the diffusion of durables: a study of the role of price and adoption influence processes via tests of nested models", International Journal of Research in Marketing, 5, 1-13.

78. Karshenas, M. and Stoneman, P. (1993), "Rank, Stock, Order and Epidemic Effects in the Diffusion of New Process Technologies: an Empirical Model", Rand Journal of Economics, 1993, 24, 503-528.

79. Karshenas, M. and Stoneman, P. (1995), Technological Diffusion, in Stoneman, P., ed., Handbook of the Economics of Innovation and Technological Change, Oxford: Blackwell, 265-297.

80. Kauppila, O.P. (2008), "Strategic innovation- and customer- orientation: An examination in the context of business environment and organizational structure", Executive Summary, Helsinki School of Economics.

81. Kaplan, B. and Duchon, D. (1988), "Combining Qualitative and Quantitative Methods in Information Systems Research: A Case Study", MIS Quarterly, 12(4), 571-587.

82. Kast, F.E. and Rosenzweig, J.E. (1972), "General Systems Theory: Applications for Organizations and Management", Academy of Management Journal, 15(4), 447-465.

83. Katz, D. and Kahn, R.L. (1966), *The Social Psychology of Organizations*, New York: John Wiley & Sons.

84. Kim, D.H. (1990), *Introduction to Systems Thinking*, Waltham, MA: Pegasus Communications.

85. Kim, D.H. (1994), *Systems Thinking Tools: A User's Reference Guide*, Waltham, MA: Pegasus Communications.

86. Kim, N. and Srivastava, R.K. (2005), "Modeling cross-price effects on inter-category dynamics: The case of three computing platforms", Omega, 35(3), 290-301.

87. Kimberly, J.R. and Evanisko, M.J. (1981), "Organizational innovation: the influence of individual, organizational, and contextual factors on hospital adoption of technological and administrative innovation", Academy of Management Journal, 24, 689-713.

88. King, C.W, Jr. (1963), "Fashion Adoption: A Rebuttal to the 'Trickle Down' Theory", in S.A. Greyser, Ed., Proceedings of the American Marketing Association, Chicago: American Marketing Association, 108-125.

89. Krasner, O.J. (1982), "The role of entrepreneurs in innovation", in Kent, C.A., Sexton, D.L., Vesper, K.H., Encyclopedia of Entrepreneurship, Upper Saddle River, NJ: Prentice Hall.

90. Kumar, U. and Kumar V. (1992), "Technological Innovation Diffusion: The Proliferation of Substitution Models and Easing the User's Dilemma", IEEE Transactions on Engineering Management, 39(2), 158-168.

91. Lange, R., McDade, S. and Oliva, T.A. (2004), "The Estimation of a Cusp Model to Describe the Adoption of Word for Windows", Journal of Product Innovation Management, 21(1), 15-32.

92. Langlois, R., & Robertson, P. (1989), Explaining vertical integration: Lessons from the American automobile industry, Journal of Economic History, 49(2), 361–375.

93. Lawrence, P.R. and Lorsch, J.W. (1967), *Organization and Environment*, Cambridge, MA: Harvard University Press.

94. Lawton, S.B. and Lawton, W.H. (1979), "An Autocatalytic Model for the Diffusion of Educational Innovations", Educational Administration Quarterly, 15(1), 19-46.

95. Lee, A. S. (1991), "Integrating Positivist and Interpretive Approaches to Organizational Research", Organization Science, 2(4), 342-365.

96. Lekvall, P. and Wahlbin, C. (1973), "A Study of Some Assumptions Underlying Innovation Diffusion Functions", The Swedish Journal of Economics, 75(4), 362-377.

97. Leonard-Barton, D. (1985), "Experts as negative opinion leaders in the diffusion of a technological innovation", Journal of Consumer Research, 11(4), 914-926.

98. Lilien, Gary L. and Rangaswamy, A. (1998), *Marketing Engineering*, Reading, MA: Addison Wesley.

99. Lin, C., Tung, C. and Huang, C. (2006), Elucidating the industrial cluster effect from a system dynamics perspective, Technovation, 26(4), 473–482.

100. Lowe, P. (1995), *The Management of Technology: Perception and opportunities*, Paul Lowe, UK: Chapman & Hall.

101. Luecke, R. and Katz, R. (2003), *Managing Creativity and Innovation*, Boston, MA: Harvard Business School Press.

102. Mahajan, V., Muller, E. and Bass, F.M. (1990), "New Product Diffusion Models in Marketing: A Review and Directions for Research", Journal of Marketing, 54(1), 1-26.

103. Mahajan, V., Muller, E. and Wind, Y., eds. (2000), *New-Product Diffusion Models*, Norwell, MA: Kluwer Academic Publishers.

104. Markus, M.L. (1987), "Toward a 'critical mass' theory of interactive media: Universal access, interdependence and diffusion", Communication Research, 14(5), 491–511.

105. Mansfield, E. (1961), "Technical Change and the Rate of Imitation", Econometric a, 29(4), 741-766.

106. Mansfield, E. (1989), "The Diffusion of Industrial Robots in Japan and the United States", Research Policy, 18(4), 183-192.

107. Mansfield, E. (1993), "The Diffusion of Flexible Manufacturing Systems in Japan, Europe, and the United States", Management Science, 39(2), 149-159.

108. Mansfield, E. (1996), "Book review of Silverberg, Gerald and Luc Soete. The economic of growth and technical change: technologies, nations, agents", Journal of Economic Literature, 34(1), 179-181.

109. Mansfield, E. (1998), "Academic research and industrial innovation: An update of empirical findings", Research Policy, 26(7-8), 773-776.

110. Mansfield, E., Rapoport, J., Romeo, A., Wagner, S. and Beardsley, G. (1977), "Social and Private Rates of Return from Industrial Innovations", The Quarterly Journal of Economics, 91(2), 221-240.

111. Mansfield, E., Schwartz, M. and Wagner, S. (1981), "Imitation Costs and Patents: An Empirical Study", The Economic Journal, 91(364), 907-918.

112. Mazzoleni, R. (1997), "Learning and path-dependence in the diffusion of innovations: comparative evidence on numerically controlled machine tools", Research Policy, 26, 425-428.

113. McCarthy, C. and Ryan, J. (1976), "An econometric model of television ownership", Economic and Social Review, 7, 256–277.

114. Meade, N. (1989), "Technological Substitution: A Framework of Stochastic Models", Technology Forecasting and Social Change, 36(4), 389-400.

115. Meade N. and Islam, T. (2006), "Modeling and forecasting the diffusion of innovation – A 25-year review", International Journal of Forecasting, 22 (3), 519-545.

116. Meadows, D.H. (1989), "System dynamics meets the press", System dynamics Review, 5(1), 68-80.

117. Meadows, D. H., Meadows, D.L. and Randers, J. (1992), *Beyond the Limits: Confronting Global Collapse, Envisioning a Sustainable Future*, Post Mills, VT: Chelsea Green Publishing Co.

118. Meier, J.D., Farre, C., Bansode, P., Barber, S. and Rea, D. (2007), *Performance Testing Guidance for Web Applications*, Seattle: Microsoft Press.

119. Meredith, J.R., Raturi, A., Amoako-Gyampah, K. and Kaplan, B. (1989), "Alternative research paradigms in operations", Journal of Operations Management, 8(4), 297-326.

120. Metcalfe, J.S. (1994), "Evolutionary Economics and Technology Policy", The Economic Journal, 104(425), 931-944.

121. Midgley, D.F. and Dowling, G.R. (1978), "Innovativeness: the concept and its measurement", Journal of Consumer Research, 4(4), 229-242.

122. Midgley, D.F. and Dowling, G.R. (1993), "A longitudinal study of product form innovation: the interaction between predisposition and social messages", Journal of Consumer Research, 19, 611-625.

123. Milbergs, E., Speech posted in IBM April 2006 Business Leadership Forum, cited in "Technology's role in innovation", from World Wide Web http://ideaflow.corante.com/archives/2006/04/17/technologys_role_in_innovation.php, 2006

124. Milling, P.M. (2002), "Understanding and managing innovation processes", System Dynamics Review, 18(1), 73-86.

125. Mingers, J. (2001), "Combining IS Research Methods: Towards a Pluralist Methodology", Information Systems Research, 12(3), 240-259.

126. MIT web site, http://web.mit.edu/sdg/www/what_is_sd.html, Retrieved on August 10, 2006.

127. Moore, G.A. (1999), *Crossing the Chasm: Marketing and Selling High-Tech Products to Mainstream Customer (revised edition)*, New York: HarperCollins.

128. Moore, G.C. and Benbasat, I. (1991), "Development of an instrument to measure the perceptions of adopting an information technology innovation", Information Systems Research, 2(3), 192-222.

129. Myers, M. D. (1997), "Qualitative Research in Information Systems", MIS Quarterly, 21(2), 241-242.

130. Nevers, J. V. (1972), "Extensions of a New Product Growth Model", Sloan Management Review, 13(2), 77-91.

131. Nooteboom, B. (1999), "Innovation, learning and industrial organization", Cambridge Journal of Economics, 23, 127–150.

132. OECD 1997 The Oslo Manual: Proposed Guidelines for Collecting and Interpreting Technological Innovation Data, Paris, OECD

133. OECD (1997), *The OECD STAN Database 1970-1995*, Economic Analysis and Statistics Division: Paris

134. Oliver, R.M. (1987), "A Bayesian Model to Predict Saturation and Logistic Growth", The Journal of the Operational Research Society, 38(1), 49-56.

135. Olshavsky, R.W. (1980), "Time and the Rate of Adoptions of Innovations", Journal of Consumer Research, 6(4), 425-428.

136. Parker, J.E.S. (1978). *The Economics of Innovation: The National and Multinational Enterprise in Technological Change ($2^{nd}$ Edition)*, London: Longman.

137. Pickett, J.P., et al., ed. (2006), The American Heritage Dictionary of the English Language ($4^{th}$ Edition), Boston, MA: Houghton Mifflin.

138. Plazo, J.R. (2006), *Maximum Influence Advantage: Persuasion Workshop*, New York, NY: Booksurge Llc.

139. Poppo, L., & Zenger, T. (1998), "Testing alternative theories of the firm: Transaction cost, knowledge-based, and measurement explanations for make-or-buy decisions in information services", Strategic Management Journal, 19(9), 853–877.

140. Porter, M.E. (1979), "The structure within industries and companies' performance", Review of Economics and Statistics, 61(2), 214-227.

141. Porter, M.E. (1980), *Competitive Strategy*, New York, NY: Free Press.

142. Porter, M.E. (1990), *The Competitive Advantage of Nations*, London: MacMillan, 1990.

143. Prahalad, C. and Hamel, G. (1990), "The Core Competence of the Corporation", Harvard Business Review, 68(3), 79–91.

144. Quirmbach, H.J. (1986), "The Diffusion of New Technology and the Market for an Innovation", The RAND Journal of Economics, 17(1), 33-47.

145. Ragin, C.C. (1987), *The Comparative Method: Moving Beyond Qualitative and Quantitative Strategies*, Berkeley and Los Angeles, CA: University of California Press.

146. Raghavan, S.A. and Chand, D.R. (1989), "Diffusing Sofware-Engineering Methods", IEEE Software, 6(4), 1981-1990.

147. Ramamurthy, K. and Premkumar, G. (1995), "Determinants and Outcomes of Electronic Data Interchange Diffusion", IEEE Transactions on Engineering Management, 42(4), 332-351.

148. Rao, A.G and Yamada, M. (1988), "Forecasting With a Repeat Purchase Diffusion Model", Management Science, 34(6), 734-752.

149. Rao, A.G. (2006), "A framework for implementing information and communication technologies in agricultural development in India", Technological Forecasting and Social Change, 74(4), 491-518.

150. Ray, G.F. (1989), "Full Circle: The Diffusion of Technology", Research Policy, 18(1), 1-18.

151. Reinganum, J.F. (1981), "On the Diffusion of New Technology: A Game Theoretic Approach", Review of Economic Studies, 48(3), 395-405.

152. Reinganum, J.F. (1981), "Market Structure and the Diffusion of New Technology", The Bell Journal of Economics, 12(2), 618-624.

153. Richmond, B. (1993), "Systems thinking: critical thinking skills for the 1990s and beyond", System Dynamics Review, 9(2), 113-133.

154. Richmond, B. (2000), *The Thinking in Systems Thinking: An Overview of Seven Skills*, Waltham, MA: Pegasus Communications.

155. Robinson, B. and Lakhani, C. (1975), "Dynamic Price Models for New-Product Planning", Management Science, 21(10), 1113-1122.

156. Rogers, E.M. (1962), *Diffusion of Innovations*, New York, NY: The Free Press, 1962.

157. Rogers, E.M. (2003), *Diffusion of Innovations (5$^{th}$ Edition)*, New York, NY: The Free Press.

158. Rogers, E.M., Medina, U.E., Rivera, M.A. and Wiley, C.J. (2005), Complex Adaptive Systems And The Diffusion Of Innovations, The Innovation Journal: The Public Sector Innovation Journal, Volume 10(3), Article 30.

159. Rose, N.L. and Joskow, P.L. (1990), "The Diffusion of New Technologies: Evidence from the Electric Utility Industry", Rand Journal of Economics, 21(3), 354-373.

160. Rosenberg, N. (1976), "On Technological Expectations", Economic Journal, 86(343), 523-535.

161. Ryan, B. and N. Gross (1943), "The Diffusion of Hybrid Seed Corn in Two Iowa Communities", Rural Sociology, 8(1), 15-24.

162. Saffer, D., *Jumping Barriers Using Design to Aid Technology Adoption*, http://www.odannyboy.com/blog/images/jumpingbarriers.pdf, April 2006.

163. Senge, P.M. (1990), *The Fifth Discipline: The Art & Practice of the Learning Organization*, New York, NY: Currency Doubleday.

164. Schon, D. (1971), *Beyond the Stable State*, New York, NY: Norton.

165. Schumpeter, J. A. (1934), *Theory of Economic Development: an inquiry into profits, capital, credit, interest, and the business cycle*, Cambridge, MA: Harvard University Press.

166. Scotchmer, S. (2004), *Innovation and Incentives*, Cambridge, MA: MIT Press.

167. Scott, J. (1991), "Networks of Corporate Power: A Comparative Assessment", Annual Review of Sociology, 17, 181-203.

168. Scott, W.R. (2002), *Organizations: Rational, Natural, and Open Systems (5th Edition)*, Englewood Cliffs, NJ: Prentice-Hall.

169. Sector Info, *Association of Automotive Parts & Components Manufacturers:* http://www.taysad.org.tr, 19$^{th}$ May 2008.

170. Sharif, M. N. and Islam, M. N. (1980), "The Weibull distribution as a general model for forecasting technological change", Technological Forecasting and Social Change, 18(3), 247–256.

171. Singleton, R. and Straits, B.C. (2004), *Approaches to Social Research (4$^{th}$ Edition)*, New York, NY: Oxford University Press.

172. Sonnenwald, D.H., Maglaughlin, K., and Whitton, M.C. (2001), *Using Innovation Diffusion Theory to Guide Collaboration Technology Evaluation: Work in Progress*, Proceedings of the 10th IEEE International Workshops on Enabling Technologies: Infrastructure for Collaborative Enterprises, p.114-119, June 20-22, 2001

173. Souder, W.E. and Chakrabarti, A.K. (1978), "The R&D/Marketing Interface: Results from an Empirical Study of Innovation Projects", IEEE Transactions on Engineering Management, 25(4), 88-93.

174. Soydan, I. and Oner, M.A (2004)., "Resource Allocation between R&D and Marketing", Unpublished Paper, Yeditepe University, Istanbul.

175. Spender, J.-C. and Grant, R.M. (1996), "Knowledge and the Firm: Overview", Strategic Management Journal, 17(1), 5-9.

176. Sterman, J.D. (2001), System Dynamics Modeling: Tools for Learning in a Complex World, California Management Review, 43(4), 8-25.

177. Sterman, J.D. (2002), "All models are wrong: reflections on becoming a systems scientist", System Dynamics Review, 18(4), 501-531.

178. Stoneman, P. (2002), *The Economics of Technological Diffusion.* Oxford, UK: Blackwell Publishers, 2002

179. Stoneman, P. And Ireland, N.J. (1983), "The Role of Supply Factors in the Diffusion of New Process Technology", The Economic Journal, 93(Supplement: Conference Papers), 66-78.

180. Stoneman, P. and Ireland, N. (1986), "Technological Diffusion, Expectations and Welfare", Oxford Economic Papers, 38(2), 283-304.

181. System Dynamics Society, http://www.systemdynamics.org/, Retrieved on November 15, 2005.

182. System Dynamics, The System Dynamics Society Official Web Site: http://www.systemdynamics.org , 2006

183. Swanepoel, M. (2005), "Digital repositories: all hype and no substance?", New Review of Information Networking, 11(1), 13-25.

184. Swann, G.M.P. (2001), "Sales practice and market evolution: the case of virtual reality", International Journal of Industrial Organization, 19, 1119-1139.

185. Tam, K.Y. and Hui, K.L. (1999), "Price Elasticity and The Growth of Computer Spending", IEEE Transactions on Engineering Management, 46(2), 190-200.

186. Tarde, G. (1903), *The Laws of Imitation*. New York, NY: Henry Holt.

187. Teng, T.C., Grover, V. and Güttler, W. (2002), "Information Technology Innovations: General Diffusion Patterns and Its Relationships to Innovation Characteristics", IEEE Transactions on Engineering Management, 49(1), 13-25.

188. Thacker, C. and Handscombe, B. (2003), "Innovation, Competitive Position and Industry Attractiveness: A Tool to Assist SMEs", Creativity and Innovation Management, 12(4), 230-239.

189. Tigert, D. and Farivar, B. (1981), "The Bass New Product Growth Model: A Sensitivity Analysis for a High Technology Product", Journal of Marketing, 45(4), 81-90.

190. Thurow, L.C. (1984), "Building a world class economy", Society, 22(1), 16-29.

191. Tidd, J., Pessant, J., Pavitt, K. (2005), *Managing innovation: Integrating technological, market and organizational change (3rd Edition)*, London: John Wiley & Sons.

192. Tung, L.L. and Rieck, O. (2005), "Adoption of electronic government services among business organizations in Singapore", Journal of Strategic Information Systems, 14(4), 417–440.

193. Tushman, M. and Rosenkopf, L. (1992), "Organizational Determinants of Technological Change", In Staw, B.M. and Cummings, L.L. (Eds.), *Research in Organizational Behavior*, Vol. 14:311-347, Greenwich, CT: JAI Press.

194. Ulwick, A. (2002), "Turn Customer Input into Innovation", Harvard Business Review, 80(1), 5-11.

195. Utterback, J. (1973), "The process of technological innovation with in the firm", In Rowe, L. and Boise, W., *Organizational and Managerial Innovation*, Goodyear Publishing, Pacific Palisades, CA: 1973

196. Utterback, J.M. and Abernathy, W.J. (1975), "A dynamic model of product and process innovation", Omega, 3(6), 639-656.

197. Van de Ven, A.H. (1986), "Central Problems in the Management of Innovation", Management Science, 32(5), 590-607.

198. Van Everdingen, Y.M., Aghina, W.B., Fok, D. (2005), "Forecasting cross-population innovation diffusion: A Bayesian approach", International Journal of Research in Marketing, 22(3), 293-308.

199. Vennix, J.A.M. (1999), "Group model-building: tackling messy problems", System Dynamics Review, 15(4), 379-401.

200. Vickery, G. and Blau, E. (1989), *Government Policies and the Diffusion of Microelectronics*, Paris: Organisation for Economic Co-operation and Development.

201. Von Hippel, E. (1988), *The Sources of Innovation*, London: Oxford University Press.

202. Webster Dictionary, 2008.

203. Wejnert, B. (2002), "Integrating of Models of Diffusion of Innovations: A Conceptual Framework, Annual Review Sociology", 28, 297–326.

204. Wheelen, T. L., & Hunger, D. J. (2004). *Strategic Management and Business Policy (9th Edition)*, Upper Saddle River, NJ: Pearson Education.

205. Wind, J. and Mahajan, V. (1987), "Marketing hype: a new perspective for new product research and introduction", Journal of Product Innovation Management, 4(1), 43-49.

206. Wolter, C. and Veloso, F.M., "The Effects of Innovation on Vertical Structure: Perspectives on Transaction Costs and Competences, Academy of Management Review, 2008, Vol. 33, No. 3, 586–605.

207. Woodward, J. (1965), *Industrial Organization: Theory and Practice*, London: Oxford University Press.

208. Yang, J. and Liu, C.Y. (2006), "New Product Development: An innovation diffusion perspective", Journal of High Technology Management Research, 17(1), 17-26.

209. Yi, Youjae (1991), "A Critical Review of Consumer Satisfaction", In Zeithmal, V.A (Ed.), *Review of Marketing 1989*, Chicago, IL: American Marketing Association.

210. Yim, N.H., Kim, S.H., Kim, H.W. and Kwahk, K.Y., Knowledge based decision making on higher level strategic concerns: system dynamics approach, Expert Systems with Applications, 27(1), 143-158, 2004.
211. Zuscovitch, E., Heraud, J.A., Cohendet, P. (1988), Innovation diffusion from a qualitative standpoint, Futures, 20 (3), 266-306.

## APPENDIX I: Model Equations

(01)  ALLOCATION FRACTION= 0.8

   Units: Dmnl

(02)  awareness discrepancy= 1-Customer awareness/desired awareness

   Units: Dmnl

(03)  Backlog= INTEG (orders received-production,0)

   Units: unit

(04)  BACKLOG CORRECTION= 1

   Units: 1/Month

(05)  BASE PRODUCTION COST FACTOR= 3

   Units: EUR/unit

(06)  budget allocation to marketing= Total expenditure budget*MARKETING BUDGET FRACTION

   Units: EUR/Month

(07)  budget allocation to production= PRODUCTION BUDGET FRACTION*Total expenditure budget

   Units: EUR/Month

(08)  "budget allocation to R&D"= Total expenditure budget*"R&D budget fraction"

   Units: EUR/Month

(09)  budget increase=revenue*ALLOCATION FRACTION

   Units: EUR/Month

(10)  Capacity= INTEG (INTEGER( investment-reductions ),2)

   Units: unit/Month

(11)  capacity adjustment= IF THEN ELSE( target capacity - Capacity -capacity step >0, capacity step, 0)/time to adjust capacity

   Units: unit/(Month*Month)

(12)  capacity life= 25

Units: Month

(13) capacity step= 40

Units: unit/Month

(14) contacts of noncustomers with customers = contacts with customers*potential customer concentration

Units: contact/Month

(15) contacts with customers = Number of firms using new technology*sociability

Units: contact/Month

(16) Customer awareness= INTEG (+increase awareness-decrease awareness,0.6)

Units: Dmnl

(17) CUSTOMER AWARENESS ADJUSTMENT TIME= 6

Units: Month

(18) decrease awareness= Customer awareness*FORGETTING FRACTION

Units: 1/Month

(19) DELAY IN CUSTOMER PAYMENTS= 4

Units: Month

(20) demand from advertising= Number of firms not using new technology*EFFECT OF CUSTOMER AWARENESS ON ADOPTION(Customer awareness)

Units: company/Month

(21) desired awareness= 1

Units: Dmnl

(22) desired backlog= Capacity

Units: unit/Month

(23) desired process quality= 0.99

Units: Dmnl

(24) desired production= DELAY1( use of production budget/production cost of unit new technology, PRODUCTION LEAD TIME )

Units: unit/Month

(25) EFFECT OF CUSTOMER AWARENESS ON ADOPTION([(0,0)-(1,0.02)],(0,0),(0.1,0.0012),(0.2,0.0032),(0.3,0.0056),(0.4,0.0084),(0.5,0.0113),(0.6,0.0142),(0.7,0.0164),(0.8,0.0181),(0.9,0.0195),(1,0.0197))

Units: 1/Month

(26) EFFECT OF MARKETING BUDGET RATIO ON AWARENESS([(0,0)-(1.5,1.2)],(0,0.2),(0.15,0.23),(0.3,0.31),(0.45,0.39),(0.6,0.52),(0.75,0.67),(0.9,0.84),(1.05,1),(1.2,1.11),(1.35,1.17),(1.5,1.19))

Units: Dmnl

(27) "EFFECT OF R&D PROCESS BUDGET ON QUALITY"([(0,0)-(2,1)],(0.3,0),(0.4,0.05),(0.5,0.1),(0.6,0.15),(0.7,0.2),(0.8,0.25),(0.9,0.3),(1,0.35),(1.1,0.45),(1.2,0.5),(1.3,0.55),(1.4,0.6),(1.5,0.65),(1.5,0.65),(1.6,0.7),(1.7,0.8),(1.8,0.85),(1.9,0.9),(1.95,0.95),(2,1))

Units: 1/Month

(28) FINAL TIME = 120

Units: Month

The final time for the simulation.

(29) FORGETTING FRACTION= 0.01

Units: 1/Month

(30) FRACTION OF MARKETING BUDGET USAGE= 1

Units: 1/Month

(31) FRACTION OF PRODUCTION BUDGET USAGE= 1

Units: 1/Month

(32) "FRACTION OF R&D PRODUCT BUDGET USAGE"= 0

Units: 1/Month

(33) fruitfulness= 0.01

Units: company/contact

(34) FRUITFULNESS ADJUSTMENT= 0.1

Units: company/contact

(35) increase awareness= effect of marketing budget ratio on awareness(marketing budget ratio)*awareness discrepancy/CUSTOMER AWARENESS ADJUSTMENT TIME

Units: 1/Month

(36) INITIAL TIME = 0

Units: Month

The initial time for the simulation.

(37) "INITIAL USE OF R&D PROCESS BUDGET"= 10

Units: EUR/Month

(38) investment= capacity adjustment

Units: unit/(Month*Month)

(39) Marketing budget= INTEG (budget allocation to marketing-use of marketing budget,10)

Units: EUR

(40) MARKETING BUDGET FRACTION= 0.1

Units: 1/Month

(41) marketing budget ratio= use of marketing budget/previous marketing budget

Units: Dmnl

(42) new customers= INTEGER( word of mouth demand + demand from advertising)

Units: company/Month

(43) number of firms industry= Number of firms not using new technology+Number of firms using new technology

Units: company

(44) Number of firms not using new technology= INTEG (- new customers, 1000)

Units: company

(45) Number of firms using new technology= INTEG (new customers, 10)

Units: company

(46) OPTIMUM PRICE= 10

Units: EUR/unit

(47) orders received= IF THEN ELSE( Backlog/desired backlog<1, new customers*technology per customer, 0.9*new customers*technology per customer )

Units: unit/Month

(47) potential customer concentration= Number of firms not using new technology/number of firms industry

Units: Dmnl

(48) potential production= Capacity

Units: unit/Month

(49) previous marketing budget= DELAY FIXED( use of marketing budget, 1 , 10 )

Units: EUR/Month

(50) "previous R&D process budget allocation"= DELAY FIXED ("use of R&D process budget" , 1 , "INITIAL USE OF R&D PROCESS BUDGET")

Units: EUR/Month

(51) price per unit= OPTIMUM PRICE*(1+EXP( -Time / TIME STEP))

Units: EUR/unit

(52) Process Quality= INTEG (process quality inflow-process quality outflow, 0.6)

Units: Dmnl

(53) process quality balance= Process Quality/desired process quality

Units: Dmnl

(54) process quality inflow= (1-process quality balance)*"EFFECT OF R&D PROCESS BUDGET ON QUALITY"("R&D process budget ratio")

Units: 1/Month

(55) process quality outflow= Process Quality*PROCESS QUALITY OUTFLOW FRACTION

Units: 1/Month

(56) PROCESS QUALITY OUTFLOW FRACTION= 0.01

Units: 1/Month

(57) production= MIN(MIN(INTEGER( desired production), potential production) , Backlog*BACKLOG CORRECTION)

Units: unit/Month

(58)  Production budget= INTEG (budget allocation to production-use of production budget,50)

   Units: EUR

(59)  PRODUCTION BUDGET FRACTION= 0.5

   Units: 1/Month

(60)  production cost factor= BASE PRODUCTION COST FACTOR/Process Quality

   Units: EUR/unit

(61)  production cost of unit new technology= 1*production cost factor

   Units: EUR/unit

(62)  PRODUCTION LEAD TIME= 12

   Units: Month

(63)  "R&D budget fraction"= "REFERENCE R&D BUDGET FRACTION"/process quality balance

   Units: 1/Month

(64)  "R&D budget"= INTEG ( "budget allocation to R&D"-"use of R&D process budget"-"use of R&D product budget", 10)

   Units: EUR

(65)  "R&D process budget ratio"= "use of R&D process budget"/"previous R&D process budget allocation"

   Units: Dmnl

(66)  reductions= Capacity/(capacity life*12)

   Units: unit/(Month*Month)

(67)  "REFERENCE R&D BUDGET FRACTION"= 0.15

   Units: 1/Month

(68)  REFERENCE TIME TO ADJUST CAPACITY= 0.4

   Units: Month*Month/unit

(69)  revenue= DELAY1( price per unit*unit sales , DELAY IN CUSTOMER PAYMENTS )

   Units: EUR/Month

(70)　SALES FRACTION= 1

　　　Units: 1/Month

(71)　SAVEPER  = TIME STEP

　　　Units: Month [0,?]

　　　The frequency with which output is stored.

(72)　sociability= 3

　　　Units: contact/company/Month

(73)　target capacity= Backlog*BACKLOG CORRECTION

　　　Units: unit/Month

(74)　technology per customer= 1

　　　Units: unit/company

(75)　TIME STEP  = 1

　　　Units: Month [0,?]

　　　The time step for the simulation.

(76)　time to adjust capacity= capacity step*REFERENCE TIME TO ADJUST CAPACITY

　　　Units: Month

(77)　Total expenditure budget= INTEG (budget increase-budget allocation to production-"budget allocation to R&D"-budget allocation to marketing, 100)

　　　Units: EUR

(78)　unit sales= Units in stock*SALES FRACTION

　　　Units: unit/Month

(79)　Units in stock= INTEG (production-unit sales, 10)

　　　Units: unit

(80)　use of marketing budget= Marketing budget*FRACTION OF MARKETING BUDGET USAGE

　　　Units: EUR/Month

(81)　use of production budget= FRACTION OF PRODUCTION BUDGET USAGE*Production budget

Units: EUR/Month

(82) "use of R&D process budget"= "R&D budget"*(1-"FRACTION OF R&D PRODUCT BUDGET USAGE")

Units: EUR/Month

(83) "use of R&D product budget"= "R&D budget"*"FRACTION OF R&D PRODUCT BUDGET USAGE"

Units: EUR/Month

(84) word of mouth demand= contacts of noncustomers with customers*fruitfulness

Units: company/Month

# APPENDIX II: Sensitivity Analysis Outputs of Comprehensive Results

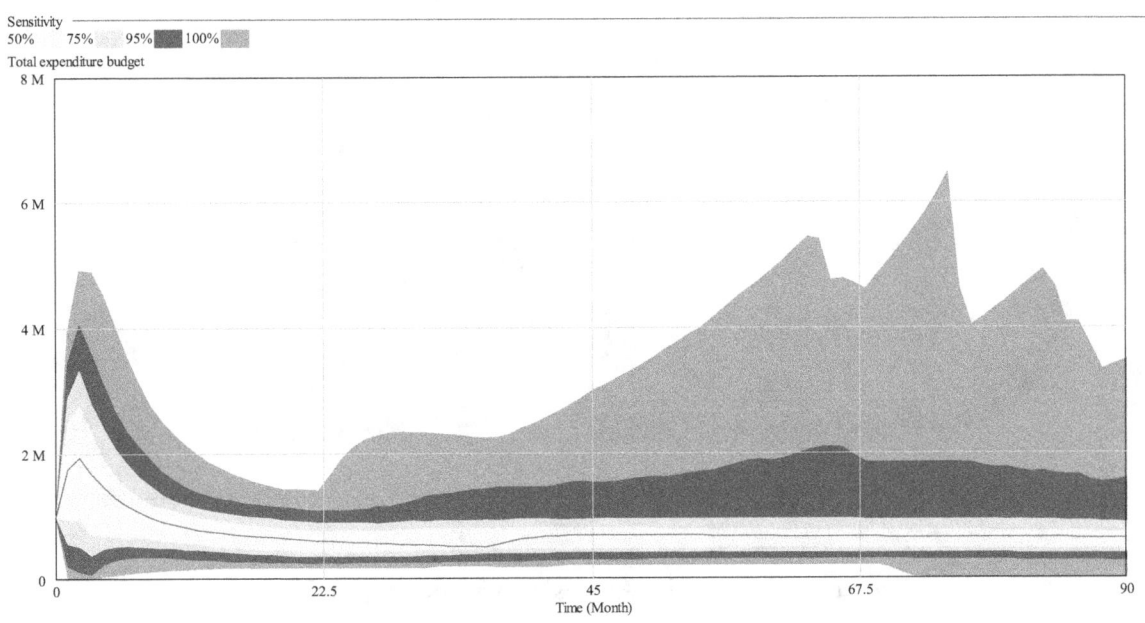

**Figure 149** Sensitivity Analysis on Total Expenditure Budget

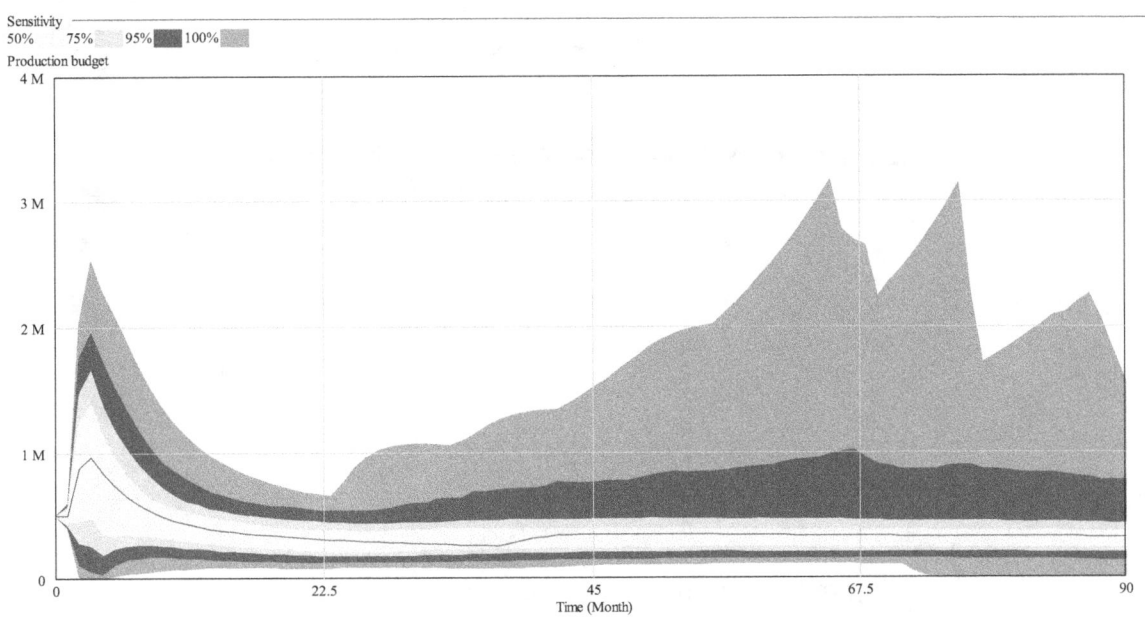

**Figure 150** Sensitivity Analysis on Production Budget

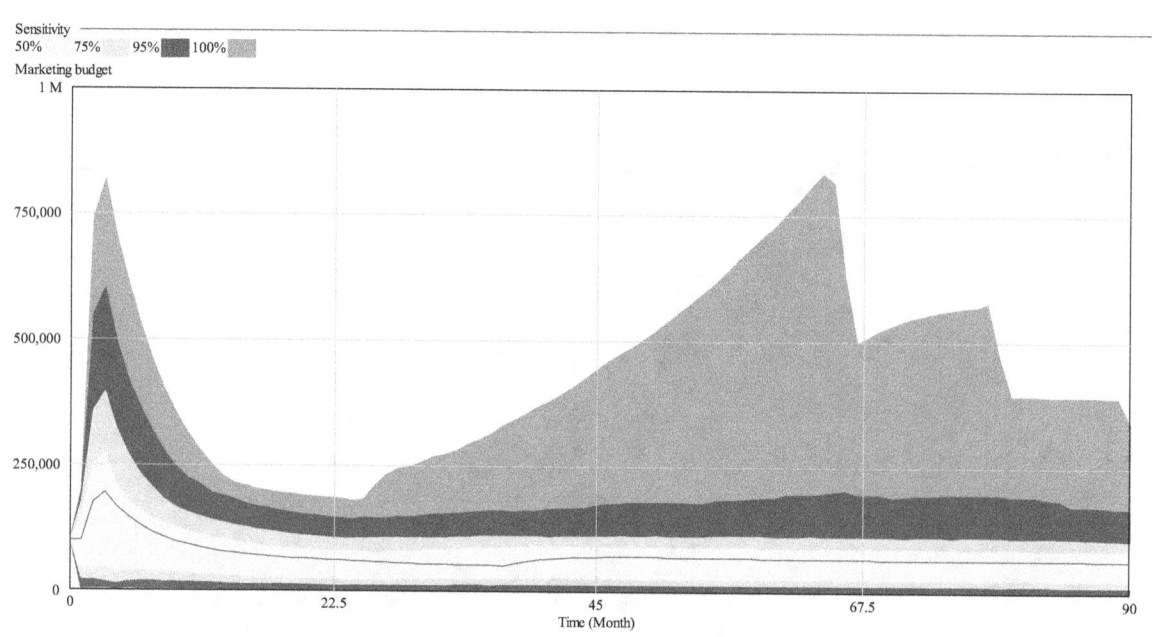

**Figure 151** Sensitivity Analysis on Marketing Budget

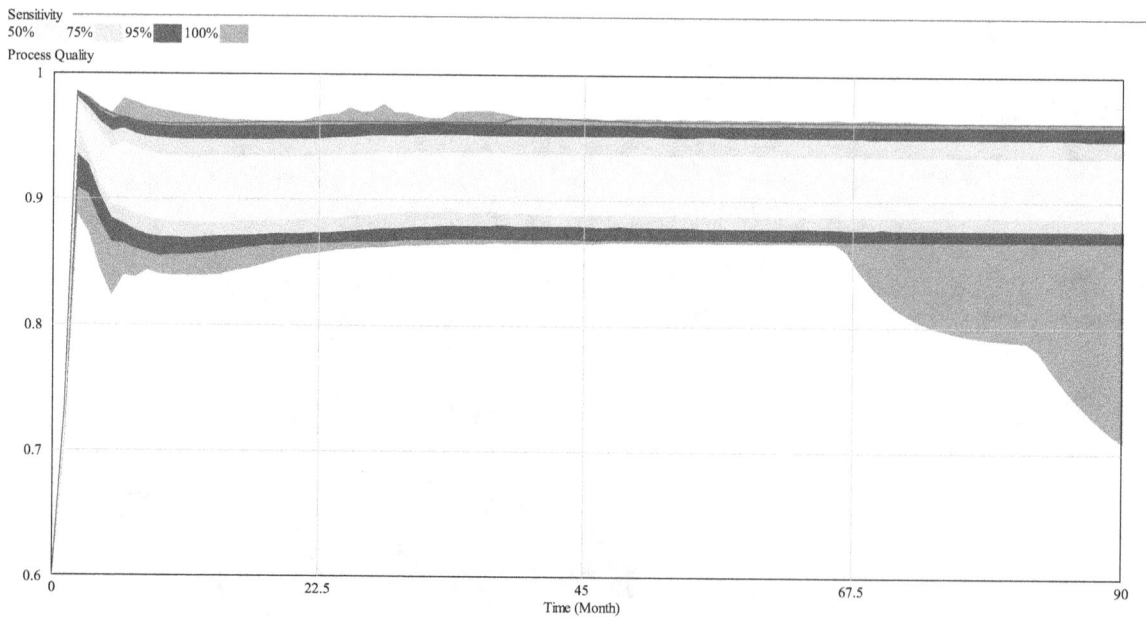

**Figure 152** Sensitivity Analysis on Process Quality

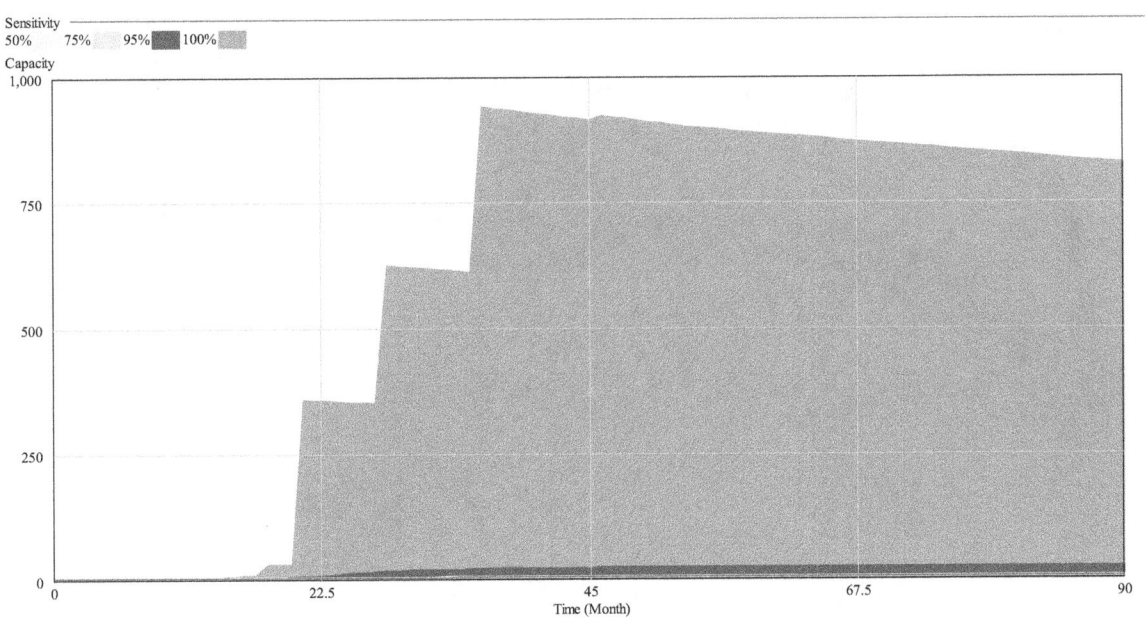

**Figure 153** Sensitivity Analysis on Capacity

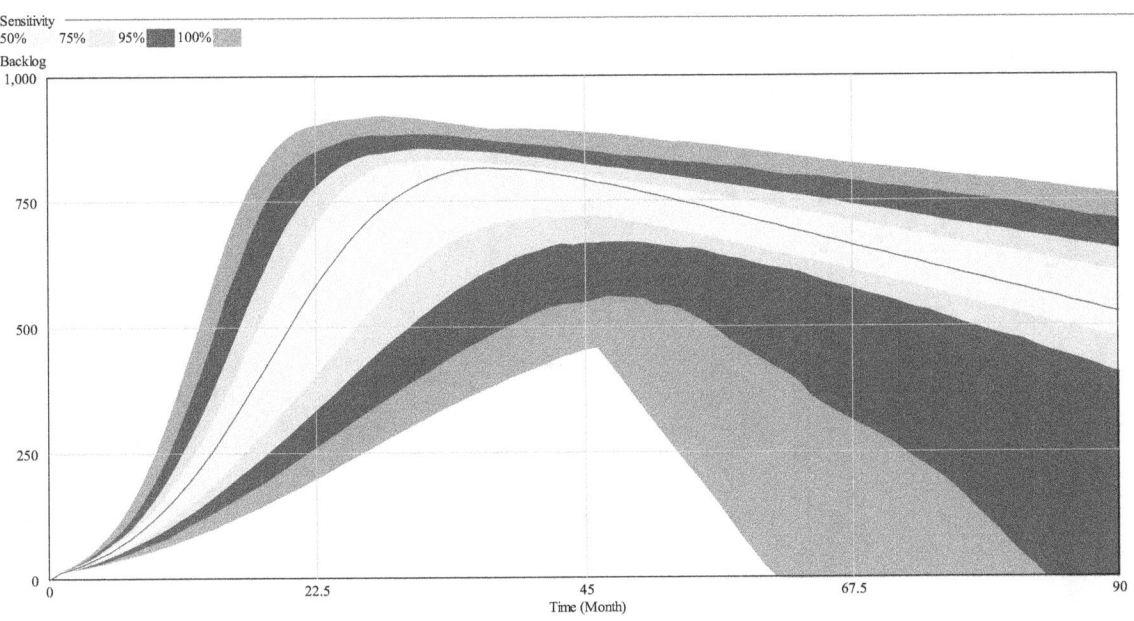

**Figure 154** Sensitivity Analysis on Backlog

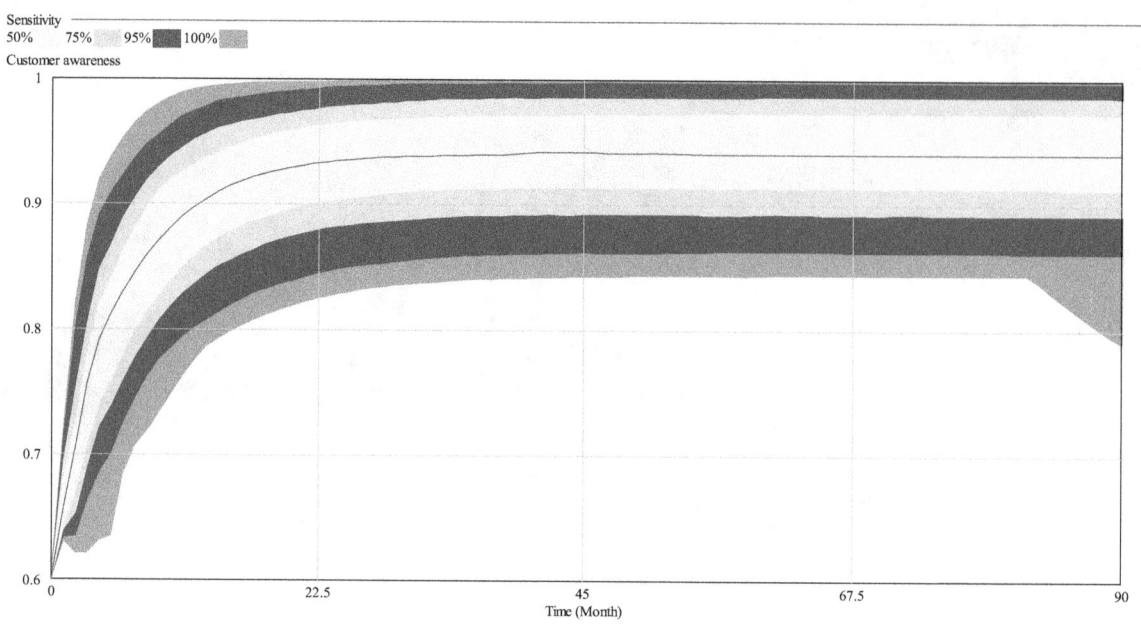

**Figure 155** Sensitivity Analysis on Customer Awareness

# APPENDIX III: Sensitivity Analysis Outputs of Extended Model

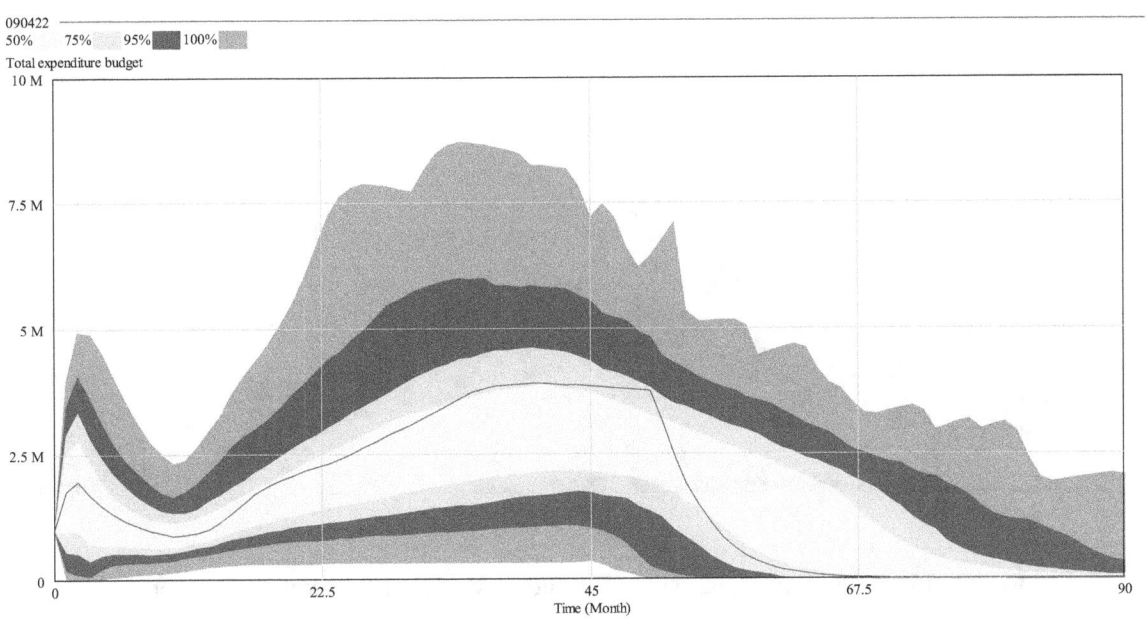

**Figure 156** Sensitivity Analysis of Extended Model on Total Expenditure Budget

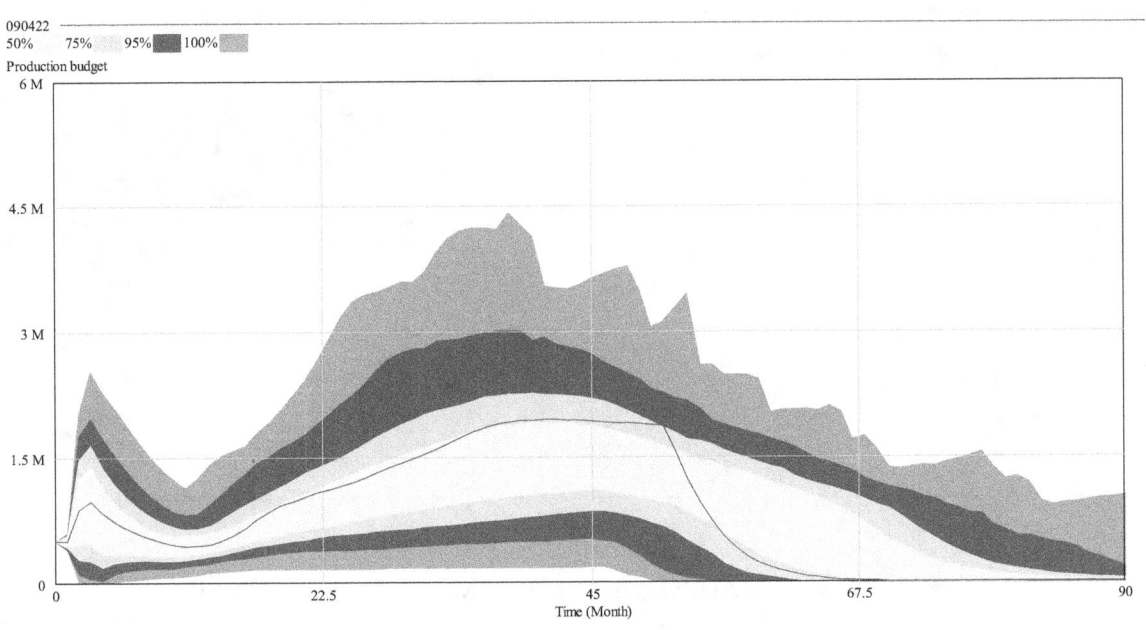

**Figure 157** Sensitivity Analysis of Extended Model on Production Budget

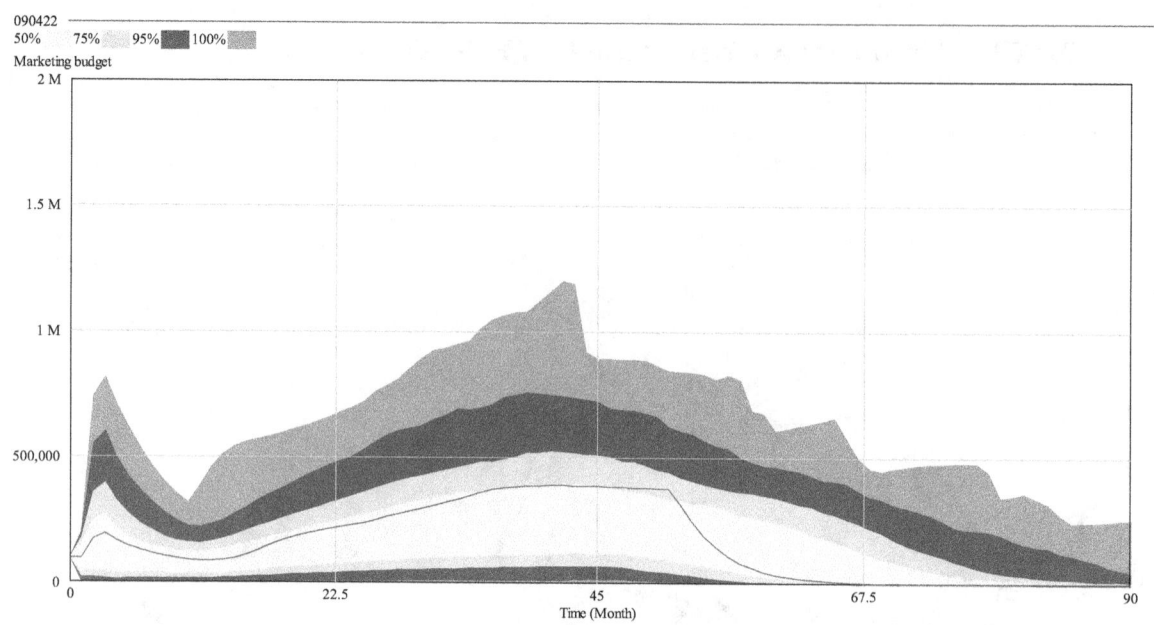

**Figure 158** Sensitivity Analysis of Extended Model on Marketing Budget

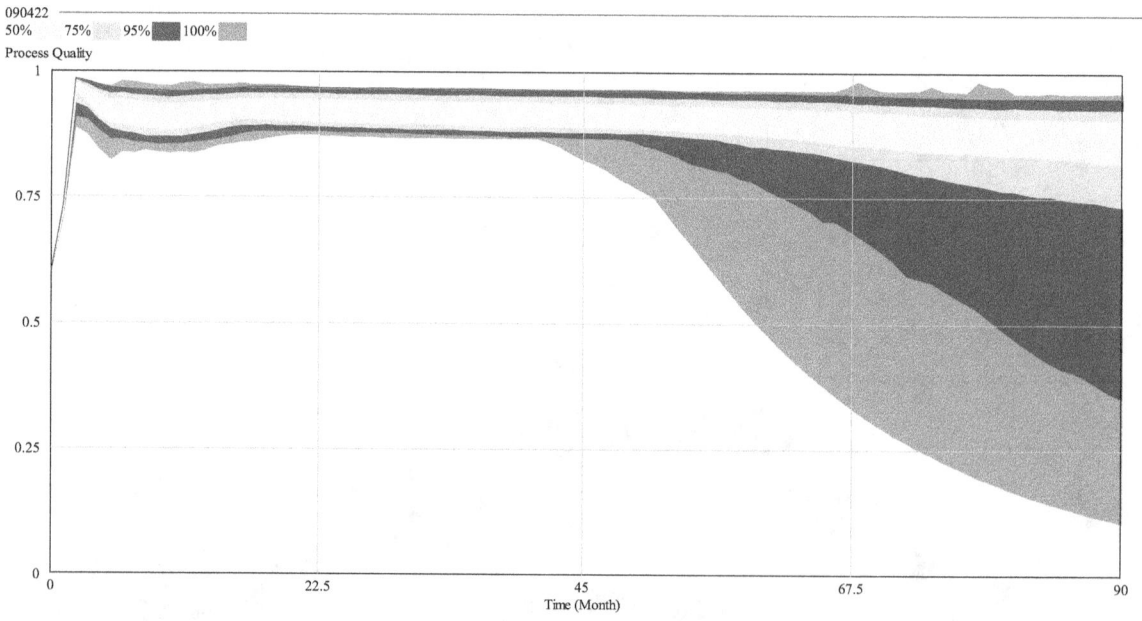

**Figure 159** Sensitivity Analysis of Extended Model on Process Quality

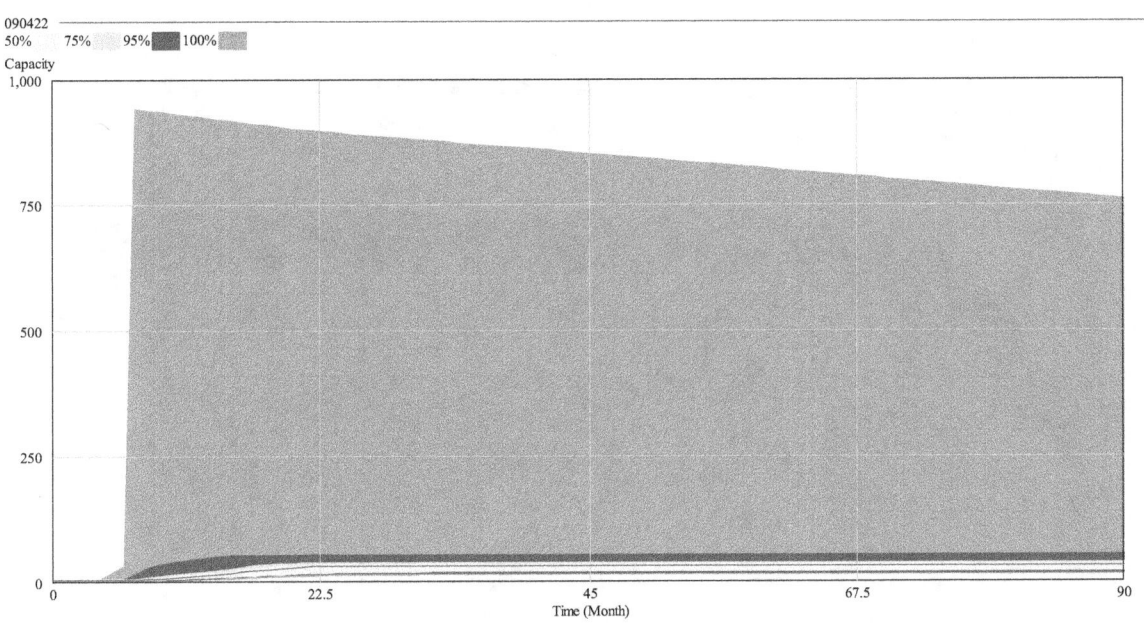

**Figure 160** Sensitivity Analysis of Extended Model on Capacity

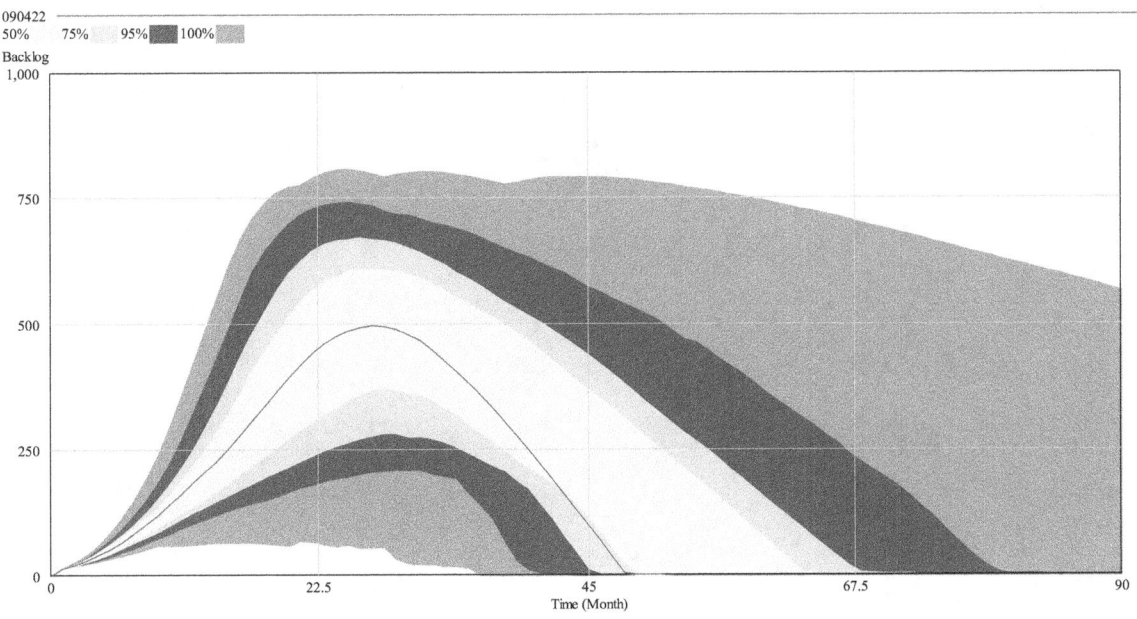

**Figure 161** Sensitivity Analysis of Extended Model on Backlog

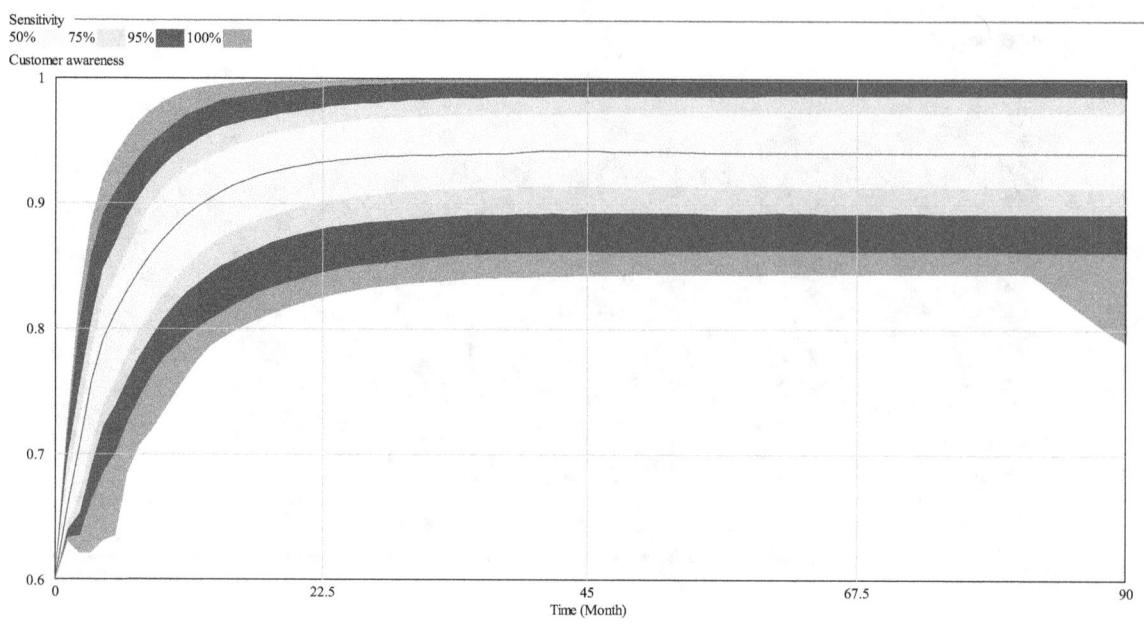

**Figure 162** Sensitivity Analysis of Extended Model on Customer Awareness

www.ingramcontent.com/pod-product-compliance
Lightning Source LLC
Chambersburg PA
CBHW080956170526
45158CB00010B/2815